Emeril Lagasse Power Air Fryer 360 ==COOKBOOK==

800 Easy and Delicious Fryer Recipes to Fry, Grill, Roast, and Bake for You and Your Family on Every Occasion

By James Cluck

Copyright© 2021 By James Cluck All Rights Reserved

The content contained within this book may not be reproduced, duplicated or transmitted without direct written permission from the author or the publisher.

Under no circumstances will any blame or legal responsibility be held against the publisher, or author, for any damages, reparation, or monetary loss due to the information contained within this book, either directly or indirectly.

Legal Notice:

This book is copyright protected. It is only for personal use. You cannot amend, distribute, sell, use, quote or paraphrase any part of the content within this book, without the consent of the author or publisher.

Disclaimer Notice:

Please note the information contained within this document is for educational and entertainment purposes only. All effort has been executed to present accurate, up to date, reliable, complete information. No warranties of any kind are declared or implied. Readers acknowledge that the author is not engaged in the rendering of legal, financial, medical or professional advice. The content within this book has been derived from various sources. Please consult a licensed professional before attempting any techniques outlined in this book.

Paperback ISBN: 979-8-537712749

Table of Content

Introduction 1

Chapter 1 The Emeril Lagasse Power Air Fryer 360 2

Performance of the Emeril Lagasse Power Air Fryer 360 3
Benefits of the Emeril Lagasse Power Air Fryer 360 4
Using the Accessories 5
Cleaning the Emeril Lagasse Power Air Fryer 360 7
About the Recipes and Cookbook 7

Chapter 2 Breakfasts 9

Strawberry Toast 9
Bacon and Cheese Muffin Sandwiches 9
Sweet Potato Chips with Cinnamon 9
Vanilla Granola with Syrup 9
Homemade Biscuits 10
Ham and Tomato Sandwiches with Cheese 10
Sausage and Cheese Tater Tots 10
Shrimp and Spinach Rice Frittata 11
Egg Cheese Bread 11
Tomato Corn Frittata with Avocado 11
Eggs in Bell Pepper Rings 12
Spinach and Bacon Cheese Roll-ups 12
Spinach and Bacon Cheese Muffins 12
Sausage and Apple Patties 13
Syrupy Bacon Knots 13
Ham and Cheese Toast 13
Bourbon French Toast 14
Asparagus Cheese Strata 14
Buttermilk Biscuits 14
Cheesy Ham Hash Brown Cups 15
Ham Cheese Omelet 15
Bacon and Egg Cheese Cups 15
Cheese Grits 16
Banana and Chocolate Bread 16
Cheesy Hash Brown Casserole 16
Cornmeal Pancake 17
Chicken Sausages with Apple 17
Banana and Oat Bread Pudding 17
Mushroom and Spinach Cheese Frittata .. 18
Coconut Brown Rice Porridge with Dates .. 18
Carrot and Pepper Frittata 18
Broccoli Cheese Quiche 19
Bacon and Cheese Casserole 19
Kale Cheese Eggs 19
Creamy Sausage and Cheese Quiche 20
Egg and Avocado Cheese Burrito 20
Blueberry Cobbler 20
Potato with Peppers 21
Chili Brown Rice Cheese Quiches 21
Banana and Oat Bread Pudding 21
Avocado and Egg with Cheese 22
Blueberry Muffins 22
Cheese Egg Florentine with Spinach 22
Carrot and Banana Muffins 23
Mixed Berry Pancake 23
Walnut Butter Pancake 23
Brown Sugar Butter Rolls 24
Artichoke Mushroom Cheese Frittata 24

Chapter 3 Vegan and Vegetarian 26

Squash and Parsnip 26
Carrots with Dill 26
Lemony Wax Beans 26
Turnip and Zucchini 26
Brussels Sprouts with Cheese 27
Pecan Granola with Maple Syrup 27
Glazed Red Potato and Mushrooms 27
Zucchini Cheese Quesadilla 28
Broccoli with Sauce 28
Cheesy Broccoli Tots 28
Cauliflower with Paprika 29
Asparagus with Eggs and Tomatoes 29
Brussels Sprouts with Tomatoes 29
Butternut Squash with Cheese 30
Cabbage and Peas with Mango 30
Carrot Tofu with Peanuts 30
Cauliflower with Yogurt and Cashew 31
Carrot and Potato with Thyme 31
Okra with Sour Cream 31
Zucchini and Carrot with Cheese 32
Tofu Carrot and Cauliflower Rice 32
Breaded Zucchini Chips 32

Celery Roots with Butter......................33
Eggplant with Basil 33
Bell Peppers with Garlic 33
Black Beans Cheese Tacos with Salsa 34
Rosemary Beets with Glaze...................34
Glazed Cauliflower 34
Kale with Tahini and Lemon...................35
Breaded Eggplant Slices 35
Tomato Stuffed Mushrooms with Cheese..35
Pea and Mushroom with Rice.................36
Crispy Tofu Strips 36
Lemony Chickpea Oat Meatballs 36
Garlicky Carrots 37
Brussels Sprouts with Chili Sauce 37
Roast Mushrooms 37
Asparagus Spears................................38
Walnut and Cheese Stuffed Mushrooms ...38
Broccoli with Cheese............................38
Egg and Spinach with Basil 39
Eggplant with Yogurt............................39
Cabbage Wedges with Cheese 39
Zucchini and Tomato Ratatouille 40
Garlic Stuffed Mushrooms.....................40
Baked Tofu 40
Squash and Mushroom Mélange............41
Broccoli with Peppercorn......................41
Panko-Crusted Cheese Green Beans........41

Chapter 4 Vegetable Sides...43

Brussels Sprouts with Sage...................43
Air Fried Zucchini Sticks 43
Broccoli with Cheese............................43
Sweet Potato with Lime 44
Green Beans with Sesame Seeds...........44
Peppers with Sauce 44
Asparagus with Garlic 45
Brussels Sprouts with Sauce 45
Butternut Squash Croquettes 45
Carrot with Glaze 46
Panko Cheese Asparagus 46
Corn on the Cob...................................46
Broccoli with Hot Sauce........................47
Cabbage with Red Pepper 47
Cheesy Broccoli Gratin 47
Squash with Cinnamon.........................48
Corn Cheese Casserole.........................48
Potato with Yogurt...............................48
Zucchini Crisps....................................49
Rosemary Potato 49
Creamy Potato 49

Chapter 5 Fish and Seafood 51

Salmon Spring Rolls with Carrot 51
Snapper with Tomato and Olives 51
Panko Fish Fillets.................................52
Cod Fillets with Parsley........................52
Salmon with Teriyaki Sauce...................52
Mustard Sole Fillets..............................53
Breaded Fish Strips..............................53
Tuna and Pineapple Kebabs..................53
Tuna and Lettuce Wraps with Mayo 54
Tilapia and Coleslaw Tacos 54
Salmon Patties 54
Tuna Cubes over Rice...........................55
Tuna Casserole....................................55
Snapper with Plums.............................55
Salmon Patties 56
Beer Cod Fillets...................................56
Basil Salmon with Tomato.....................56
Salmon and Asparagus.........................57
Salmon Steaks with Butter....................57
Swordfish Steaks with Lemon................57
Garlicky Cod Fillets..............................58
Salmon with Asparagus 58
Catfish Fillets with Pecan 58
Salmon Bowl with Salsa........................59
Breaded Catfish Nuggets......................59
Halibut Fillets with Cheese 59
Halibut Steaks with Vermouth 60
Lemony Cod Fillets...............................60
Red Snapper with Lemon......................60
Sole and Cauliflower Fritters 61
Tuna Patties with Cheese Sauce............61
Tilapia Meunière with Potato 62
Potato and Tuna Nicoise Salad 62

Chapter 6 Poultry 64

Italian Herby Chicken with Tomatoes.......64
Crispy Chili Chicken Skin 64
Cajun Chicken Drumsticks 64
Mozzarella Pepperoni and Chicken Pizza...65
Barbecue Chicken Drumsticks 65
Bacon-Wrapped Spiced Chicken Rolls 65
Chicken Drumettes with Buffalo Sauce 66
Bacon-Wrapped Cheesy Chicken Breast ...66

Baked Garlicky Whole Chicken 66
Hawaiian Glazed Chicken Bites 67
Parmesan Breaded Chicken Cutlets 67
Panko-Crusted Chicken Livers 67
Bruschetta Stuffed Chicken 68
Stuffed Chicken Rolls with Bell Peppers ...68
Chicken Goulash....................................68
Baked Turkey and Cauliflower Meatloaf....69
Air-Fried Duck Leg 69
Turkey Scotch Eggs................................69
Chicken Breast Nuggets.........................70
Air-Fried Chicken Wings.........................70
Maple-Mustard Turkey Breast 70
Tangy Chicken Breast with Cilantro 71
Chinese Spiced Turkey Thighs 71
Sweet-Sour Chicken Nuggets 71
Strawberry Puréed-Glazed Turkey Breast .72
Orange-Balsamic Glazed Duck Breasts.....72
Bacon-Wrapped Balsamic Turkey with Carrots 72
Panko-Crusted Chicken Fingers...............73
Parmesan Chicken with Roasted Peanuts..73
Honey-Glazed Chicken 73
Chicken Breast with Veggies and Beans ...74
Air-Fried Apricot-Glazed Drumsticks 74
Cherry Sauce-Glazed Duck.....................75
Pomegranate-Glazed Chicken with Couscous Salad..75
Hearty Chicken Rochambeau with Mushroom Sauce 76
Chicken Tostadas with Coleslaw Topping ..76
Honey Chicken Thighs on Waffles............77
Lettuce-Wrapped Chicken with Peanut Sauce 77
Teriyaki Chicken with Lemony Snow Peas.78
Herby Turkey with Dijon Sauce 78
Cheddar Turkey Burgers 79
Curried Chicken and Sweet Potato 79
Korean-Inspired Chicken Wings 80
Paprika Chicken Skewers with Satay Sauce 80
Oregano-Balsamic Chicken Breast..........81
Parmesan Chicken Ciabatta Sandwiches...81
Lettuce Turkey and Mushroom Taco.........82
Roasted Chicken and Sausage with Peppers 82
Fried Thai Hens with Vegetable Salad 83
Breaded Chicken Schnitzel 83
Chicken and Peppers Skewers with Corn ..84
Air-Fried Chicken and Fingerling Potato....84
Ham-Chicken Meatballs with Lemony Mustard 85
Tandoori Drumsticks 85
Spanish Chicken and Sweet Pepper.........86
Japanese Skewered Chicken (Yakitori).....86

Chapter 7 Appetizers and Snacks..88

Parmesan Ranch Snack Mix....................88
Fish Sticks..88
Buttermilk Fried Chicken Wings 88
Sweet and Spicy Roasted Walnuts...........89
Polenta Fries with Tangy Chili Mayonnaise 89
Coated Pickle Spears.............................89
Parma Prosciutto-Wrapped Pears 90
Small Hush Puppies 90
Buttery Snack Mix 90
Breaded Green Tomatoes with Horseradish 91
Double Cheese Sausage Balls..................91
Breaded Zucchini Tots 91
Homemade Potato Chips........................92
Deviled Eggs wiih Paprika 92
Smoky Sausage and Mushroom Empanadas 92
Roasted Walnuts, Pecans, and Almonds ...93
Apple Chips 93
Sesame Kale Chips 93
Brie Pear Sandwiches............................93
Mozzarella Chicken Sausage Pizza...........94
Panko- Crusted Artichoke Bites...............94
Ham and Cheese Stuffed Mushroom........94
Cuban Pork and Turkey Sandwiches 95
Hot Chickpeas......................................95
Muffuletta with Mozzarella Olives Topping 95
Bruschetta with Parmesan Tomato 96
Turkey Bacon-Wrapped Almond Stuffed Dates..96
Tuna Melts Sandwiches..........................96
Edamame...97
Caramelized Cinnamon Peaches..............97
Italian Cheesy Rice Balls........................97
Ricotta Capers with Lemon Zest..............98
Shrimp Toasts with Thai Chili Sauce 98
Cinnamon Apple Chips 98
Cinnamon Apple Wedges with Yogurt.......99
Spicy Corn Tortilla Chips 99
Spinach and Mushroom Cheese Calzones .99
Air-Fried Old Bay Chicken Wings...........100
Lime Avocado Chips............................100
Corn and Black Bean Chunky Salsa 100

Chapter 8 Desserts 102

Peach and Blueberry Galette 102
Apple-Cinnamon Fritters 102
Mixed Berry Crisp with Coconut Chips.... 103
S'mores 103
Desiccated Coconut-Pineapple Sticks 103
Chocolate Bread Pudding 103
Pistachio and Walnut Baklava 104
Ricotta Cheesecake 104
Cinnamon Candy Covered Apple 104
Walnut-Coconut Tart 105
Butter Shortbread 105
Coffee-Coconut Cake 105
Vanilla Chocolate and Coconut Cake 106
Strawberry and Rhubarb Crisp 106
Tangy Coconut Cake 106
Raspberry Muffins 107
Apple-Peach Crumble with Oatmeal....... 107
Mixed Berries with Mixed Nuts Streusel . 107
Bourbon Chocolate Pecan Pie 108
White Chocolate Cookies 108
Coconut Flake-Coated Pineapple Rings .. 108
Apple-Peach Crisp 109
Pecan-Coconut Cookies 109
Caramelized Fruity Kebabs 109
Apple Wedges with Apricots and Cinnamon 110
Pound Cake 110
Ultimate Chocolate Cheesecake 110
Pumpkin Pudding with Vanilla Wafers Topping 111
Blackberry Goden Cobbler 111
Black and White Chocolate Cake 111
Caramelized Peach with Blueberry Yogurt 112
Maple Blackberry and Peach Cobbler 112
Triple Berry Crisp 112
Fudgy Brownies 113
Fried Banana with Chocolate Sauce 113
Blackberry Almond Muffins 113
Southern Fudge Pie 114
Blackberry Brownie 114
Blueberry Chocolate Cupcakes 114
Pear Tart with Caramel Sauce 115
Chocolate Chip and Oat Cookies 115
Sweet Chocolate Cookies 116
Monk Fruit and Hazelnut Cake 116
Blueberry and Peach Tart 117
Chocolate-Coconut Cake 117

Chapter 9 Wraps and Sandwiches 119

Avocado and Cabbage Slaw Taco 119
Tilapia Fillet Tacos 119
Mushroom, Veggies and Noodle Spring Rolls 120
Beef and Red Onion Taco 120
Salsa Bacon and Egg Cheese Wraps 121
Cod Fillet Taco with Salsa 121
Avocado and Tomato Egg Rolls Wrappers 121
Beef and Bell Pepper Cheese Fajitas 122
Mexican Cheese Potato Taquitos 122
Eggplant Parmesan Hoagies 122
Mozzarella Chicken and Yogurt Taquitos . 123
Thai Curried Pork Burgers 123
Pork and Carrot Momos 123
Turkey and Leek Hamburger 124
Greek Lamb and Feta Hamburgers 124
Curried Shrimp and Zucchini Potstickers 124
English Pea and Potato Samosas 125
Cream Cheese Wontons 125
Potato, Spinach and Black Bean Burritos 126
Prawn and Cabbage Egg Wrappers 126
Spinach and Tomato Pockets 127
Vegetable Spring Rolls 127
Chicken and Cabbage Egg Rolls 128
Chicken and Spring Onion Wraps 128
Beer-Battered Cod Tacos 129
Philly Cheese Steaks 129
Crab Meat and Cream Cheese Wontons .. 130
Japanese Pork and Cabbage Gyoza 130
Turkey Sliders with Chive Mayonnaise ... 131
Cheesy Vegetable Wraps 131
Montreal Steak Hamburgers 132
Korean Bulgogi Burgers 132
Mexican Spiced Chicken Burgers 133
Empanadas de Pollo Verde 133

Chapter 10 Casseroles, Frittata, and Quiche 135

Pimento and Turkey Casserole 135
Creamy Cauliflower and Pumpkin Casserole 135
Pastrami and Bell Pepper Casserole 136
Ranch Cheddar Broccoli Casserole 136
Mushroom and Spinach Frittata 136
Half-and-Half Frittata 136
Sausage and Broccoli Egg Casserole 137
Ritzy Seafood Casserole 137
Beef and Mushroom Casserole 137
Corn Kernels and Bell Pepper Casserole . 138
Asparagus and Grits Casserole 138

Breakfast Sausage and Colorful Peppers Casserole 138
Double Cheese Green Bean Casserole ... 139
Smoky Trout and Crème Fraiche Frittata 139
Asparagus and Goat Cheese Frittata 139
Okra and Cauliflower Casserole 140
Chicken Broccoli Divan 140
Beef and Green Chile Casserole 140
Swiss Chicken and Ham Casserole 141
Classic Mediterranean Quiche 141
Beef and Cannellini Casserole 141
Chicken and Veggies Casserole 142
Shrimp and Baby Spinach Frittata 142
Spinach, Chickpea and Tomato Casserole 142
Broccoli, Tomato, and Carrot Quiche 143
Pork Gratin 143
Chorizo, Potato, and Corn Frittata 143
Lush Veggies Frittata 144
Keto Cheesy Quiche 144

Chapter 11 Holiday Specials 146

Mexican Churros 146
Buttermilk Banana Cake 146
Pork, Cabbage and Mushroom Egg Rolls 147
Blistered Cherry Tomatoes 147
Baked Butter Cake 148
Chocolate Glazed Custard Donut Holes .. 148
Pickle Spears with Buttermilk Dressing . 149
Marinated Olive Stromboli 149
Mini Crescent Dogs 150
Coconut Chocolate Macaroons 150
Blintzes 150
Arancini Balls 151
Nuggets 151
Cream Glazed Cinnamon Rolls 152
Brazilian Cheese Bread 152
Panko-Kale Salad Sushi Rolls 153
Sweet Pecan Tart 153
Sriracha Panko-Crusted Shrimp 154
Teriyaki Panko-Shrimp Skewers 154
Risotto Croquettes 155

Chapter 12 Fast and Easy Everyday Favorites 157

Quick Edamame 157
Okra Chips 157
Cinnamon-Sugar Chickpeas 157
Hot Chicken Wings 157
Crunchy Tortilla Chips 158
Blistered Shishito Peppers 158
Canadian Poutine 158
Crispy Zucchini 159
Beer Battered Onion Rings 159
Fast Corn on the Cob 159
Butternut Squash with Fried-Hazelnuts .. 160
Jalapeño Cheddar Cornbread 160
Maple Bacon Pinwheels 160
French Fries with Ketchup 161
Greek Spinach Pie with Feta 161
Parmesan Cauliflower Patties 161
Candy Coated Pecans 162
Panko-Green Tomatoes Slices 162
Buttered Knots with Parsley 162
Parsnip Fries with Creamy Yogurt Dip 163
Potato Latkes 163
Southwest Lemony Corn and Bell Pepper 163
Cherry Tomato with Basil 164
Air-Fried Brussels Sprouts 164
Vanilla Cinnamon Toast 164
Manchego Cheese Wafers 165
Parmesan Shrimps 165
Chips with Lemony Cream Dip 165
Shrimp, Sausage and Corn Bake 166
Lime Avocado Wedge 166

Chapter 13 Basic Sauce and Dressing 168

Roast Mushrooms with Butter 168
Teriyaki Sauce 168
Enchilada Sauce 168
Spice Mix with Cumin 169
Tomato Marinara Sauce 169
Baked Rice 169
Chile Seasoning 169
Easy Dipping Sauce 170
Salad Dressing 170
Polenta with Butter 170

Appendix 1 Measurement Conversion Chart 171
Appendix 2: Air Fryer Cooking Timetable 172
Appendix 3: Recipe Index 174

Introduction

If you are looking for a great way to prepare healthy meals for you and your family, then air fryers are the way to go. They are fast becoming one of the most important modern kitchen appliances. On this note, you definitely can't go wrong with The Emeril Lagasse Power Air Fryer 360. It offers you modern and easy ways to prepare healthy meals for the whole family. By now you are probably aware of the fact that fryers are especially helpful when you want to fry your foods without the messiness of using oil. Before now, you can get that crispy, fried, and crunchy flavor you love so much if you don't deep fry in oil or fat. However, with the introduction of air fryers, you can now enjoy juicy, crispy, and oil-free meals. You can say goodbye to the unhealthy and messy turbo cyclonic air surrounding your food.

Air fryers are perfect for preparing some of your favorite foods like French fries, cakes, doughnuts, and more.

They work much in the same way as conventional ovens, circulating hot to give you crunchy fried foods containing less fat and calories. In other words, you can eat healthier with the help of an air fryer.

You can introduce your family to great-tasting foods free of unnecessary calories by using the Emeril Lagasse Power Air Fryer 360.

This book is for anyone looking to improve their health by eating healthier meals. It is also for those who want to cook and eat without all the troubles associated with frying with oil. Enjoy oil-free pizzas, fries, and chicken!

If you have been looking for fun and flexibility in the ways to prepare your meals, then you can't go wrong with the Power Air Fryer 360 cookbook. you will even discover that there is more than one way of preparing many recipes in this book. The Emeril Lagasse Power Air Fryer 360 is everything you need to spice up your cooking experience and get you preparing tasty and delicious meals for yourself and your family.

It is a cookbook to guide you on your daily cooking, providing you with new ideas and cooking techniques. You will also discover tips on how you can spice up some of your favorite and classic recipes. The author believes that the time spends in the kitchen should be enjoyable and fun. You can say goodbye to the same old boring recipes. No matter the season, time, occasion, or mode, you can always find a recipe to go with it. If you are looking for a fryer to prepare your meals quickly, then this is it.

Enjoy every bite of your meal, crunchy, or spicy. These invaluable recipes have you covered no matter your preference or that of your family.

Chapter 1

The Emeril Lagasse Power Air Fryer 360

The Emeril Lagasse Power Air Fryer 360 is not just about air frying. it can also perform the functions of conventional ovens, food dehydrators, toasters, and slow cookers. Other things you can do with it include cooking pizzas, warm your foods. What this tells you is that when you get the Emeril Lagasse Power Air Fryer 360, you get a multifunctional kitchen appliance that can do more than you can imagine. It features up to 12 preset cooking functions that you can use in crisping French fries, baking deserts, drying or dehydrating slices of fruits, roasting turkey, reheating leftovers, slow-cooking roasts, and toasting bread.

The Emeril Lagasse Power Air Fryer 360 is one of the few air fryers in the market that comes with an easy-to-read LCD screen that Illuminates blue when in standby or selection mode and illuminates orange when a program is actively operating. This makes it easy to see your settings in real-time.

You can easily set your air fryer to whatever setting you need to prepare your meals thanks to its intuitive controls. The control also includes a knob you can use to change between its preset programs depending on the recipe or meal you want to prepare. The installed presets are especially helpful if you are using the product for the first time and don't know what to do. All you have to do is choose a preset according to what you want to prepare and you are good to go.

Other design and features that make the Emeril Lagasse Power Air Fryer 360 a standout air fryer includes the brightly lighted interior and guide marking which you can see on the door. The purpose of the guide is to help you identify the appropriate rack height suitable for a specific function.

The Emeril Lagasse Power Air Fryer 360 comes with what is called 360° Quick Cook Technology as well as 5 heating elements situated at the top and bottom of the unit fan. Hot air is circulated around your food with the help of a fan. Thanks to its preset cooking functions, you don't have to worry about setting the time and temperature to suit what you want to want to cook.

The manual also made things easier for me as it contains a preset chart filled with lists of time ranges and temperature for all the cooking modes on the Emeril Lagasse Power Air Fryer 360. You can also change the temperature unit from Fahrenheit to Celsius, of and on the interior light, and put of the conventional fan.

The Power Air Fryer 360 also comes with several accessories which are especially helpful in making tasty meals. They include a baking pan, and rotisserie spit, a crisper tray, a drip tray, and a pizza rack. You can prepare or cook multiple trays simultaneously, as it features three rack placements. If you want to dehydrate several fruits at the same time or make French fries, then you may have to buy extra crisper trays separately.

Performance of the Emeril Lagasse Power Air Fryer 360

There are very few air fryers that can beat the Emeril Lagasse Power Air Fryer 360 When it comes to Performance. powerful and efficiency are the two words that describe its performance. On testing one of the fries recipes in this book I discovered that it performs even better than a standard oven. I loaded the crisper tray with a single serving of frozen steak fries and set the Emeril Lagasse Power Air Fryer 360 to the air fryer function which has a set of 400 degrees and an 18-minute timer. The end result was crisp fries with golden exteriors and tender insides. Other preset functions work much, in the same way, resulting in delicious and healthy oil-free meals. You can experience cooking in a whole new and better way.

Dehydrate

The dehydrating function of the Emeril Lagasse Power Air Fryer 360 is just as good as any standalone dehydrator. It is perfect for dehydrating fruits such as apples and bananas. You can enjoy the crispy and delicious taste of banana chips and apple chips. If you love to dehydrate and store your fruits and vegetables then you would definitely love the Emeril Lagasse Power Air Fryer 360 – I was certainly happy with the result I got dehydrating some fruits and vegetables. You can use either use the pizza rack to dehydrate some extra layer of foods, or you can get an additional crisper tray.

Rotisserie

The rotisserie is perfect for dehydrating chicken. You can try out the chicken recipe contained in the Emeril Lagasse Power Air Fryer 360 cookbook and see the amazing result you will get. You don't have to worry if it doesn't go well on your first try.

Bake

This is another excellent preset function of the Emeril Lagasse Power Air Fryer 360. You may have to read the manual to know how you can turn off the air frying fan when using the baking functionality. Turning off the fan allows your appliance to bake in silence. The Emeril Lagasse Power Air Fryer 360 is excellent when it comes to baking cupcakes and other tasty treats.

Pizza

All you have to do to get your pizza prepared is to get your ingredients together and then place the pizza tray before putting it in the unit. The pizza recipe in this book is a great place to start on your pizza-making journey with your appliance. Cleaning after you are done should be easy thanks to the design of the Emeril Lagasse Power Air Fryer 360.

Slow Cook

There are several recipes in the Emeril Lagasse Power Air Fryer 360 cookbook that were initially designed to be prepared with a slow cooker. The Emeril Lagasse Power Air Fryer 360 can also work in much the same way as a slow cooker. This means you can test out many of the recipes in this book. All you have to do is put in your food and choose the appropriate function.

Toast

The toast or bagel preset makes it especially easy to use the Emeril Lagasse Power Air Fryer 360 to toast anything you want. You can adjust the level of toast by using the Temp/Darkness dial and the number of slices with the Time/Slices dial. The machine simply determines the required times and temperature depending on your input and begins toasting. Your toast is ready at the beep.

To get the timing of whatever you are baking right, you have to put the food in the air fryer at the same time it's preheating. This is because the air fryer begins its timer automatically immediately after the oven is heated.

Benefits of the Emeril Lagasse Power Air Fryer 360

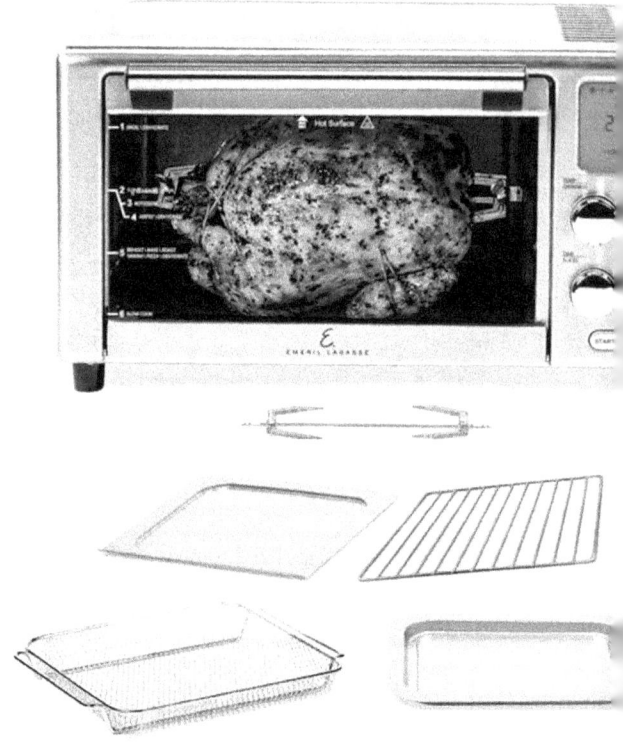

The Emeril Lagasse Power Air Fryer 360 is made with food-grade silicone. This means it is 100% safe to use and is non-toxic.

Easy Cleanup - the container and the air element are designed to be separated from each other. This makes taking them apart easy. The element is designed to be removable. This makes it easy to clean. It also makes it easier to clean, along with the sponge that comes with it.

Food Sealing Mechanism - The food sealing mechanism is a patented airtight seal. This means that your food is airtight and keeps in the freshness and taste of your food.

Temperature Control - The temperature control is made so that the air can be adjusted. For example, you can set a high temperature for frying eggs or something that needs higher heat. You can also monitor the air temperature with a thermometer.

Timer Design - the timer is designed with indicator lights and sound a beep to let you know when the meal is done. The timer can be set to come on every 30 minutes, 1 hour, or an hour and a half.

True Air Frying - Air Frying is the process of using hot air for cooking your food. This cooking method is designed to move the air inside the compartment to be able to cook your food fast.

Compact Design - The Emeril Lagasse Power Air Fryer is compact and small. This can be a benefit if you travel and need to pack light. It makes it easy to travel with. Also, it is easy to keep in small areas.

Material - The Emeril Lagasse Power Air Fryer is made with food-grade silicone. This makes it safe and non-toxic.

User Friendly - With its user-friendly design, you will be able to cook your food while staying within your kitchen. There is little to no mess since the meal drips back into the bowl. Also, there are no cooking smells since there are no open flames.

Using the Accessories

Using the Pizza Rack

- place the drip tray under the heating elements at the bottom of the appliance

- look through the marking or guide on the door to know the recommended shelf position for what you want to prepare.

- place the pizza rack into the recommended position for what you have to prepare. then put your food into the pizza rack.

Using the Baking Pan

- Place the drip tray under the heating elements at the bottom of the appliance
- Look through the marking or guide on the door, to know the recommended shelf position for what you want to prepare.
- Put the baking pan on top of the pizza rack followed by the food you want to bake.

Using the Crisper Tray

- Place the drip tray under the heating elements at the bottom of the appliance
- Look through the marking or guide on the door, to know the recommended shelf position for what you want to prepare. out the food, you want to cook into the crisper tray then place it into the recommended slot.
- Place the baking pan underneath the rack or tray to catch the dripping juices when cooking foods containing more moisture with the crisper tray or pizza rack.

Using the Rotisserie Spit

- Place the drip tray under the heating elements at the bottom of the appliance
- Remove the forks and push the rotisserie spit into the length of the food through its center
- Move the forks into the sides of the spit and make sure they are secured by increasing the tightness of the two screws.
- Insert the rotisserie forks at different angles into the food you want to cook, to properly secure the food on the rotisserie spit.
- Ensure that you are holding the rotisserie spit you have put together at a slight angle – the right side should be higher than the left. Then put the left side of the rotisserie spit into the connection made for it in the appliance.
- When the left side is secured, gently lower the right side into the connection located on the right side of your appliance.
- Push a large fork into the food then twist to the left. Remove the spit from the left slot by slightly raising the spit. Then remove your food by lifting it from the unit. Place the food on a serving plate.

Another feature of the Power Air Fryer 360 I loved is the fact that it comes with a stainless steel visualization window through which you can examine whatever you put in the oven and watch as it cooks.

Cleaning the Emeril Lagasse Power Air Fryer 360

Another great aspect of the Emeril Lagasse Power Air Fryer 360 is that it is easy to clean. You won't have much trouble cleaning thanks to its removable drip pan and cooking trays. Although you may have to line the drip tray with foil to make your cleaning quicker and easier otherwise everything else involving cleaning is simple. Makes sure to remove the power cord from the socket and it is properly cooled before cleaning.

To clean, begin from the door scrubbing both sides with soapy water and a wet cloth – don't submerge or wash with a dishwasher. Then clean the inside with hot water containing a mild detergent using a non-abrasive sponge. Ensure you do not scrub the heating coils. Doing so might damage the coils because they are fragile. Proceed to rinse the appliances with a damp cloth, until no water is left.

With your cleaning time reduced, you can reduce the amount of time you spend in the kitchen and have time for other activities.

About the Recipes and Cookbook

The Emeril Lagasse Power Air Fryer 360 cookbook comes with some excellent and tasty recipes to go with the Emeril Lagasse Power Air Fryer 360. You can say goodbye to your days of crying for a quality fryer that can do the job it's meant to do the right way. No more worrying if you are going to like what's going to come out of the fryer. The perfect combination of the recipes in this book and the Emeril Lagasse Power Air Fryer 360 will get you looking forward to your next time in the kitchen.

The recipes are provided with simple step-by-step instructions you can follow to prepare delicious meals. You are going to be ready to gift your friends and family this book by the time you are done. Every recipe is designed to provide you with all the nutrients and energy you need to stay strong and healthy. All you need to do follow the instructions and make use of the Emeril Lagasse Power Air Fryer 360 to prepare each recipe. Each ingredient has been chosen to fill your mouth with a burst of flavors, that will get you wanting more.

Chapter 2 Breakfasts

Strawberry Toast

Prep time: 5 minutes | Cook time: 8 minutes | Makes 4 toasts

4 slices bread, ½-inch thick
1 cup sliced strawberries
1 teaspoon sugar
Cooking spray

1. On a clean work surface, lay the bread slices and spritz one side of each slice of bread with cooking spray.
2. Place the bread slices in the air fryer basket, sprayed side down. Top with the strawberries and a sprinkle of sugar.
3. Select Air Fry, Super Convection, set temperature to 375°F (190°C), and set time to 8 minutes. Select Start/Stop to begin preheating.
4. Once preheated, place the basket on the air fry position.
5. When cooking is complete, the toast should be well browned on each side. Remove from the oven to a plate and serve.

Bacon and Cheese Muffin Sandwiches

Prep time: 5 minutes | Cook time: 8 minutes | Serves 4

4 English muffins, split
8 slices Canadian bacon
4 slices cheese
Cooking spray

1. Make the sandwiches: Top each of 4 muffin halves with 2 slices of Canadian bacon, 1 slice of cheese, and finish with the remaining muffin half.
2. Put the sandwiches in the air fryer basket and spritz the tops with cooking spray.
3. Select Bake, Super Convection, set temperature to 370°F (188°C), and set time to 8 minutes. Select Start/Stop to begin preheating.
4. Once preheated, place the basket on the bake position. Flip the sandwiches halfway through the cooking time.
5. When cooking is complete, remove the basket from the oven. Divide the sandwiches among four plates and serve warm.

Sweet Potato Chips with Cinnamon

Prep time: 5 minutes | Cook time: 8 minutes | Makes 6 to 8 slices

1 small sweet potato, cut into ⅜ inch-thick slices
2 tablespoons olive oil
1 to 2 teaspoon ground cinnamon

1. Add the sweet potato slices and olive oil in a bowl and toss to coat. Fold in the cinnamon and stir to combine.
2. Lay the sweet potato slices in a single layer in the air fryer basket.
3. Select Air Fry, Super Convection, set temperature to 390°F (199°C), and set time to 8 minutes. Select Start/Stop to begin preheating.
4. Once preheated, place the basket on the air fry position. Stir the potato slices halfway through the cooking time.
5. When cooking is complete, the chips should be crisp. Remove the basket from the oven. Allow to cool for 5 minutes before serving.

Vanilla Granola with Syrup

Prep time: 5 minutes | Cook time: 40 minutes | Serves 4

1 cup rolled oats
3 tablespoons maple syrup
1 tablespoon sunflower oil
1 tablespoon coconut sugar
¼ teaspoon vanilla
¼ teaspoon cinnamon
¼ teaspoon sea salt

1. Mix together the oats, maple syrup, sunflower oil, coconut sugar, vanilla, cinnamon, and sea salt in a medium bowl and stir to combine. Transfer the mixture to a baking pan.
2. Select Bake, Super Convection, set temperature to 248°F (120°C) and set time to 40 minutes. Select Start/Stop to begin preheating.
3. Once preheated, place the pan on the bake position. Stir the granola four times during cooking.
4. When cooking is complete, the granola will be mostly dry and lightly browned.
5. Let the granola stand for 5 to 10 minutes before serving.

Homemade Biscuits

Prep time: 5 minutes | Cook time: 8 minutes | Serves 4

1 (8-ounce / 227-g) can refrigerated biscuits
3 tablespoons melted unsalted butter
¼ cup white sugar
3 tablespoons brown sugar
½ teaspoon cinnamon
⅛ teaspoon nutmeg

1. On a clean work surface, cut each biscuit into 4 pieces.
2. In a shallow bowl, place the melted butter. In another shallow bowl, stir together the white sugar, brown sugar, cinnamon, and nutmeg until combined.
3. Dredge the biscuits, one at a time, in the melted butter, then roll them in the sugar mixture to coat well. Spread the biscuits evenly in a baking pan.
4. Select Bake, Super Convection, set temperature to 350ºF (180ºC) and set time to 8 minutes. Select Start/Stop to begin preheating.
5. Once the oven has preheated, place the pan on the bake position.
6. When cooked, the biscuits should be golden brown.
7. Cool for 5 minutes before serving.

Ham and Tomato Sandwiches with Cheese

Prep time: 5 minutes | Cook time: 8 minutes | Serves 2

1 teaspoon butter, softened
4 slices bread
4 slices smoked country ham
4 slices Cheddar cheese
4 thick slices tomato

1. Spoon ½ teaspoon of butter onto one side of 2 slices of bread and spread it all over.
2. Assemble the sandwiches: Top each of 2 slices of unbuttered bread with 2 slices of ham, 2 slices of cheese, and 2 slices of tomato. Place the remaining 2 slices of bread on top, butter-side up.
3. Lay the sandwiches in the air fryer basket, buttered side down.
4. Select Bake, Super Convection, set temperature to 370ºF (188ºC), and set time to 8 minutes. Select Start/Stop to begin preheating.
5. Once preheated, place the basket on the bake position. Flip the sandwiches halfway through the cooking time.
6. When cooking is complete, the sandwiches should be golden brown on both sides and the cheese should be melted. Remove from the oven. Allow to cool for 5 minutes before slicing to serve.

Sausage and Cheese Tater Tots

Prep time: 5 minutes | Cook time: 17 to 18 minutes | Serves 4

4 eggs
1 cup milk
Salt and pepper, to taste
12 ounces (340 g) ground chicken sausage
1 pound (454 g) frozen tater tots, thawed
¾ cup grated Cheddar cheese
Cooking spray

1. Whisk together the eggs and milk in a medium bowl. Season with salt and pepper to taste and stir until mixed. Set aside.
2. Place a skillet over medium-high heat and spritz with cooking spray. Place the ground sausage in the skillet and break it into smaller pieces with a spatula or spoon. Cook for 3 to 4 minutes until the sausage Start/Stops to brown, stirring occasionally. Remove from heat and set aside.
3. Coat a baking pan with cooking spray. Arrange the tater tots in the baking pan.
4. Select Bake, Super Convection, set temperature to 400ºF (205ºC) and set time to 14 minutes. Select Start/Stop to begin preheating.
5. Once preheated, place the pan on the bake position.
6. After 6 minutes, remove the pan from the oven. Stir the tater tots and add the egg mixture and cooked sausage. Return the pan to the oven and continue cooking.
7. After another 6 minutes, remove the pan from the oven. Scatter the cheese on top of the tater tots. Return the pan to the oven and continue to cook for 2 minutes more.
8. When done, the cheese should be bubbly and melted.
9. Let the mixture cool for 5 minutes and serve warm.

Shrimp and Spinach Rice Frittata

Prep time: 15 minutes | Cook time: 16 minutes | Serves 4

4 eggs
Pinch salt
½ cup cooked rice
½ cup chopped cooked shrimp
½ cup baby spinach
½ cup grated Monterey Jack cheese
Nonstick cooking spray

1. Spritz a baking pan with nonstick cooking spray.
2. Whisk the eggs and salt in a small bowl until frothy.
3. Place the cooked rice, shrimp, and baby spinach in the baking pan. Pour in the whisked eggs and scatter the cheese on top.
4. Select Bake, Super Convection, set temperature to 320ºF (160ºC) and set time to 16 minutes. Select Start/Stop to begin preheating.
5. Once the oven has preheated, place the pan on the bake position.
6. When cooking is complete, the frittata should be golden and puffy.
7. Let the frittata cool for 5 minutes before slicing to serve.

Egg Cheese Bread

Prep time: 5 minutes | Cook time: 5 minutes | Serves 1

1 slice bread
1 teaspoon butter, softened
1 egg
Salt and pepper, to taste
1 tablespoon shredded Cheddar cheese
2 teaspoons diced ham

1. On a flat work surface, cut a hole in the center of the bread slice with a 2½-inch-diameter biscuit cutter.
2. Spread the butter evenly on each side of the bread slice and transfer to a baking dish.
3. Crack the egg into the hole and season as desired with salt and pepper. Scatter the shredded cheese and diced ham on top.
4. Select Bake, Super Convection, set temperature to 330ºF (166ºC), and set time to 5 minutes. Select Start/Stop to begin preheating.
5. Once preheated, place the baking dish on the bake position.
6. When cooking is complete, the bread should be lightly browned and the egg should be set. Remove from the oven and serve hot.

Tomato Corn Frittata with Avocado

Prep time: 10 minutes | Cook time: 20 minutes | Serves 2 or 3

½ cup cherry tomatoes, halved
Kosher salt and freshly ground black pepper, to taste
6 large eggs, lightly beaten
½ cup fresh corn kernels
¼ cup milk
1 tablespoon finely chopped fresh dill
½ cup shredded Monterey Jack cheese

Avocado Dressing:
1 ripe avocado, pitted and peeled
2 tablespoons fresh lime juice
¼ cup olive oil
1 scallion, finely chopped
8 fresh basil leaves, finely chopped

1. Put the tomato halves in a colander and lightly season with salt. Set aside for 10 minutes to drain well. Pour the tomatoes into a large bowl and fold in the eggs, corn, milk, and dill. Sprinkle with salt and pepper and stir until mixed.
2. Pour the egg mixture into a baking pan.
3. Select Bake, Super Convection, set temperature to 300ºF (150ºC) and set time to 15 minutes. Select Start/Stop to begin preheating.
4. Once the oven has preheated, place the pan on the bake position.
5. When done, remove the pan from the oven. Scatter the cheese on top.
6. Select Bake, Super Convection, set temperature to 315ºF (157ºC) and set time to 5 minutes. Return the pan to the oven.
7. Meanwhile, make the avocado dressing: Mash the avocado with the lime juice in a medium bowl until smooth. Mix in the olive oil, scallion, and basil and stir until well incorporated.
8. When cooking is complete, the frittata will be puffy and set. Let the frittata cool for 5 minutes and serve alongside the avocado dressing.

Eggs in Bell Pepper Rings

Prep time: 5 minutes | Cook time: 7 minutes | Serves 4

1 large red, yellow, or orange bell pepper, cut into four ¾-inch rings
4 eggs
Salt and freshly ground black pepper, to taste
2 teaspoons salsa
Cooking spray

1. Coat a baking pan lightly with cooking spray.
2. Put 4 bell pepper rings in the prepared baking pan. Crack one egg into each bell pepper ring and sprinkle with salt and pepper. Top each egg with ½ teaspoon of salsa.
3. Select Air Fry, Super Convection, set temperature to 350ºF (180ºC) and set time to 7 minutes. Select Start/Stop to begin preheating.
4. Once preheated, place the pan on the air fry position.
5. When done, the eggs should be cooked to your desired doneness.
6. Remove the rings from the pan to a plate and serve warm.

Spinach and Bacon Cheese Roll-ups

Prep time: 5 minutes | Cook time: 8 to 9 minutes | Serves 4

4 flour tortillas (6- or 7-inch size)
4 slices Swiss cheese
1 cup baby spinach leaves
4 slices turkey bacon

Special Equipment:
4 toothpicks, soak in water for at least 30 minutes

1. On a clean work surface, top each tortilla with one slice of cheese and ¼ cup of spinach, then tightly roll them up.
2. Wrap each tortilla with a strip of turkey bacon and secure with a toothpick.
3. Arrange the roll-ups in the air fryer basket, leaving space between each roll-up.
4. Select Air Fry, Super Convection, set temperature to 390ºF (199ºC), and set time to 8 minutes. Select Start/Stop to begin preheating.
5. Once preheated, place the basket on the air fry position.
6. After 4 minutes, remove the basket from the oven. Flip the roll-ups with tongs and rearrange them for more even cooking. Return to the oven and continue cooking for another 4 minutes.
7. When cooking is complete, the bacon should be crisp. If necessary, continue cooking for 1 minute more. Remove the basket from the oven. Rest for 5 minutes and remove the toothpicks before serving.

Spinach and Bacon Cheese Muffins

Prep time: 5 minutes | Cook time: 10 minutes | Serves 4

2 strips turkey bacon, cut in half crosswise
2 whole-grain English muffins, split
1 cup fresh baby spinach, long stems removed
¼ ripe pear, peeled and thinly sliced
4 slices Provolone cheese

1. Put the turkey bacon strips in the air fryer basket.
2. Select Air Fry, Super Convection, set temperature to 390ºF (199ºC), and set time to 6 minutes. Select Start/Stop to begin preheating.
3. Once preheated, place the basket on the air fry position. Flip the strips halfway through the cooking time.
4. When cooking is complete, the bacon should be crisp.
5. Remove from the oven and drain on paper towels. Set aside.
6. Put the muffin halves in the air fryer basket.
7. Select Air Fry and set time to 2 minutes. Return the basket to the oven. When done, the muffin halves will be lightly browned.
8. Remove the basket from the oven. Top each muffin half with ¼ of the baby spinach, several pear slices, a strip of turkey bacon, followed by a slice of cheese.
9. Select Bake, Super Convection, set temperature to 360ºF (182ºC), and set time to 2 minutes. Place the basket back to the oven. When done, the cheese will be melted.
10. Serve warm.

Sausage and Apple Patties

Prep time: 5 minutes | Cook time: 10 minutes | Serves 4

1 tablespoon chopped fresh thyme
1 tablespoon chopped fresh sage
1¼ teaspoons kosher salt
1 teaspoon chopped fennel seeds
¾ teaspoon smoked paprika
½ teaspoon onion powder
½ teaspoon garlic powder
⅛ teaspoon crushed red pepper flakes
⅛ teaspoon freshly ground black pepper
1 pound (454 g) 93% lean ground turkey
½ cup finely minced sweet apple (peeled)

1. Thoroughly combine the thyme, sage, salt, fennel seeds, paprika, onion powder, garlic powder, red pepper flakes, and black pepper in a medium bowl.
2. Add the ground turkey and apple and stir until well incorporated. Divide the mixture into 8 equal portions and shape into patties with your hands, each about ¼ inch thick and 3 inches in diameter.
3. Place the patties in the air fryer basket in a single layer.
4. Select Air Fry, Super Convection, set temperature to 400°F (205°C), and set time to 10 minutes. Select Start/Stop to begin preheating.
5. Once preheated, place the basket on the air fry position. Flip the patties halfway through the cooking time.
6. When cooking is complete, the patties should be nicely browned and cooked through. Remove from the oven to a plate and serve warm.

Syrupy Bacon Knots

Prep time: 5 minutes | Cook time: 7 to 8 minutes | Serves 6

1 pound (454 g) maple smoked center-cut bacon
¼ cup maple syrup
¼ cup brown sugar
Coarsely cracked black peppercorns, to taste

1. On a clean work surface, tie each bacon strip in a loose knot.
2. Stir together the maple syrup and brown sugar in a bowl. Generously brush this mixture over the bacon knots.
3. Place the bacon knots in the air fryer basket and sprinkle with the coarsely cracked black peppercorns.
4. Select Air Fry, Super Convection, set temperature to 390°F (199°C), and set time to 8 minutes. Select Start/Stop to begin preheating.
5. Once preheated, place the basket on the air fry position.
6. After 5 minutes, remove the basket from the oven and flip the bacon knots. Return the basket to the oven and continue cooking for 2 to 3 minutes more.
7. When cooking is complete, the bacon should be crisp. Remove from the oven to a paper towel-lined plate. Let the bacon knots cool for a few minutes and serve warm.

Ham and Cheese Toast

Prep time: 5 minutes | Cook time: 6 minutes | Serves: 1

1 slice bread
1 teaspoon butter, at room temperature
1 egg
Salt and freshly ground black pepper, to taste
2 teaspoons diced ham
1 tablespoon grated Cheddar cheese

1. On a clean work surface, use a 2½-inch biscuit cutter to make a hole in the center of the bread slice with about ½-inch of bread remaining.
2. Spread the butter on both sides of the bread slice. Crack the egg into the hole and season with salt and pepper to taste. Transfer the bread to the air fryer basket.
3. Select Air Fry, Super Convection, set temperature to 325°F (163°C), and set time to 6 minutes. Select Start/Stop to begin preheating.
4. Once preheated, place the basket on the air fry position.
5. After 5 minutes, remove the basket from the oven. Scatter the cheese and diced ham on top and continue cooking for an additional 1 minute.
6. When cooking is complete, the egg should be set and the cheese should be melted. Remove the toast from the oven to a plate and let cool for 5 minutes before serving.

Bourbon French Toast

Prep time: 15 minutes | Cook time: 6 minutes | Serves 4

2 large eggs
2 tablespoons water
2/3 cup whole or 2% milk
1 tablespoon butter, melted
2 tablespoons bourbon
1 teaspoon vanilla extract
8 (1-inch-thick) French bread slices
Cooking spray

1. Line the air fryer basket with parchment paper and spray it with cooking spray.
2. Beat the eggs with the water in a shallow bowl until combined. Add the milk, melted butter, bourbon, and vanilla and stir to mix well.
3. Dredge 4 slices of bread in the batter, turning to coat both sides evenly. Transfer the bread slices onto the parchment paper.
4. Select Bake, Super Convection, set temperature to 320ºF (160ºC) and set time to 6 minutes. Select Start/Stop to begin preheating.
5. Once the oven has preheated, place the basket on the bake position. Flip the slices halfway through the cooking time.
6. When cooking is complete, the bread slices should be nicely browned.
7. Remove from the oven to a plate and serve warm.

Asparagus Cheese Strata

Prep time: 10 minutes | Cook time: 17 minutes | Serves 4

6 asparagus spears, cut into 2-inch pieces
1 tablespoon water
2 slices whole-wheat bread, cut into ½-inch cubes
4 eggs
3 tablespoons whole milk
2 tablespoons chopped flat-leaf parsley
½ cup grated Havarti or Swiss cheese
Pinch salt
Freshly ground black pepper, to taste
Cooking spray

1. Add the asparagus spears and 1 tablespoon of water in a baking pan.
2. Select Bake, Super Convection, set temperature to 330ºF (166ºC) and set time to 4 minutes. Select Start/Stop to begin preheating.
3. Once preheated, place the pan on the bake position.
4. When cooking is complete, the asparagus spears will be crisp-tender.
5. Remove the asparagus from the pan and drain on paper towels.
6. Spritz the pan with cooking spray. Place the bread and asparagus in the pan.
7. Whisk together the eggs and milk in a medium mixing bowl until creamy. Fold in the parsley, cheese, salt, and pepper and stir to combine. Pour this mixture into the baking pan.
8. Select Bake, Super Convection and set time to 13 minutes. Place the pan back to the oven. When done, the eggs will be set and the top will be lightly browned.
9. Let cool for 5 minutes before slicing and serving.

Buttermilk Biscuits

Prep time: 5 minutes | Cook time: 18 minutes | Makes 16 biscuits

2½ cups all-purpose flour
1 tablespoon baking powder
1 teaspoon kosher salt
1 teaspoon sugar
½ teaspoon baking soda
8 tablespoons (1 stick) unsalted butter, at room temperature
1 cup buttermilk, chilled

1. Stir together the flour, baking powder, salt, sugar, and baking powder in a large bowl.
2. Add the butter and stir to mix well. Pour in the buttermilk and stir with a rubber spatula just until incorporated.
3. Place the dough onto a lightly floured surface and roll the dough out to a disk, ½ inch thick. Cut out the biscuits with a 2-inch round cutter and re-roll any scraps until you have 16 biscuits.
4. Arrange the biscuits in the air fryer basket in a single layer.
5. Select Bake, Super Convection, set temperature to 325ºF (163ºC), and set time to 18 minutes. Select Start/Stop to begin preheating.
6. Once preheated, place the basket on the bake position.
7. When cooked, the biscuits will be golden brown.
8. Remove from the oven to a plate and serve hot.

Cheesy Ham Hash Brown Cups

Prep time: 10 minutes | Cook time: 9 minutes | Serves 6

4 eggs, beaten
2¼ cups frozen hash browns, thawed
1 cup diced ham
½ cup shredded Cheddar cheese
½ teaspoon Cajun seasoning
Cooking spray

1. Lightly spritz a 12-cup muffin tin with cooking spray.
2. Combine the beaten eggs, hash browns, diced ham, cheese, and Cajun seasoning in a medium bowl and stir until well blended.
3. Spoon a heaping 1½ tablespoons of egg mixture into each muffin cup.
4. Select Bake, Super Convection, set temperature to 350°F (180°C) and set time to 9 minutes. Select Start/Stop to begin preheating.
5. Once preheated, place the muffin tin on the bake position.
6. When cooked, the muffins will be golden brown.
7. Allow to cool for 5 to 10 minutes on a wire rack and serve warm.

Ham Cheese Omelet

Prep time: 5 minutes | Cook time: 20 minutes | Serves 2

¼ cup chopped bell pepper, green or red
¼ cup chopped onion
¼ cup diced ham
1 teaspoon butter
4 large eggs
2 tablespoons milk
⅛ teaspoon salt
¾ cup shredded sharp Cheddar cheese

1. Put the bell pepper, onion, ham, and butter in a baking pan and mix well.
2. Select Air Fry, Super Convection, set temperature to 390°F (199°C) and set time to 5 minutes. Select Start/Stop to begin preheating.
3. Once the oven has preheated, place the pan on the air fry position.
4. After 1 minute, remove the pan from the oven. Stir the mixture. Return the pan to the oven and continue to cook for another 4 minutes.
5. When done, the veggies should be softened.
6. Whisk together the eggs, milk, and salt in a bowl. Pour the egg mixture over the veggie mixture.
7. Select Bake, Super Convection, set temperature to 360°F (182°C) and set time to 15 minutes. Place the pan on the bake position.
8. After 14 minutes, remove the pan from the oven. Scatter the omelet with the shredded cheese. Return the pan to the oven and continue to cook for another 1 minute.
9. When cooking is complete, the top will be lightly golden browned, the eggs will be set and the cheese will be melted.
10. Let the omelet cool for 5 minutes before serving.

Bacon and Egg Cheese Cups

Prep time: 10 minutes | Cook time: 10 minutes | Serves 4

4 (3-by-4-inch) crusty rolls
4 thin slices Gouda or Swiss cheese mini wedges
5 eggs
2 tablespoons heavy cream
3 strips precooked bacon, chopped
½ teaspoon dried thyme
Pinch salt
Freshly ground black pepper, to taste

1. On a clean work surface, cut the tops off the rolls. Using your fingers, remove the insides of the rolls to make bread cups, leaving a ½-inch shell. Place a slice of cheese onto each roll bottom.
2. Whisk together the eggs and heavy cream in a medium bowl until well combined. Fold in the bacon, thyme, salt, and pepper and stir well.
3. Scrape the egg mixture into the prepared bread cups. Arrange the bread cups in the air fryer basket.
4. Select Bake, Super Convection, set temperature to 330°F (166°C) and set time to 10 minutes. Select Start/Stop to begin preheating.
5. Once preheated, place the basket on the bake position.
6. When cooked, the eggs should be cooked to your preference.
7. Serve warm.

Cheese Grits

Prep time: 10 minutes | Cook time: 11 minutes | Serves 4

2/3 cup instant grits
1 teaspoon salt
1 teaspoon freshly ground black pepper
¾ cup whole or 2% milk
3 ounces (85 g) cream cheese, at room temperature
1 large egg, beaten
1 tablespoon butter, melted
1 cup shredded mild Cheddar cheese
Cooking spray

1. Mix the grits, salt, and black pepper in a large bowl. Add the milk, cream cheese, beaten egg, and melted butter and whisk to combine. Fold in the Cheddar cheese and stir well.
2. Spray a baking pan with cooking spray. Spread the grits mixture into the baking pan.
3. Select Air Fry, Super Convection, set temperature to 400°F (205°C) and set time to 11 minutes. Select Start/Stop to begin preheating.
4. Once preheated, place the pan on the air fry position. Stir the mixture halfway through the cooking time.
5. When done, a knife inserted in the center should come out clean.
6. Rest for 5 minutes and serve warm.

Banana and Chocolate Bread

Prep time: 10 minutes | Cook time: 30 minutes | Serves 4

¼ cup cocoa powder
6 tablespoons plus 2 teaspoons all-purpose flour, divided
½ teaspoon kosher salt
¼ teaspoon baking soda
1½ ripe bananas
1 large egg, whisked
¼ cup vegetable oil
½ cup sugar
3 tablespoons buttermilk or plain yogurt (not Greek)
½ teaspoon vanilla extract
6 tablespoons chopped white chocolate
6 tablespoons chopped walnuts

1. Mix together the cocoa powder, 6 tablespoons of the flour, salt, and baking soda in a medium bowl.
2. Mash the bananas with a fork in another medium bowl until smooth. Fold in the egg, oil, sugar, buttermilk, and vanilla, and whisk until thoroughly combined. Add the wet mixture to the dry mixture and stir until well incorporated.
3. Combine the white chocolate, walnuts, and the remaining 2 tablespoons of flour in a third bowl and toss to coat. Add this mixture to the batter and stir until well incorporated. Pour the batter into a baking pan and smooth the top with a spatula.
4. Select Bake, Super Convection, set temperature to 310°F (154°C) and set time to 30 minutes. Select Start/Stop to begin preheating.
5. Once the oven has preheated, place the pan on the bake position.
6. When done, a toothpick inserted into the center of the bread should come out clean.
7. Remove from the oven and allow to cool on a wire rack for 10 minutes before serving.

Cheesy Hash Brown Casserole

Prep time: 15 minutes | Cook time: 30 minutes | Serves 4

3½ cups frozen hash browns, thawed
1 teaspoon salt
1 teaspoon freshly ground black pepper
3 tablespoons butter, melted
1 (10.5-ounce / 298-g) can cream of chicken soup
½ cup sour cream
1 cup minced onion
½ cup shredded sharp Cheddar cheese
Cooking spray

1. Put the hash browns in a large bowl and season with salt and black pepper. Add the melted butter, cream of chicken soup, and sour cream and stir until well incorporated. Mix in the minced onion and cheese and stir well.
2. Spray a baking pan with cooking spray.
3. Spread the hash brown mixture evenly into the baking pan.
4. Select Bake, Super Convection, set temperature to 325°F (163°C) and set time to 30 minutes. Select Start/Stop to begin preheating.
5. Once the oven has preheated, place the pan on the bake position.
6. When cooked, the hash brown mixture will be browned.
7. Cool for 5 minutes before serving.

Cornmeal Pancake

Prep time: 10 minutes | Cook time: 6 minutes | Serves 4

1½ cups yellow cornmeal
½ cup all-purpose flour
2 tablespoons sugar
1 teaspoon salt
1 teaspoon baking powder
1 cup whole or 2% milk
1 large egg, lightly beaten
1 tablespoon butter, melted
Cooking spray

1. Line the air fryer basket with parchment paper.
2. Stir together the cornmeal, flour, sugar, salt, and baking powder in a large bowl. Mix in the milk, egg, and melted butter and whisk to combine.
3. Drop tablespoonfuls of the batter onto the parchment paper for each pancake. Spray the pancakes with cooking spray.
4. Select Bake, Super Convection, set temperature to 350ºF (180ºC) and set time to 6 minutes. Select Start/Stop to begin preheating.
5. Once the oven has preheated, place the basket on the bake position. Flip the pancakes and spray with cooking spray again halfway through the cooking time.
6. When cooking is complete, remove the pancakes from the oven to a plate.
7. Cool for 5 minutes and serve immediately.

Chicken Sausages with Apple

Prep time: 15 minutes | Cook time: 10 minutes | Makes 8 patties

1 Granny Smith apple, peeled and finely chopped
2 tablespoons apple juice
2 garlic cloves, minced
1 egg white
1/3 cup minced onion
3 tablespoons ground almonds
⅛ teaspoon freshly ground black pepper
1 pound (454 g) ground chicken breast

1. Combine all the ingredients except the chicken in a medium mixing bowl and stir well.
2. Add the chicken breast to the apple mixture and mix with your hands until well incorporated.
3. Divide the mixture into 8 equal portions and shape into patties. Arrange the patties in the air fry basket.
4. Select Air Fry, Super Convection, set temperature to 330ºF (166ºC) and set time to 10 minutes. Select Start/Stop to begin preheating.
5. Once the oven has preheated, place the air fry basket on the air fry position.
6. When done, a meat thermometer inserted in the center of the chicken should reach at least 165ºF (74ºC).
7. Remove from the oven to a plate. Let the chicken cool for 5 minutes and serve warm.

Banana and Oat Bread Pudding

Prep time: 10 minutes | Cook time: 16 minutes | Serves 4

2 medium ripe bananas, mashed
½ cup low-fat milk
2 tablespoons maple syrup
2 tablespoons peanut butter
1 teaspoon vanilla extract
1 teaspoon ground cinnamon
2 slices whole-grain bread, cut into bite-sized cubes
¼ cup quick oats
Cooking spray

1. Spritz a baking dish lightly with cooking spray.
2. Mix the bananas, milk, maple syrup, peanut butter, vanilla, and cinnamon in a large mixing bowl and stir until well incorporated.
3. Add the bread cubes to the banana mixture and stir until thoroughly coated. Fold in the oats and stir to combine.
4. Transfer the mixture to the baking dish. Wrap the baking dish in aluminum foil.
5. Select Air Fry, Super Convection, set temperature to 350ºF (180ºC) and set time to 16 minutes. Select Start/Stop to begin preheating.
6. Once the oven has preheated, place the baking dish on the air fry position.
7. After 10 minutes, remove the baking dish from the oven. Remove the foil. Return the baking dish to the oven and continue to cook another 6 minutes.
8. When done, the pudding should be set.
9. Let the pudding cool for 5 minutes before serving.

Mushroom and Spinach Cheese Frittata

Prep time: 10 minutes | Cook time: 22 minutes | Serves 2

4 large eggs
4 ounces (113 g) baby bella mushrooms, chopped
1 cup (1 ounce / 28-g) baby spinach, chopped
½ cup (2 ounces / 57-g) shredded Cheddar cheese
⅓ cup (from 1 large) chopped leek, white part only
¼ cup halved grape tomatoes
1 tablespoon 2% milk
¼ teaspoon dried oregano
¼ teaspoon garlic powder
½ teaspoon kosher salt
Freshly ground black pepper, to taste
Cooking spray

1. Lightly spritz a baking dish with cooking spray.
2. Whisk the eggs in a large bowl until frothy. Add the mushrooms, baby spinach, cheese, leek, tomatoes, milk, oregano, garlic powder, salt, and pepper and stir until well blended. Pour the mixture into the prepared baking dish.
3. Select Bake, Super Convection, set temperature to 300ºF (150ºC) and set time to 22 minutes. Select Start/Stop to begin preheating.
4. Once the oven has preheated, place the dish on the bake position.
5. When cooked, the center will be puffed up and the top will be golden brown.
6. Let the frittata cool for 5 minutes before slicing to serve.

Coconut Brown Rice Porridge with Dates

Prep time: 5 minutes | Cook time: 23 minutes | Serves 1 or 2

½ cup cooked brown rice
1 cup canned coconut milk
¼ cup unsweetened shredded coconut
¼ cup packed dark brown sugar
4 large Medjool dates, pitted and roughly chopped
½ teaspoon kosher salt
¼ teaspoon ground cardamom
Heavy cream, for serving (optional)

1. Place all the ingredients except the heavy cream in a baking pan and stir until blended.
2. Select Bake, Super Convection, set temperature to 375ºF (190ºC) and set time to 23 minutes. Select Start/Stop to begin preheating.
3. Once the oven has preheated, place the pan on the bake position. Stir the porridge halfway through the cooking time.
4. When cooked, the porridge will be thick and creamy.
5. Remove from the oven and ladle the porridge into bowls.
6. Serve hot with a drizzle of the cream, if desired.

Carrot and Pepper Frittata

Prep time: 10 minutes | Cook time: 12 minutes | Serves 4

½ cup chopped red bell pepper
⅓ cup grated carrot
⅓ cup minced onion
1 teaspoon olive oil
1 egg
6 egg whites
⅓ cup 2% milk
1 tablespoon shredded Parmesan cheese

1. Mix together the red bell pepper, carrot, onion, and olive oil in a baking pan and stir to combine.
2. Select Bake, Super Convection, set temperature to 350ºF (180ºC) and set time to 12 minutes. Select Start/Stop to begin preheating.
3. Once preheated, place the pan on the bake position.
4. After 3 minutes, remove the pan from the oven. Stir the vegetables. Return the pan to the oven and continue cooking.
5. Meantime, whisk together the egg, egg whites, and milk in a medium bowl until creamy.
6. After 3 minutes, remove the pan from the oven. Pour the egg mixture over the top and scatter with the Parmesan cheese. Return the pan to the oven and continue cooking for additional 6 minutes.
7. When cooking is complete, the eggs will be set and the top will be golden around the edges.
8. Allow the frittata to cool for 5 minutes before slicing and serving.

Broccoli Cheese Quiche

Prep time: 5 minutes | Cook time: 10 minutes | Serves 4

1 cup broccoli florets
¾ cup chopped roasted red peppers
1¼ cups grated Fontina cheese
6 eggs
¾ cup heavy cream
½ teaspoon salt
Freshly ground black pepper, to taste
Cooking spray

1. Spritz a baking pan with cooking spray
2. Add the broccoli florets and roasted red peppers to the pan and scatter the grated Fontina cheese on top.
3. In a bowl, beat together the eggs and heavy cream. Sprinkle with salt and pepper. Pour the egg mixture over the top of the cheese. Wrap the pan in foil.
4. Select Air Fry, Super Convection, set temperature to 325ºF (163ºC) and set time to 10 minutes. Select Start/Stop to begin preheating.
5. Once preheated, place the pan on the air fry position.
6. After 8 minutes, remove the pan from the oven. Remove the foil. Return the pan to the oven and continue to cook another 2 minutes.
7. When cooked, the quiche should be golden brown.
8. Rest for 5 minutes before cutting into wedges and serve warm.

Bacon and Cheese Casserole

Prep time: 10 minutes | Cook time: 16 minutes | Serves 4

6 slices bacon
6 eggs
Salt and pepper, to taste
Cooking spray
½ cup chopped green bell pepper
½ cup chopped onion
¾ cup shredded Cheddar cheese

1. Place the bacon in a skillet over medium-high heat and cook each side for about 4 minutes until evenly crisp. Remove from the heat to a paper towel-lined plate to drain. Crumble it into small pieces and set aside.
2. Whisk the eggs with the salt and pepper in a medium bowl.
3. Spritz a baking pan with cooking spray.
4. Place the whisked eggs, crumbled bacon, green bell pepper, and onion in the prepared pan.
5. Select Bake, Super Convection, set temperature to 400ºF (205ºC) and set time to 8 minutes. Select Start/Stop to begin preheating.
6. Once preheated, place the pan on the bake position.
7. After 6 minutes, remove the pan from the oven. Scatter the Cheddar cheese all over. Return the pan to the oven and continue to cook another 2 minutes.
8. When cooking is complete, let sit for 5 minutes and serve on plates.

Kale Cheese Eggs

Prep time: 5 minutes | Cook time: 11 minutes | Serves 2

1 cup roughly chopped kale leaves, stems and center ribs removed
¼ cup grated pecorino cheese
¼ cup olive oil
1 garlic clove, peeled
3 tablespoons whole almonds
Kosher salt and freshly ground black pepper, to taste
4 large eggs
2 tablespoons heavy cream
3 tablespoons chopped pitted mixed olives

1. Place the kale, pecorino, olive oil, garlic, almonds, salt, and pepper in a small blender and blitz until well incorporated.
2. One at a time, crack the eggs in a baking pan. Drizzle the kale pesto on top of the egg whites. Top the yolks with the cream and swirl together the yolks and the pesto.
3. Select Bake, Super Convection, set temperature to 300ºF (150ºC) and set time to 11 minutes. Select Start/Stop to begin preheating.
4. Once preheated, place the pan on the bake position.
5. When cooked, the top should begin to brown and the eggs should be set.
6. Allow the eggs to cool for 5 minutes. Scatter the olives on top and serve warm.

Creamy Sausage and Cheese Quiche

Prep time: 5 minutes | Cook time: 25 minutes | Serves 4

12 large eggs
1 cup heavy cream
Salt and black pepper, to taste
12 ounces (340 g) sugar-free breakfast sausage
2 cups shredded Cheddar cheese
Cooking spray

1. Coat a casserole dish with cooking spray.
2. Beat together the eggs, heavy cream, salt and pepper in a large bowl until creamy. Stir in the breakfast sausage and Cheddar cheese.
3. Pour the sausage mixture into the prepared casserole dish.
4. Select Bake, Super Convection, set temperature to 375ºF (190ºC) and set time to 25 minutes. Select Start/Stop to begin preheating.
5. Once the oven has preheated, place the dish on the bake position.
6. When done, the top of the quiche should be golden brown and the eggs will be set.
7. Remove from the oven and let sit for 5 to 10 minutes before serving.

Egg and Avocado Cheese Burrito

Prep time: 10 minutes | Cook time: 4 minutes | Serves 4

4 low-sodium whole-wheat flour tortillas
Filling:
1 hard-boiled egg, chopped
2 hard-boiled egg whites, chopped
1 ripe avocado, peeled, pitted, and chopped
1 red bell pepper, chopped
1 (1.2-ounce / 34-g) slice low-sodium, low-fat American cheese, torn into pieces
3 tablespoons low-sodium salsa, plus additional for serving (optional)

Special Equipment:
4 toothpicks (optional), soaked in water for at least 30 minutes

1. Make the filling: Combine the egg, egg whites, avocado, red bell pepper, cheese, and salsa in a medium bowl and stir until blended.
2. Assemble the burritos: Arrange the tortillas on a clean work surface and place ¼ of the prepared filling in the middle of each tortilla, leaving about 1½-inch on each end unfilled. Fold in the opposite sides of each tortilla and roll up. Secure with toothpicks through the center, if needed.
3. Transfer the burritos to the air fry basket.
4. Select Air Fry, Super Convection, set temperature to 390ºF (199ºC) and set time to 4 minutes. Select Start/Stop to begin preheating.
5. Once the oven has preheated, place the air fry basket on the air fry position.
6. When cooking is complete, the burritos should be crisp and golden brown.
7. Allow to cool for 5 minutes and serve with salsa, if desired.

Blueberry Cobbler

Prep time: 5 minutes | Cook time: 15 minutes | Serves 4

¾ teaspoon baking powder
⅓ cup whole-wheat pastry flour
Dash sea salt
⅓ cup unsweetened nondairy milk
2 tablespoons maple syrup
½ teaspoon vanilla
Cooking spray
½ cup blueberries
¼ cup granola
Nondairy yogurt, for topping (optional)

1. Spritz a baking pan with cooking spray.
2. Mix together the baking powder, flour, and salt in a medium bowl. Add the milk, maple syrup, and vanilla and whisk to combine.
3. Scrape the mixture into the prepared pan. Scatter the blueberries and granola on top.
4. Select Bake, Super Convection, set temperature to 347ºF (175ºC) and set time to 15 minutes. Select Start/Stop to begin preheating.
5. Once preheated, place the pan on the bake position.
6. When done, the top should begin to brown and a knife inserted in the center should come out clean.
7. Let the cobbler cool for 5 minutes and serve with a drizzle of nondairy yogurt.

Potato with Peppers

Prep time: 10 minutes | Cook time: 35 minutes | Serves 4

1 pound (454 g) red potatoes, cut into ½-inch dices
1 large red bell pepper, cut into ½-inch dices
1 large green bell pepper, cut into ½-inch dices
1 medium onion, cut into ½-inch dices
1½ tablespoons extra-virgin olive oil
1¼ teaspoons kosher salt
¾ teaspoon sweet paprika
¾ teaspoon garlic powder
Freshly ground black pepper, to taste

1. Mix together the potatoes, bell peppers, onion, oil, salt, paprika, garlic powder, and black pepper in a large mixing and toss to coat.
2. Transfer the potato mixture to the air fry basket.
3. Select Air Fry, Super Convection, set temperature to 350ºF (180ºC) and set time to 35 minutes. Select Start/Stop to begin preheating.
4. Once preheated, place the air fry basket on the air fry position. Stir the potato mixture three times during cooking.
5. When done, the potatoes should be nicely browned.
6. Remove from the oven to a plate and serve warm.

Chili Brown Rice Cheese Quiches

Prep time: 10 minutes | Cook time: 14 minutes | Serves 6

4 ounces (113 g) diced green chilies
3 cups cooked brown rice
1 cup shredded reduced-fat Cheddar cheese, divided
½ cup egg whites
⅓ cup fat-free milk
¼ cup diced pimiento
½ teaspoon cumin
1 small eggplant, cubed
1 bunch fresh cilantro, finely chopped
Cooking spray

1. Spritz a 12-cup muffin pan with cooking spray.
2. In a large bowl, stir together all the ingredients, except for ½ cup of the cheese.
3. Scoop the mixture evenly into the muffin cups and sprinkle the remaining ½ cup of the cheese on top.
4. Select Bake, Super Convection, set temperature to 400ºF (205ºC) and set time to 14 minutes. Select Start/Stop to begin preheating.
5. Once the unit has preheated, place the pan on the bake position.
6. When cooking is complete, remove the pan and check the quiches. They should be set.
7. Carefully transfer the quiches to a platter and serve immediately.

Banana and Oat Bread Pudding

Prep time: 10 minutes | Cook time: 18 minutes | Serves 4

2 medium ripe bananas, mashed
½ cup low-fat milk
2 tablespoons maple syrup
2 tablespoons peanut butter
1 teaspoon vanilla extract
1 teaspoon ground cinnamon
2 slices whole-grain bread, torn into bite-sized pieces
¼ cup quick oats
Cooking spray

1. Spritz the sheet pan with cooking spray.
2. In a large bowl, combine the bananas, milk, maple syrup, peanut butter, vanilla extract and cinnamon. Use an immersion blender to mix until well combined.
3. Stir in the bread pieces to coat well. Add the oats and stir until everything is combined.
4. Transfer the mixture to the sheet pan. Cover with the aluminum foil.
5. Select Air Fry, Super Convection, set temperature to 375ºF (190ºC) and set time to 18 minutes. Select Start/Stop to begin preheating.
6. Once the unit has preheated, place the pan on the air fry position.
7. After 10 minutes, remove the foil and continue to cook for 8 minutes.
8. Serve immediately.

Avocado and Egg with Cheese

Prep time: 5 minutes | Cook time: 9 minutes | Serves 2

1 large avocado, halved and pitted
2 large eggs
2 tomato slices, divided
½ cup nonfat Cottage cheese, divided
½ teaspoon fresh cilantro, for garnish

1. Line the sheet pan with the aluminium foil.
2. Slice a thin piece from the bottom of each avocado half so they sit flat. Remove a small amount from each avocado half to make a bigger hole to hold the egg.
3. Arrange the avocado halves on the pan, hollow-side up. Break 1 egg into each half. Top each half with 1 tomato slice and ¼ cup of the Cottage cheese.
4. Select Bake, Super Convection, set temperature to 425ºF (220ºC) and set time to 9 minutes. Select Start/Stop to begin preheating.
5. Once the unit has preheated, place the pan on the bake position.
6. When cooking is complete, remove the pan from the oven. Garnish with the fresh cilantro and serve.

Blueberry Muffins

Prep time: 5 minutes | Cook time: 25 minutes | Makes 8 muffins

½ cup unsweetened applesauce
½ cup plant-based milk
½ cup maple syrup
1 teaspoon vanilla extract
2 cups whole-wheat flour
½ teaspoon baking soda
1 cup blueberries
Cooking spray

1. Spritz a 8-cup muffin pan with cooking spray.
2. In a large bowl, stir together the applesauce, milk, maple syrup and vanilla extract. Whisk in the flour and baking soda until no dry flour is left and the batter is smooth. Gently mix in the blueberries until they are evenly distributed throughout the batter.
3. Spoon the batter into the muffin cups, three-quarters full.
4. Select Bake, Super Convection, set temperature to 375ºF (190ºC) and set time to 25 minutes. Select Start/Stop to begin preheating.
5. Once preheated, place the pan on the bake position.
6. When cooking is complete, remove the pan and check the muffins. You can stick a knife into the center of a muffin and it should come out clean.
7. Let rest for 5 minutes before serving.

Cheese Egg Florentine with Spinach

Prep time: 10 minutes | Cook time: 15 minutes | Serves 4

3 cups frozen spinach, thawed and drained
2 tablespoons heavy cream
¼ teaspoon kosher salt
⅛ teaspoon freshly ground black pepper
4 ounces (113 g) Ricotta cheese
2 garlic cloves, minced
½ cup panko bread crumbs
3 tablespoons grated Parmesan cheese
2 teaspoons unsalted butter, melted
4 large eggs

1. In a medium bowl, whisk together the spinach, heavy cream, salt, pepper, Ricotta cheese and garlic.
2. In a small bowl, whisk together the bread crumbs, Parmesan cheese and butter. Set aside.
3. Spoon the spinach mixture on the sheet pan and form four even circles.
4. Select Roast, Super Convection, set temperature to 375ºF (190ºC) and set time to 15 minutes. Select Start/Stop to begin preheating.
5. Once the unit has preheated, place the pan on the roast position.
6. After 8 minutes, remove the pan from the oven. The spinach should be bubbling. With the back of a large spoon, make indentations in the spinach for the eggs. Crack the eggs into the indentations and sprinkle the panko mixture over the surface of the eggs. Return the pan to the oven to continue cooking.
7. When cooking is complete, remove the pan from the oven. Serve hot.

Carrot and Banana Muffins

Prep time: 10 minutes | Cook time: 20 minutes | Serves 12

1½ cups whole-wheat flour
1 cup grated carrot
1 cup mashed banana
½ cup bran
½ cup low-fat buttermilk
2 tablespoons agave nectar
2 teaspoons baking powder
1 teaspoon vanilla
1 teaspoon baking soda
½ teaspoon nutmeg
Pinch cloves
2 egg whites

1. Line a muffin pan with 12 paper liners.
2. In a large bowl, stir together all the ingredients. Mix well, but do not over beat.
3. Scoop the mixture into the muffin cups.
4. Select Bake, Super Convection, set temperature to 400ºF (205ºC) and set time to 20 minutes. Select Start/Stop to begin preheating.
5. Once the unit has preheated, place the pan on the bake position.
6. When cooking is complete, remove the pan and let rest for 5 minutes.
7. Serve warm or at room temperature.

Mixed Berry Pancake

Prep time: 10 minutes | Cook time: 14 minutes | Serves 4

1 tablespoon unsalted butter, at room temperature
1 egg
2 egg whites
½ cup 2% milk
½ cup whole-wheat pastry flour
1 teaspoon pure vanilla extract
1 cup sliced fresh strawberries
½ cup fresh raspberries
½ cup fresh blueberries

1. Grease a baking pan with the butter.
2. Using a hand mixer, beat together the egg, egg whites, milk, pastry flour, and vanilla in a medium mixing bowl until well incorporated.
3. Pour the batter into the pan.
4. Select Bake, Super Convection, set temperature to 330ºF (166ºC) and set time to 14 minutes. Select Start/Stop to begin preheating.
5. Once the oven has preheated, place the pan on the bake position.
6. When cooked, the pancake should puff up in the center and the edges should be golden brown
7. Allow the pancake to cool for 5 minutes and serve topped with the berries.

Walnut Butter Pancake

Prep time: 10 minutes | Cook time: 20 minutes | Serves 4

3 tablespoons melted butter, divided
1 cup flour
2 tablespoons sugar
1½ teaspoons baking powder
¼ teaspoon salt
1 egg, beaten
¾ cup milk
1 teaspoon pure vanilla extract
½ cup roughly chopped walnuts
Maple syrup or fresh sliced fruit, for serving

1. Grease a baking pan with 1 tablespoon of melted butter.
2. Mix together the flour, sugar, baking powder, and salt in a medium bowl. Add the beaten egg, milk, the remaining 2 tablespoons of melted butter, and vanilla and stir until the batter is sticky but slightly lumpy.
3. Slowly pour the batter into the greased baking pan and scatter with the walnuts.
4. Select Bake, Super Convection, set temperature to 330ºF (166ºC) and set time to 20 minutes. Select Start/Stop to begin preheating.
5. Once preheated, place the pan on the bake position.
6. When cooked, the pancake should be golden brown and cooked through.
7. Let the pancake rest for 5 minutes and serve topped with the maple syrup or fresh fruit, if desired.

Brown Sugar Butter Rolls

Prep time: 5 minutes | Cook time: 25 minutes | Makes 18 rolls

1/3 cup light brown sugar
2 teaspoons cinnamon
1 (9-by-9-inch) frozen puff pastry sheet, thawed
All-purpose flour, for dusting
6 teaspoons unsalted butter, melted, divided

1. In a small bowl, stir together the brown sugar and cinnamon.
2. On a clean work surface, lightly dust with the flour and lay the puff pastry sheet. Using a rolling pin, press the folds together and roll the dough out in one direction so that it measures about 9 by 11 inches. Cut it in half to form two squat rectangles of about 5½ by 9 inches.
3. Brush 2 teaspoons of the butter over each pastry half. Sprinkle with 2 tablespoons of the cinnamon sugar. Pat it down lightly with the palm of your hand to help it adhere to the butter.
4. Starting with the 9-inch side of one rectangle. Using your hands, carefully roll the dough into a cylinder. Repeat with the other rectangle. To make slicing easier, refrigerate the rolls for 10 to 20 minutes.
5. Using a sharp knife, slice each roll into nine 1-inch pieces. Transfer the rolls to the center of the sheet pan. They should be very close to each other, but not quite touching. Drizzle the remaining 2 teaspoons of the butter over the rolls and sprinkle with the remaining cinnamon sugar.
6. Select Bake, Super Convection, set temperature to 350°F (180°C) and set time to 25 minutes. Select Start/Stop to begin preheating.
7. Once the unit has preheated, place the pan on the bake position.
8. When cooking is complete, remove the pan and check the rolls. They should be puffed up and golden brown.
9. Let the rolls rest for 5 minutes and transfer them to a wire rack to cool completely. Serve.

Artichoke Mushroom Cheese Frittata

Prep time: 10 minutes | Cook time: 15 minutes | Serves 6

8 eggs
½ teaspoon kosher salt
¼ cup whole milk
¾ cup shredded Mozzarella cheese, divided
2 tablespoons unsalted butter, melted
1 cup coarsely chopped artichoke hearts
¼ cup chopped onion
½ cup mushrooms
¼ cup grated Parmesan cheese
¼ teaspoon freshly ground black pepper

1. In a medium bowl, whisk together the eggs and salt. Let rest for a minute or two, then pour in the milk and whisk again. Stir in ½ cup of the Mozzarella cheese.
2. Grease the sheet pan with the butter. Stir in the artichoke hearts and onion and toss to coat with the butter.
3. Select Roast, Super Convection, set temperature to 375°F (190°C) and set time to 12 minutes. Select Start/Stop to begin preheating.
4. Once the unit has preheated, place the pan on the roast position.
5. After 5 minutes, remove the pan. Spread the mushrooms over the vegetables. Pour the egg mixture on top. Stir gently just to distribute the vegetables evenly. Return the pan to the oven and continue cooking for 5 to 7 minutes, or until the edges are set. The center will still be quite liquid.
6. Select Broil, Super Convection, set temperature to Low and set time to 3 minutes. Place the pan on the broil position.
7. After 1 minute, remove the pan and sprinkle the remaining ¼ cup of the Mozzarella and Parmesan cheese over the frittata. Return the pan to the oven and continue cooking for 2 minutes.
8. When cooking is complete, the cheese should be melted with the top completely set but not browned. Sprinkle the black pepper on top and serve.

Chapter 3 Vegan and Vegetarian

Squash and Parsnip

Prep time: 5 minutes | Cook time: 16 minutes | Serves 2

1 parsnip, sliced
1 cup sliced butternut squash
1 small red onion, cut into wedges
½ chopped celery stalk
1 tablespoon chopped fresh thyme
2 teaspoons olive oil
Salt and black pepper, to taste

1. Toss all the ingredients in a large bowl until the vegetables are well coated.
2. Transfer the vegetables to the air fry basket.
3. Select Air Fry, Super Convection, set temperature to 380ºF (193ºC), and set time to 16 minutes. Select Start/Stop to begin preheating.
4. Once preheated, place the basket on the air fry position. Stir the vegetables halfway through the cooking time.
5. When cooking is complete, the vegetables should be golden brown and tender. Remove from the oven and serve warm.

Lemony Wax Beans

Prep time: 5 minutes | Cook time: 12 minutes | Serves 4

2 pounds (907 g) wax beans
2 tablespoons extra-virgin olive oil
Salt and freshly ground black pepper, to taste
Juice of ½ lemon, for serving

1. Line a baking sheet with aluminum foil.
2. Toss the wax beans with the olive oil in a large bowl. Lightly season with salt and pepper.
3. Spread out the wax beans on the sheet pan.
4. Select Roast, Super Convection, set temperature to 400ºF (205ºC), and set time to 12 minutes. Select Start/Stop to begin preheating.
5. Once preheated, place the baking sheet on the roast position.
6. When done, the beans will be caramelized and tender. Remove from the oven to a plate and serve sprinkled with the lemon juice.

Carrots with Dill

Prep time: 5 minutes | Cook time: 12 minutes | Serves 4

1 pound (454 g) baby carrots
2 tablespoons olive oil
1 tablespoon honey
1 teaspoon dried dill
Salt and black pepper, to taste

1. Place the carrots in a large bowl. Add the olive oil, honey, dill, salt, and pepper and toss to coat well.
2. Transfer the carrots to the air fry basket.
3. Select Roast, Super Convection, set temperature to 350ºF (180ºC), and set time to 12 minutes. Select Start/Stop to begin preheating.
4. Once preheated, place the basket on the roast position. Stir the carrots once during cooking.
5. When cooking is complete, the carrots should be crisp-tender. Remove from the oven and serve warm.

Turnip and Zucchini

Prep time: 5 minutes | Cook time: 18 minutes | Serves 4

3 turnips, sliced
1 large zucchini, sliced
1 large red onion, cut into rings
2 cloves garlic, crushed
1 tablespoon olive oil
Salt and black pepper, to taste

1. Put the turnips, zucchini, red onion, and garlic in a baking pan. Drizzle the olive oil over the top and sprinkle with the salt and pepper.
2. Select Bake, Super Convection, set temperature to 330ºF (166ºC), and set time to 18 minutes. Select Start/Stop to begin preheating.
3. Once preheated, place the pan on the bake position.
4. When cooking is complete, the vegetables should be tender. Remove from the oven and serve on a plate.

Brussels Sprouts with Cheese

Prep time: 10 minutes | Cook time: 20 minutes | Serves 4

1 pound (454 g) fresh Brussels sprouts, trimmed
1 tablespoon olive oil
½ teaspoon salt
⅛ teaspoon pepper
¼ cup grated Parmesan cheese

1. In a large bowl, combine the Brussels sprouts with olive oil, salt, and pepper and toss until evenly coated.
2. Spread the Brussels sprouts evenly in the air fry basket.
3. Select Air Fry, Super Convection, set temperature to 330ºF (166ºC), and set time to 20 minutes. Select Start/Stop to begin preheating.
4. Once preheated, place the air fry basket on the air fry position. Stir the Brussels sprouts twice during cooking.
5. When cooking is complete, the Brussels sprouts should be golden brown and crisp. Remove the basket from the oven. Sprinkle the grated Parmesan cheese on top and serve warm.

Pecan Granola with Maple Syrup

Prep time: 5 minutes | Cook time: 20 minutes | Serves 4

1½ cups rolled oats
¼ cup maple syrup
¼ cup pecan pieces
1 teaspoon vanilla extract
½ teaspoon ground cinnamon

1. Line a baking sheet with parchment paper.
2. Mix together the oats, maple syrup, pecan pieces, vanilla, and cinnamon in a large bowl and stir until the oats and pecan pieces are completely coated. Spread the mixture evenly on the baking sheet.
3. Select Bake, Super Convection, set temperature to 300ºF (150ºC), and set time to 20 minutes. Select Start/Stop to begin preheating.
4. Once preheated, place the baking sheet on the bake position. Stir once halfway through the cooking time.
5. When done, remove from the oven and cool for 30 minutes before serving. The granola may still be a bit soft right after removing, but it will gradually firm up as it cools.

Glazed Red Potato and Mushrooms

Prep time: 15 minutes | Cook time: 20 minutes | Makes 3 cups

Glaze:
2 tablespoons raw honey
2 teaspoons minced garlic
¼ teaspoon dried marjoram
¼ teaspoon dried basil
¼ teaspoon dried oregano
⅛ teaspoon dried sage
⅛ teaspoon dried rosemary
⅛ teaspoon dried thyme
½ teaspoon salt
¼ teaspoon ground black pepper

Veggies:
3 to 4 medium red potatoes, cut into 1- to 2-inch pieces
1 small zucchini, cut into 1- to 2-inch pieces
1 small carrot, sliced into ¼-inch rounds
1 (10.5-ounce / 298-g) package cherry tomatoes, halved
1 cup sliced mushrooms
3 tablespoons olive oil

1. Combine the honey, garlic, marjoram, basil, oregano, sage, rosemary, thyme, salt, and pepper in a small bowl and stir to mix well. Set aside.
2. Place the red potatoes, zucchini, carrot, cherry tomatoes, and mushroom in a large bowl. Drizzle with the olive oil and toss to coat.
3. Pour the veggies into the air fry basket.
4. Select Roast, Super Convection, set temperature to 380ºF (193ºC) and set time to 15 minutes. Select Start/Stop to begin preheating.
5. Once preheated, place the basket on the roast position. Stir the veggies halfway through.
6. When cooking is complete, the vegetables should be tender.
7. When ready, transfer the roasted veggies to the large bowl. Pour the honey mixture over the veggies, tossing to coat.
8. Spread out the veggies in a baking pan and place in the oven.
9. Increase the temperature to 390ºF (199ºC) and set time to 5 minutes on Roast, Super Convection. Place the basket on the roast position.
10. When cooking is complete, the veggies should be tender and glazed. Serve warm.

Zucchini Cheese Quesadilla

Prep time: 5 minutes | Cook time: 10 minutes | Serves 1

1 teaspoon olive oil
2 flour tortillas
¼ zucchini, sliced
¼ yellow bell pepper, sliced
¼ cup shredded gouda cheese
1 tablespoon chopped cilantro
½ green onion, sliced

1. Coat the air fry basket with 1 teaspoon of olive oil.
2. Arrange a flour tortilla in the air fry basket and scatter the top with zucchini, bell pepper, gouda cheese, cilantro, and green onion. Place the other flour tortilla on top.
3. Select Air Fry, Super Convection, set temperature to 390ºF (199ºC), and set time to 10 minutes. Select Start/Stop to begin preheating.
4. Once preheated, place the basket on the air fry position.
5. When cooking is complete, the tortillas should be lightly browned and the vegetables should be tender. Remove from the oven and cool for 5 minutes before slicing into wedges.

Broccoli with Sauce

Prep time: 10 minutes | Cook time: 15 to 20 minutes | Serves 4

½ teaspoon olive oil, plus more for greasing
1 pound (454 g) fresh broccoli, cut into florets
½ tablespoon minced garlic
Salt, to taste
Sauce:
1½ tablespoons soy sauce
2 teaspoons hot sauce or sriracha
1½ teaspoons honey
1 teaspoon white vinegar
Freshly ground black pepper, to taste

1. Grease the air fry basket with olive oil.
2. Add the broccoli florets, ½ teaspoon of olive oil, and garlic to a large bowl and toss well. Season with salt to taste.
3. Put the broccoli in the air fry basket in a single layer.
4. Select Air Fry, Super Convection, set temperature to 400ºF (205ºC), and set time to 15 minutes. Select Start/Stop to begin preheating.
5. Once preheated, place the air fry basket on the air fry position. Stir the broccoli florets three times during cooking.
6. Meanwhile, whisk together all the ingredients for the sauce in a small bowl until well incorporated. If the honey doesn't incorporate well, microwave the sauce for 10 to 20 seconds until the honey is melted.
7. When cooking is complete, the broccoli should be lightly browned and crispy. Continue cooking for 5 minutes, if desired. Remove from the oven to a serving bowl. Pour over the sauce and toss to combine. Add more salt and pepper, if needed. Serve warm.

Cheesy Broccoli Tots

Prep time: 20 minutes | Cook time: 15 minutes | Serves 4

12 ounces (340 g) frozen broccoli, thawed, drained, and patted dry
1 large egg, lightly beaten
½ cup seasoned whole-wheat bread crumbs
¼ cup shredded reduced-fat sharp Cheddar cheese
¼ cup grated Parmesan cheese
1½ teaspoons minced garlic
Salt and freshly ground black pepper, to taste
Cooking spray

1. Spritz the air fry basket lightly with cooking spray.
2. Place the remaining ingredients into a food processor and process until the mixture resembles a coarse meal. Transfer the mixture to a bowl.
3. Using a tablespoon, scoop out the broccoli mixture and form into 24 oval "tater tot" shapes with your hands.
4. Put the tots in the prepared basket in a single layer, spacing them 1 inch apart. Mist the tots lightly with cooking spray.
5. Select Air Fry, Super Convection, set temperature to 375ºF (190ºC), and set time to 15 minutes. Select Start/Stop to begin preheating.
6. Once preheated, place the air fry basket on the air fry position. Flip the tots halfway through the cooking time.
7. When done, the tots will be lightly browned and crispy. Remove from the oven and serve on a plate.

Cauliflower with Paprika

Prep time: 10 minutes | Cook time: 20 minutes | Serves 4

1 large head cauliflower, broken into small florets
2 teaspoons smoked paprika
1 teaspoon garlic powder
Salt and freshly ground black pepper, to taste
Cooking spray

1. Spray the air fry basket with cooking spray.
2. In a medium bowl, toss the cauliflower florets with the smoked paprika and garlic powder until evenly coated. Sprinkle with salt and pepper.
3. Place the cauliflower florets in the air fry basket and lightly mist with cooking spray.
4. Select Air Fry, Super Convection, set temperature to 400ºF (205ºC), and set time to 20 minutes. Select Start/Stop to begin preheating.
5. Once preheated, place the air fry basket on the air fry position. Stir the cauliflower four times during cooking.
6. Remove the cauliflower from the oven and serve hot.

Asparagus with Eggs and Tomatoes

Prep time: 10 minutes | Cook time: 12 minutes | Serves 4

2 pounds (907 g) asparagus, trimmed
3 tablespoons extra-virgin olive oil, divided
1 teaspoon kosher salt, divided
1 pint cherry tomatoes
4 large eggs
¼ teaspoon freshly ground black pepper

1. Put the asparagus on the sheet pan and drizzle with 2 tablespoons of olive oil, tossing to coat. Season with ½ teaspoon of kosher salt.
2. Select Roast, Super Convection, set temperature to 375ºF (190ºC), and set time to 12 minutes. Select Start/Stop to begin preheating.
3. Once preheated, place the pan on the roast position.
4. Meanwhile, toss the cherry tomatoes with the remaining 1 tablespoon of olive oil in a medium bowl until well coated.
5. After 6 minutes, remove the pan and toss the asparagus. Evenly spread the asparagus in the middle of the sheet pan. Add the tomatoes around the perimeter of the pan. Return the pan to the oven and continue cooking.
6. After 2 minutes, remove the pan from the oven.
7. Carefully crack the eggs, one at a time, over the asparagus, spacing them out. Season with the remaining ½ teaspoon of kosher salt and the pepper. Return the pan to the oven and continue cooking. Cook for an additional 3 to 7 minutes, or until the eggs are cooked to your desired doneness.
8. When done, divide the asparagus and eggs among four plates. Top each plate evenly with the tomatoes and serve.

Brussels Sprouts with Tomatoes

Prep time: 15 minutes | Cook time: 20 minutes | Serves 4

1 pound (454 g) Brussels sprouts, trimmed and halved
1 tablespoon extra-virgin olive oil
Sea Salt and freshly ground black pepper, to taste
½ cup sun-dried tomatoes, chopped
2 tablespoons freshly squeezed lemon juice
1 teaspoon lemon zest

1. Line a large baking sheet with aluminum foil.
2. Toss the Brussels sprouts with the olive oil in a large bowl. Sprinkle with salt and black pepper.
3. Spread the Brussels sprouts in a single layer on the baking sheet.
4. Select Roast, Super Convection, set temperature to 400ºF (205ºC), and set time to 20 minutes. Select Start/Stop to begin preheating.
5. Once preheated, place the baking sheet on the roast position.
6. When done, the Brussels sprouts should be caramelized. Remove from the oven to a serving bowl, along with the tomatoes, lemon juice, and lemon zest. Toss to combine. Serve immediately.

Butternut Squash with Cheese

Prep time: 5 minutes | Cook time: 20 minutes | Serves 2

1 pound (454 g) butternut squash, cut into wedges
2 tablespoons olive oil
1 tablespoon dried rosemary
Salt, to salt
1 cup crumbled goat cheese
1 tablespoon maple syrup

1. Toss the squash wedges with the olive oil, rosemary, and salt in a large bowl until well coated.
2. Transfer the squash wedges to the air fry basket, spreading them out in as even a layer as possible.
3. Select Air Fry, Super Convection, set temperature to 350ºF (180ºC), and set time to 20 minutes. Select Start/Stop to begin preheating.
4. Once preheated, place the air fry basket on the air fry position.
5. After 10 minutes, remove from the oven and flip the squash. Return the basket to the oven and continue cooking for 10 minutes.
6. When cooking is complete, the squash should be golden brown. Remove the basket from the oven. Sprinkle the goat cheese on top and serve drizzled with the maple syrup.

Cabbage and Peas with Mango

Prep time: 10 minutes | Cook time: 8 minutes | Serves 4

1 small head Napa cabbage, shredded, divided
1 medium carrot, cut into thin coins
8 ounces (227 g) snow peas
1 red or green bell pepper, sliced into thin strips
1 tablespoon vegetable oil
2 tablespoons soy sauce
1 tablespoon sesame oil
2 tablespoons brown sugar
2 tablespoons freshly squeezed lime juice
2 teaspoons red or green Thai curry paste
1 serrano chile, deseeded and minced
1 cup frozen mango slices, thawed
½ cup chopped roasted peanuts or cashews

1. Put half the Napa cabbage in a large bowl, along with the carrot, snow peas, and bell pepper. Drizzle with the vegetable oil and toss to coat. Spread them evenly on the sheet pan.
2. Select Roast, Super Convection, set temperature to 375ºF (190ºC), and set time to 8 minutes. Select Start/Stop to begin preheating.
3. Once preheated, place the pan on the roast position.
4. Meanwhile, whisk together the soy sauce, sesame oil, brown sugar, lime juice, and curry paste in a small bowl.
5. When done, the vegetables should be tender and crisp. Remove the pan and put the vegetables back into the bowl. Add the chile, mango slices, and the remaining cabbage. Pour over the dressing and toss to coat. Top with the roasted nuts and serve.

Carrot Tofu with Peanuts

Prep time: 10 minutes | Cook time: 10 minutes | Serves 4

⅓ cup Asian-Style sauce
1 teaspoon cornstarch
½ teaspoon red pepper flakes, or more to taste
1 pound (454 g) firm or extra-firm tofu, cut into 1-inch cubes
1 small carrot, peeled and cut into ¼-inch-thick coins
1 small green bell pepper, cut into bite-size pieces
3 scallions, sliced, whites and green parts separated
3 tablespoons roasted unsalted peanuts

1. In a large bowl, whisk together the sauce, cornstarch, and red pepper flakes. Fold in the tofu, carrot, pepper, and the white parts of the scallions and toss to coat. Spread the mixture evenly on the sheet pan.
2. Select Roast, Super Convection, set temperature to 375ºF (190ºC), and set time to 10 minutes. Select Start/Stop to begin preheating.
3. Once preheated, place the pan on the roast position. Stir the ingredients once halfway through the cooking time.
4. When done, remove the pan from the oven. Serve sprinkled with the peanuts and scallion greens.

Cauliflower with Yogurt and Cashew

Prep time: 5 minutes | Cook time: 12 minutes | Serves 2

4 cups cauliflower florets (about half a large head)
1 tablespoon olive oil
1 teaspoon curry powder
Salt, to taste
½ cup toasted, chopped cashews, for garnish
Yogurt Sauce:
¼ cup plain yogurt
2 tablespoons sour cream
1 teaspoon honey
1 teaspoon lemon juice
Pinch cayenne pepper
Salt, to taste
1 tablespoon chopped fresh cilantro, plus leaves for garnish

1. In a large mixing bowl, toss the cauliflower florets with the olive oil, curry powder, and salt.
2. Place the cauliflower florets in the air fry basket.
3. Select Air Fry, Super Convection, set temperature to 400ºF (205ºC) and set time to 12 minutes. Select Start/Stop to begin preheating.
4. Once preheated, place the basket on the air fry position. Stir the cauliflower florets twice during cooking.
5. When cooking is complete, the cauliflower should be golden brown.
6. Meanwhile, mix all the ingredients for the yogurt sauce in a small bowl and whisk to combine.
7. Remove the cauliflower from the oven and drizzle with the yogurt sauce. Scatter the toasted cashews and cilantro on top and serve immediately.

Carrot and Potato with Thyme

Prep time: 10 minutes | Cook time: 22 minutes | Serves 4

2 carrots, sliced
2 potatoes, cut into chunks
1 rutabaga, cut into chunks
1 turnip, cut into chunks
1 beet, cut into chunks
8 shallots, halved
2 tablespoons olive oil
Salt and black pepper, to taste
2 tablespoons tomato pesto
2 tablespoons water
2 tablespoons chopped fresh thyme

1. Toss the carrots, potatoes, rutabaga, turnip, beet, shallots, olive oil, salt, and pepper in a large mixing bowl until the root vegetables are evenly coated.
2. Place the root vegetables in the air fry basket.
3. Select Air Fry, Super Convection, set temperature to 400ºF (205ºC) and set time to 22 minutes. Select Start/Stop to begin preheating.
4. Once preheated, place the basket on the air fry position. Stir the vegetables twice during cooking.
5. When cooking is complete, the vegetables should be tender.
6. Meanwhile, in a small bowl, whisk together the tomato pesto and water until smooth.
7. When ready, remove the root vegetables from the oven to a platter. Drizzle with the tomato pesto mixture and sprinkle with the thyme. Serve immediately.

Okra with Sour Cream

Prep time: 5 minutes | Cook time: 10 minutes | Serves 4

3 tablespoons sour cream
2 tablespoons flour
2 tablespoons semolina
½ teaspoon red chili powder
Salt and black pepper, to taste
1 pound (454 g) okra, halved
Cooking spray

1. Spray the air fry basket with cooking spray. Set aside.
2. In a shallow bowl, place the sour cream. In another shallow bowl, thoroughly combine the flour, semolina, red chili powder, salt, and pepper.
3. Dredge the okra in the sour cream, then roll in the flour mixture until evenly coated. Transfer the okra to the air fry basket.
4. Select Air Fry, Super Convection, set temperature to 400ºF (205ºC), and set time to 10 minutes. Select Start/Stop to begin preheating.
5. Once preheated, place the basket on the air fry position. Flip the okra halfway through the cooking time.
6. When cooking is complete, the okra should be golden brown and crispy. Remove the basket from the oven. Cool for 5 minutes before serving.

Zucchini and Carrot with Cheese

Prep time: 5 minutes | Cook time: 14 minutes | Serves 2

2 zucchinis, cut into even chunks
1 large eggplant, peeled, cut into chunks
1 large carrot, cut into chunks
6 ounces (170 g) halloumi cheese, cubed
2 teaspoons olive oil
Salt and black pepper, to taste
1 teaspoon dried mixed herbs

1. Combine the zucchinis, eggplant, carrot, cheese, olive oil, salt, and pepper in a large bowl and toss to coat well.
2. Spread the mixture evenly in the air fry basket.
3. Select Air Fry, Super Convection, set temperature to 340ºF (171ºC), and set time to 14 minutes. Select Start/Stop to begin preheating.
4. Once preheated, place the basket on the air fry position. Stir the mixture once during cooking.
5. When cooking is complete, they should be crispy and golden. Remove from the oven and serve topped with mixed herbs.

Tofu Carrot and Cauliflower Rice

Prep time: 10 minutes | Cook time: 22 minutes | Serves 4

½ block tofu, crumbled
1 cup diced carrot
½ cup diced onions
Cauliflower:
3 cups cauliflower rice
½ cup chopped broccoli
½ cup frozen peas
2 tablespoons soy sauce
1 tablespoon minced ginger
2 garlic cloves, minced
1 tablespoon rice vinegar
1½ teaspoons toasted sesame oil
2 tablespoons soy sauce
1 teaspoon turmeric

1. Mix the tofu, carrot, onions, soy sauce, and turmeric in a baking dish and stir until well incorporated.
2. Select Roast, Super Convection, set temperature to 370ºF (188ºC) and set time to 10 minutes. Select Start/Stop to begin preheating.
3. Once preheated, place the baking dish on the roast position. Flip the tofu and carrot halfway through the cooking time.
4. When cooking is complete, the tofu should be crisp.
5. Meanwhile, in a large bowl, combine all the ingredients for the cauliflower and toss well.
6. Remove the dish from the oven and add the cauliflower mixture to the tofu and stir to combine.
7. Return the baking dish to the oven and set time to 12 minutes on Roast, Super Convection. Place the baking dish on the roast position.
8. When cooking is complete, the vegetables should be tender.
9. Cool for 5 minutes before serving.

Breaded Zucchini Chips

Prep time: 5 minutes | Cook time: 14 minutes | Serves 4

2 egg whites
Salt and black pepper, to taste
½ cup seasoned bread crumbs
2 tablespoons grated Parmesan cheese
¼ teaspoon garlic powder
2 medium zucchini, sliced
Cooking spray

1. Spritz the air fry basket with cooking spray.
2. In a bowl, beat the egg whites with salt and pepper. In a separate bowl, thoroughly combine the bread crumbs, Parmesan cheese, and garlic powder.
3. Dredge the zucchini slices in the egg white, then coat in the bread crumb mixture.
4. Arrange the zucchini slices in the air fry basket.
5. Select Air Fry, Super Convection. Set temperature to 400ºF (205ºC) and set time to 14 minutes. Select Start/Stop to begin preheating.
6. Once preheated, place the basket on the air fry position. Flip the zucchini halfway through.
7. When cooking is complete, the zucchini should be tender.
8. Remove from the oven to a plate and serve.

Celery Roots with Butter

Prep time: 10 minutes | Cook time: 20 minutes | Serves 4

2 celery roots, peeled and diced
1 teaspoon extra-virgin olive oil
1 teaspoon butter, melted
½ teaspoon ground cinnamon
Sea salt and freshly ground black pepper, to taste

1. Line a baking sheet with aluminum foil.
2. Toss the celery roots with the olive oil in a large bowl until well coated. Transfer them to the prepared baking sheet.
3. Select Roast, Super Convection, set temperature to 350°F (180°C), and set time to 20 minutes. Select Start/Stop to begin preheating.
4. Once preheated, place the baking sheet on the roast position.
5. When done, the celery roots should be very tender. Remove from the oven to a serving bowl. Stir in the butter and cinnamon and mash them with a potato masher until fluffy.
6. Season with salt and pepper to taste. Serve immediately.

Eggplant with Basil

Prep time: 15 minutes | Cook time: 20 minutes | Serves 2

1 small eggplant, halved and sliced
1 yellow bell pepper, cut into thick strips
1 red bell pepper, cut into thick strips
2 garlic cloves, quartered
1 red onion, sliced
1 tablespoon extra-virgin olive oil
Salt and freshly ground black pepper, to taste
½ cup chopped fresh basil, for garnish
Cooking spray

1. Grease a nonstick baking dish with cooking spray.
2. Place the eggplant, bell peppers, garlic, and red onion in the greased baking dish. Drizzle with the olive oil and toss to coat well. Spritz any uncoated surfaces with cooking spray.
3. Select Bake, Super Convection, set temperature to 350°F (180°C), and set time to 20 minutes. Select Start/Stop to begin preheating.
4. Once preheated, place the baking dish on the bake position. Flip the vegetables halfway through the cooking time.
5. When done, remove from the oven and sprinkle with salt and pepper.
6. Sprinkle the basil on top for garnish and serve.

Bell Peppers with Garlic

Prep time: 10 minutes | Cook time: 22 minutes | Serves 4

1 green bell pepper, sliced into 1-inch strips
1 red bell pepper, sliced into 1-inch strips
1 orange bell pepper, sliced into 1-inch strips
1 yellow bell pepper, sliced into 1-inch strips
2 tablespoons olive oil, divided
½ teaspoon dried marjoram
Pinch salt
Freshly ground black pepper, to taste
1 head garlic

1. Toss the bell peppers with 1 tablespoon of olive oil in a large bowl until well coated. Season with the marjoram, salt, and pepper. Toss again and set aside.
2. Cut off the top of a head of garlic. Place the garlic cloves on a large square of aluminum foil. Drizzle the top with the remaining 1 tablespoon of olive oil and wrap the garlic cloves in foil.
3. Transfer the garlic to the air fry basket.
4. Select Roast, Super Convection, set temperature to 330°F (166°C) and set time to 15 minutes. Select Start/Stop to begin preheating.
5. Once preheated, place the basket on the roast position.
6. After 15 minutes, remove the air fry basket from the oven and add the bell peppers. Return to the oven and set time to 7 minutes.
7. When cooking is complete or until the garlic is soft and the bell peppers are tender.
8. Transfer the cooked bell peppers to a plate. Remove the garlic and unwrap the foil. Let the garlic rest for a few minutes. Once cooled, squeeze the roasted garlic cloves out of their skins and add them to the plate of bell peppers. Stir well and serve immediately.

Black Beans Cheese Tacos with Salsa

Prep time: 12 minutes | Cook time: 7 minutes | Serves 4

1 (15-ounce / 425-g) can black beans, drained and rinsed
½ cup prepared salsa
1½ teaspoons chili powder
4 ounces (113 g) grated Monterey Jack cheese
2 tablespoons minced onion
8 (6-inch) flour tortillas
2 tablespoons vegetable or extra-virgin olive oil
Shredded lettuce, for serving

1. In a medium bowl, add the beans, salsa and chili powder. Coarsely mash them with a potato masher. Fold in the cheese and onion and stir until combined.
2. Arrange the flour tortillas on a cutting board and spoon 2 to 3 tablespoons of the filling into each tortilla. Fold the tortillas over, pressing lightly to even out the filling. Brush the tacos on one side with half the olive oil and put them, oiled side down, on the sheet pan. Brush the top side with the remaining olive oil.
3. Select Air Fry, Super Convection, set temperature to 400ºF (205ºC), and set time to 7 minutes. Select Start/Stop to begin preheating.
4. Once preheated, place the pan into the oven. Flip the tacos halfway through the cooking time.
5. Remove the pan from the oven and allow to cool for 5 minutes. Serve with the shredded lettuce on the side.

Rosemary Beets with Glaze

Prep time: 5 minutes | Cook time: 10 minutes | Serves 2

Beet:
2 beets, cubed
2 tablespoons olive oil
2 springs rosemary, chopped
Salt and black pepper, to taste
Balsamic Glaze:
⅓ cup balsamic vinegar
1 tablespoon honey

1. Combine the beets, olive oil, rosemary, salt, and pepper in a mixing bowl and toss until the beets are completely coated.
2. Place the beets in the air fry basket.
3. Select Air Fry, Super Convection. Set temperature to 400ºF (205ºC) and set time to 10 minutes. Select Start/Stop to begin preheating.
4. Once preheated, place the basket on the air fry position. Stir the vegetables halfway through.
5. When cooking is complete, the beets should be crisp and browned at the edges.
6. Meanwhile, make the balsamic glaze: Place the balsamic vinegar and honey in a small saucepan and bring to a boil over medium heat. When the sauce boils, reduce the heat to medium-low heat and simmer until the liquid is reduced by half.
7. When ready, remove the beets from the oven to a platter. Pour the balsamic glaze over the top and serve immediately.

Glazed Cauliflower

Prep time: 5 minutes | Cook time: 14 minutes | Serves 4

½ cup soy sauce
⅓ cup water
1 tablespoon brown sugar
1 teaspoon sesame oil
1 teaspoon cornstarch
2 cloves garlic, chopped
½ teaspoon chili powder
1 big cauliflower head, cut into florets

1. Make the teriyaki sauce: In a small bowl, whisk together the soy sauce, water, brown sugar, sesame oil, cornstarch, garlic, and chili powder until well combined.
2. Place the cauliflower florets in a large bowl and drizzle the top with the prepared teriyaki sauce and toss to coat well.
3. Put the cauliflower florets in the air fry basket.
4. Select Air Fry, Super Convection, set temperature to 340ºF (171ºC) and set time to 14 minutes. Select Start/Stop to begin preheating.
5. Once preheated, place the basket on the air fry position. Stir the cauliflower halfway through.
6. When cooking is complete, the cauliflower should be crisp-tender.
7. Let the cauliflower cool for 5 minutes before serving.

Kale with Tahini and Lemon

Prep time: 5 minutes | Cook time: 15 minutes | Serves 2 to 4

Dressing:
¼ cup tahini
¼ cup fresh lemon juice
2 tablespoons olive oil
1 teaspoon sesame seeds
½ teaspoon garlic powder
¼ teaspoon cayenne pepper

Kale:
4 cups packed torn kale leaves (stems and ribs removed and leaves torn into palm-size pieces)
Kosher salt and freshly ground black pepper, to taste

1. Make the dressing: Whisk together the tahini, lemon juice, olive oil, sesame seeds, garlic powder, and cayenne pepper in a large bowl until well mixed.
2. Add the kale and massage the dressing thoroughly all over the leaves. Sprinkle the salt and pepper to season.
3. Place the kale in the air fry basket in a single layer.
4. Select Air Fry, Super Convection, set temperature to 350ºF (180ºC), and set time to 15 minutes. Select Start/Stop to begin preheating.
5. Once preheated, place the air fry basket on the air fry position.
6. When cooking is complete, the leaves should be slightly wilted and crispy. Remove from the oven and serve on a plate.

Breaded Eggplant Slices

Prep time: 5 minutes | Cook time: 12 minutes | Serves 4

1 cup flour
4 eggs
Salt, to taste
2 cups bread crumbs
1 teaspoon Italian seasoning
2 eggplants, sliced
2 garlic cloves, sliced
2 tablespoons chopped parsley
Cooking spray

1. Spritz the air fry basket with cooking spray. Set aside.
2. On a plate, place the flour. In a shallow bowl, whisk the eggs with salt. In another shallow bowl, combine the bread crumbs and Italian seasoning.
3. Dredge the eggplant slices, one at a time, in the flour, then in the whisked eggs, finally in the bread crumb mixture to coat well.
4. Lay the coated eggplant slices in the air fry basket.
5. Select Air Fry, Super Convection, set temperature to 390ºF (199ºC), and set time to 12 minutes. Select Start/Stop to begin preheating.
6. Once preheated, place the basket on the air fry position. Flip the eggplant slices halfway through the cooking time.
7. When cooking is complete, the eggplant slices should be golden brown and crispy. Transfer the eggplant slices to a plate and sprinkle the garlic and parsley on top before serving.

Tomato Stuffed Mushrooms with Cheese

Prep time: 5 minutes | Cook time: 8 minutes | Serves 4

4 portobello mushrooms, stem removed
1 tablespoon olive oil
1 tomato, diced
½ green bell pepper, diced
½ small red onion, diced
½ teaspoon garlic powder
Salt and black pepper, to taste
½ cup grated Mozzarella cheese

1. Using a spoon to scoop out the gills of the mushrooms and discard them. Brush the mushrooms with the olive oil.
2. In a mixing bowl, stir together the remaining ingredients except the Mozzarella cheese. Using a spoon to stuff each mushroom with the filling and scatter the Mozzarella cheese on top.
3. Arrange the mushrooms in the air fry basket.
4. Select Roast, Super Convection, set temperature to 330ºF (166ºC) and set time to 8 minutes. Select Start/Stop to begin preheating.
5. Once preheated, place the basket on the roast position.
6. When cooking is complete, the cheese should be melted.
7. Serve warm.

Pea and Mushroom with Rice

Prep time: 5 minutes | Cook time: 12 minutes | Serves 4

2 teaspoons melted butter
1 cup chopped mushrooms
1 cup cooked rice
1 cup peas
1 carrot, chopped
1 red onion, chopped
1 garlic clove, minced
Salt and black pepper, to taste
2 hard-boiled eggs, grated
1 tablespoon soy sauce

1. Coat a baking dish with melted butter.
2. Stir together the mushrooms, cooked rice, peas, carrot, onion, garlic, salt, and pepper in a large bowl until well mixed. Pour the mixture into the prepared baking dish.
3. Select Roast, Super Convection, set temperature to 380ºF (193ºC), and set time to 12 minutes. Select Start/Stop to begin preheating.
4. Once preheated, place the baking dish on the roast position.
5. When cooking is complete, remove from the oven. Divide the mixture among four plates. Serve warm with a sprinkle of grated eggs and a drizzle of soy sauce.

Crispy Tofu Strips

Prep time: 5 minutes | Cook time: 14 minutes | Serves 4

2 tablespoons olive oil, divided
½ cup flour
½ cup crushed cornflakes
Salt and black pepper, to taste
14 ounces (397 g) firm tofu, cut into ½-inch-thick strips

1. Grease the air fry basket with 1 tablespoon of olive oil.
2. Combine the flour, cornflakes, salt, and pepper on a plate.
3. Dredge the tofu strips in the flour mixture until they are completely coated. Transfer the tofu strips to the greased basket.
4. Drizzle the remaining 1 tablespoon of olive oil over the top of tofu strips.
5. Select Air Fry, Super Convection, set temperature to 360ºF (182ºC), and set time to 14 minutes. Select Start/Stop to begin preheating.
6. Once preheated, place the basket on the air fry position. Flip the tofu strips halfway through the cooking time.
7. When cooking is complete, the tofu strips should be crispy. Remove from the oven and serve warm.

Lemony Chickpea Oat Meatballs

Prep time: 15 minutes | Cook time: 18 minutes | Serves 3

½ cup grated carrots
½ cup sweet onions
2 tablespoons olive oil
1 cup rolled oats
½ cup roasted cashews
2 cups cooked chickpeas
Juice of 1 lemon
2 tablespoons soy sauce
1 tablespoon flax meal
1 teaspoon garlic powder
1 teaspoon cumin
½ teaspoon turmeric

1. Mix the carrots, onions, and olive oil in a baking dish and stir to combine.
2. Select Roast, Super Convection, set temperature to 350ºF (180ºC) and set time to 6 minutes. Select Start/Stop to begin preheating.
3. Once preheated, place the baking dish on the roast position. Stir the vegetables halfway through.
4. When cooking is complete, the vegetables should be tender.
5. Meanwhile, put the oats and cashews in a food processor or blender and pulse until coarsely ground. Transfer the mixture to a large bowl. Add the chickpeas, lemon juice, and soy sauce to the food processor and pulse until smooth. Transfer the chickpea mixture to the bowl of oat and cashew mixture.
6. Remove the carrots and onions from the oven to the bowl of chickpea mixture. Add the flax meal, garlic powder, cumin, and turmeric and stir to incorporate.
7. Scoop tablespoon-sized portions of the veggie mixture and roll them into balls with your hands. Transfer the balls to the air fry basket.
8. Increase the temperature to 370ºF (188ºC) and set time to 12 minutes on Bake, Super Convection. Place the basket on the bake position. Flip the balls halfway through the cooking time.
9. When cooking is complete, the balls should be golden brown.
10. Serve warm.

Garlicky Carrots

Prep time: 5 minutes | Cook time: 16 minutes | Serves 4 to 6

1 pound (454 g) baby carrots
1 tablespoon sesame oil
½ teaspoon dried dill
Pinch salt
Freshly ground black pepper, to taste
6 cloves garlic, peeled
3 tablespoons sesame seeds

1. In a medium bowl, drizzle the baby carrots with the sesame oil. Sprinkle with the dill, salt, and pepper and toss to coat well.
2. Place the baby carrots in the air fry basket.
3. Select Roast, Super Convection, set temperature to 380ºF (193ºC), and set time to 16 minutes. Select Start/Stop to begin preheating.
4. Once preheated, place the basket on the roast position.
5. After 8 minutes, remove the basket from the oven and stir in the garlic. Return the basket to the oven and continue roasting for 8 minutes more.
6. When cooking is complete, the carrots should be lightly browned. Remove the basket from the oven and serve sprinkled with the sesame seeds.

Brussels Sprouts with Chili Sauce

Prep time: 5 minutes | Cook time: 20 minutes | Serves 2

¼ cup Thai sweet chili sauce
2 tablespoons black vinegar or balsamic vinegar
½ teaspoon hot sauce
2 small shallots, cut into ¼-inch-thick slices
8 ounces (227 g) Brussels sprouts, trimmed (large sprouts halved)
Kosher salt and freshly ground black pepper, to taste
2 teaspoons lightly packed fresh cilantro leaves, for garnish

1. Place the chili sauce, vinegar, and hot sauce in a large bowl and whisk to combine.
2. Add the shallots and Brussels sprouts and toss to coat. Sprinkle with the salt and pepper. Transfer the Brussels sprouts and sauce to a baking pan.
3. Select Roast, Super Convection, set temperature to 390ºF (199ºC), and set time to 20 minutes. Select Start/Stop to begin preheating.
4. Once preheated, place the pan on the roast position. Stir the Brussels sprouts twice during cooking.
5. When cooking is complete, the Brussels sprouts should be crisp-tender. Remove from the oven. Sprinkle the cilantro on top for garnish and serve warm.

Roast Mushrooms

Prep time: 5 minutes | Cook time: 15 minutes | Serves 2

1 tablespoon soy sauce
2 teaspoons toasted sesame oil
3 teaspoons vegetable oil, divided
1 garlic clove, minced
7 ounces (198 g) maitake (hen of the woods) mushrooms
½ teaspoon flaky sea salt
½ teaspoon sesame seeds
½ teaspoon finely chopped fresh thyme leaves

1. Whisk together the soy sauce, sesame oil, 1 teaspoon of vegetable oil, and garlic in a small bowl.
2. Arrange the mushrooms in the air fry basket in a single layer. Drizzle the soy sauce mixture over the mushrooms.
3. Select Roast, Super Convection, set temperature to 300ºF (150ºC), and set time to 15 minutes. Select Start/Stop to begin preheating.
4. Once preheated, place the basket on the roast position.
5. After 10 minutes, remove the basket from the oven. Flip the mushrooms and sprinkle the sea salt, sesame seeds, and thyme leaves on top. Drizzle the remaining 2 teaspoons of vegetable oil all over. Return to the oven and continue roasting for an additional 5 minutes.
6. When cooking is complete, remove the mushrooms from the oven to a plate and serve hot.

Asparagus Spears

Prep time: 15 minutes | Cook time: 10 minutes | Serves 4

4 tablespoons olive oil, plus more for greasing
4 tablespoons balsamic vinegar
1½ pounds (680 g) asparagus spears, trimmed
Salt and freshly ground black pepper, to taste

1. Grease the air fry basket with olive oil.
2. In a shallow bowl, stir together the 4 tablespoons of olive oil and balsamic vinegar to make a marinade.
3. Put the asparagus spears in the bowl so they are thoroughly covered by the marinade and allow to marinate for 5 minutes.
4. Put the asparagus in the greased basket in a single layer and season with salt and pepper.
5. Select Air Fry, Super Convection, set temperature to 350ºF (180ºC), and set time to 10 minutes. Select Start/Stop to begin preheating.
6. Once preheated, place the air fry basket on the air fry position. Flip the asparagus halfway through the cooking time.
7. When done, the asparagus should be tender and lightly browned. Cool for 5 minutes before serving.

Walnut and Cheese Stuffed Mushrooms

Prep time: 5 minutes | Cook time: 10 minutes | Serves 4

4 large portobello mushrooms
1 tablespoon canola oil
½ cup shredded Mozzarella cheese
⅓ cup minced walnuts
2 tablespoons chopped fresh parsley
Cooking spray

1. Spritz the air fry basket with cooking spray.
2. On a clean work surface, remove the mushroom stems. Scoop out the gills with a spoon and discard. Coat the mushrooms with canola oil. Top each mushroom evenly with the shredded Mozzarella cheese, followed by the minced walnuts.
3. Arrange the mushrooms in the air fry basket.
4. Select Roast, Super Convection, set temperature to 350ºF (180ºC) and set time to 10 minutes. Select Start/Stop to begin preheating.
5. Once preheated, place the basket on the roast position.
6. When cooking is complete, the mushroom should be golden brown.
7. Transfer the mushrooms to a plate and sprinkle the parsley on top for garnish before serving.

Broccoli with Cheese

Prep time: 5 minutes | Cook time: 18 minutes | Serves 4

1 large-sized head broccoli, stemmed and cut into small florets
2½ tablespoons canola oil
2 teaspoons dried basil
2 teaspoons dried rosemary
Salt and ground black pepper, to taste
⅓ cup grated yellow cheese

1. Bring a pot of lightly salted water to a boil. Add the broccoli florets to the boiling water and let boil for about 3 minutes.
2. Drain the broccoli florets well and transfer to a large bowl. Add the canola oil, basil, rosemary, salt, and black pepper to the bowl and toss until the broccoli is fully coated. Place the broccoli in the air fry basket.
3. Select Air Fry, Super Convection, set temperature to 390ºF (199ºC), and set time to 15 minutes. Select Start/Stop to begin preheating.
4. Once preheated, place the air fry basket on the air fry position. Stir the broccoli halfway through the cooking time.
5. When cooking is complete, the broccoli should be crisp. Remove the basket from the oven. Serve the broccoli warm with grated cheese sprinkled on top.

Egg and Spinach with Basil

Prep time: 10 minutes | Cook time: 10 minutes | Serves 2

2 tablespoons olive oil
4 eggs, whisked
5 ounces (142 g) fresh spinach, chopped
1 medium-sized tomato, chopped
1 teaspoon fresh lemon juice
½ teaspoon ground black pepper
½ teaspoon coarse salt
½ cup roughly chopped fresh basil leaves, for garnish

1. Generously grease a baking pan with olive oil.
2. Stir together the remaining ingredients except the basil leaves in the greased baking pan until well incorporated.
3. Select Bake, Super Convection, set temperature to 280ºF (137ºC), and set time to 10 minutes. Select Start/Stop to begin preheating.
4. Once preheated, place the pan on the bake position.
5. When cooking is complete, the eggs should be completely set and the vegetables should be tender. Remove from the oven and serve garnished with the fresh basil leaves.

Eggplant with Yogurt

Prep time: 5 minutes | Cook time: 15 minutes | Serves 2

1 medium eggplant, quartered and cut crosswise into ½-inch-thick slices
2 tablespoons vegetable oil
Kosher salt and freshly ground black pepper, to taste
½ cup plain yogurt (not Greek)
2 tablespoons harissa paste
1 garlic clove, grated
2 teaspoons honey

1. Toss the eggplant slices with the vegetable oil, salt, and pepper in a large bowl until well coated.
2. Lay the eggplant slices in the air fry basket.
3. Select Air Fry, Super Convection, set temperature to 400ºF (205ºC), and set time to 15 minutes. Select Start/Stop to begin preheating.
4. Once preheated, place the air fry basket on the air fry position. Stir the slices two to three times during cooking.
5. Meanwhile, make the yogurt sauce by whisking together the yogurt, harissa paste, and garlic in a small bowl.
6. When cooking is complete, the eggplant slices should be golden brown. Spread the yogurt sauce on a platter, and pile the eggplant slices over the top. Serve drizzled with the honey.

Cabbage Wedges with Cheese

Prep time: 5 minutes | Cook time: 20 minutes | Serves 4

4 tablespoons melted butter
1 head cabbage, cut into wedges
1 cup shredded Parmesan cheese
Salt and black pepper, to taste
½ cup shredded Mozzarella cheese

1. Brush the melted butter over the cut sides of cabbage wedges and sprinkle both sides with the Parmesan cheese. Season with salt and pepper to taste.
2. Place the cabbage wedges in the air fry basket.
3. Select Air Fry, Super Convection, set temperature to 380ºF (193ºC), and set time to 20 minutes. Select Start/Stop to begin preheating.
4. Once preheated, place the air fry basket on the air fry position. Flip the cabbage halfway through the cooking time.
5. When cooking is complete, the cabbage wedges should be lightly browned. Transfer the cabbage wedges to a plate and serve with the Mozzarella cheese sprinkled on top.

Zucchini and Tomato Ratatouille

Prep time: 15 minutes | Cook time: 16 minutes | Serves 2

2 Roma tomatoes, thinly sliced
1 zucchini, thinly sliced
2 yellow bell peppers, sliced
2 garlic cloves, minced
2 tablespoons olive oil
2 tablespoons herbes de Provence
1 tablespoon vinegar
Salt and black pepper, to taste

1. Place the tomatoes, zucchini, bell peppers, garlic, olive oil, herbes de Provence, and vinegar in a large bowl and toss until the vegetables are evenly coated. Sprinkle with salt and pepper and toss again. Pour the vegetable mixture into a baking dish.
2. Select Roast, Super Convection, set temperature to 390ºF (199ºC) and set time to 16 minutes. Select Start/Stop to begin preheating.
3. Once preheated, place the baking dish on the roast position. Stir the vegetables halfway through.
4. When cooking is complete, the vegetables should be tender.
5. Let the vegetable mixture stand for 5 minutes in the oven before removing and serving.

Garlic Stuffed Mushrooms

Prep time: 5 minutes | Cook time: 12 minutes | Serves 2

18 medium-sized white mushrooms
1 small onion, peeled and chopped
4 garlic cloves, peeled and minced
2 tablespoons olive oil
2 teaspoons cumin powder
A pinch ground allspice
Fine sea salt and freshly ground black pepper, to taste

1. On a clean work surface, remove the mushroom stems. Using a spoon, scoop out the mushroom gills and discard.
2. Thoroughly combine the onion, garlic, olive oil, cumin powder, allspice, salt, and pepper in a mixing bowl. Stuff the mushrooms evenly with the mixture.
3. Place the stuffed mushrooms in the air fry basket.
4. Select Roast, Super Convection, set temperature to 345ºF (174ºC) and set time to 12 minutes. Select Start/Stop to begin preheating.
5. Once preheated, place the basket on the roast position.
6. When cooking is complete, the mushroom should be browned.
7. Cool for 5 minutes before serving.

Baked Tofu

Prep time: 5 minutes | Cook time: 10 minutes | Serves 2

1 tablespoon soy sauce
1 tablespoon water
$1/3$ teaspoon garlic powder
$1/3$ teaspoon onion powder
$1/3$ teaspoon dried oregano
$1/3$ teaspoon dried basil
Black pepper, to taste
6 ounces (170 g) extra firm tofu, pressed and cubed

1. In a large mixing bowl, whisk together the soy sauce, water, garlic powder, onion powder, oregano, basil, and black pepper. Add the tofu cubes, stirring to coat, and let them marinate for 10 minutes.
2. Arrange the tofu in the air fry basket.
3. Select Bake, Super Convection. Set temperature to 390ºF (199ºC) and set time to 10 minutes. Select Start/Stop to begin preheating.
4. Once preheated, place the basket on the bake position. Flip the tofu halfway through the cooking time.
5. When cooking is complete, the tofu should be crisp.
6. Remove from the oven to a plate and serve.

Squash and Mushroom Mélange

Prep time: 10 minutes | Cook time: 16 minutes | Serves 4

1 (8-ounce / 227-g) package sliced mushrooms
1 yellow summer squash, sliced
1 red bell pepper, sliced
3 cloves garlic, sliced
1 tablespoon olive oil
½ teaspoon dried basil
½ teaspoon dried thyme
½ teaspoon dried tarragon

1. Toss the mushrooms, squash, and bell pepper with the garlic and olive oil in a large bowl until well coated. Mix in the basil, thyme, and tarragon and toss again.
2. Spread the vegetables evenly in the air fry basket.
3. Select Roast, Super Convection, set temperature to 350ºF (180ºC), and set time to 16 minutes. Select Start/Stop to begin preheating.
4. Once preheated, place the basket on the roast position.
5. When cooking is complete, the vegetables should be fork-tender. Remove the basket from the oven. Cool for 5 minutes before serving.

Broccoli with Peppercorn

Prep time: 5 minutes | Cook time: 10 minutes | Serves 2

12 ounces (340 g) broccoli florets
2 tablespoons Asian hot chili oil
1 teaspoon ground Sichuan peppercorns (or black pepper)
2 garlic cloves, finely chopped
1 (2-inch) piece fresh ginger, peeled and finely chopped
Kosher salt and freshly ground black pepper

1. Toss the broccoli florets with the chili oil, Sichuan peppercorns, garlic, ginger, salt, and pepper in a mixing bowl until thoroughly coated.
2. Transfer the broccoli florets to the air fry basket.
3. Select Air Fry, Super Convection, set temperature to 375ºF (190ºC), and set time to 10 minutes. Select Start/Stop to begin preheating.
4. Once preheated, place the air fry basket on the air fry position. Stir the broccoli florets halfway through the cooking time.
5. When cooking is complete, the broccoli florets should be lightly browned and tender. Remove the broccoli from the oven and serve on a plate.

Panko-Crusted Cheese Green Beans

Prep time: 5 minutes | Cook time: 15 minutes | Serves 4

½ cup flour
2 eggs
1 cup panko bread crumbs
½ cup grated Parmesan cheese
1 teaspoon cayenne pepper
Salt and black pepper, to taste
1½ pounds (680 g) green beans

1. In a bowl, place the flour. In a separate bowl, lightly beat the eggs. In a separate shallow bowl, thoroughly combine the bread crumbs, cheese, cayenne pepper, salt, and pepper.
2. Dip the green beans in the flour, then in the beaten eggs, finally in the bread crumb mixture to coat well. Transfer the green beans to the air fry basket.
3. Select Air Fry, Super Convection, set temperature to 400ºF (205ºC), and set time to 15 minutes. Select Start/Stop to begin preheating.
4. Once preheated, place the basket on the air fry position. Stir the green beans halfway through the cooking time.
5. When cooking is complete, remove from the oven to a bowl and serve.

Chapter 4 Vegetable Sides

Brussels Sprouts with Sage

Prep time: 5 minutes | Cook time: 15 minutes | Serves 4

1 pound (454 g) Brussels sprouts, halved
1 cup bread crumbs
2 tablespoons grated Grana Padano cheese
1 tablespoon paprika
2 tablespoons canola oil
1 tablespoon chopped sage

1. Line the air fry basket with parchment paper. Set aside.
2. In a small bowl, thoroughly mix the bread crumbs, cheese, and paprika. In a large bowl, place the Brussels sprouts and drizzle the canola oil over the top. Sprinkle with the bread crumb mixture and toss to coat.
3. Transfer the Brussels sprouts to the prepared basket.
4. Select Roast, Super Convection, set temperature to 400°F (205°C), and set time to 15 minutes. Select Start/Stop to begin preheating.
5. Once preheated, place the basket on the roast position. Stir the Brussels a few times during cooking.
6. When cooking is complete, the Brussels sprouts should be lightly browned and crisp. Transfer the Brussels sprouts to a plate and sprinkle the sage on top before serving.

Air Fried Zucchini Sticks

Prep time: 5 minutes | Cook time: 14 minutes | Serves 4

2 small zucchini, cut into 2-inch × ½-inch sticks
3 tablespoons chickpea flour
2 teaspoons arrowroot (or cornstarch)
½ teaspoon garlic granules
¼ teaspoon sea salt
⅛ teaspoon freshly ground black pepper
1 tablespoon water
Cooking spray

1. Combine the zucchini sticks with the chickpea flour, arrowroot, garlic granules, salt, and pepper in a medium bowl and toss to coat. Add the water and stir to mix well.
2. Spritz the air fry basket with cooking spray and spread out the zucchini sticks in the basket. Mist the zucchini sticks with cooking spray.
3. Select Air Fry, Super Convection, set temperature to 392°F (200°C), and set time to 14 minutes. Select Start/Stop to begin preheating.
4. Once preheated, place the basket on the air fry position. Stir the sticks halfway through the cooking time.
5. When cooking is complete, the zucchini sticks should be crispy and nicely browned. Remove from the oven and serve warm.

Broccoli with Cheese

Prep time: 5 minutes | Cook time: 4 minutes | Serves 4

1 pound (454 g) broccoli florets
1 medium shallot, minced
2 tablespoons olive oil
2 tablespoons unsalted butter, melted
2 teaspoons minced garlic
¼ cup grated Parmesan cheese

1. Combine the broccoli florets with the shallot, olive oil, butter, garlic, and Parmesan cheese in a medium bowl and toss until the broccoli florets are thoroughly coated.
2. Place the broccoli florets in the air fry basket in a single layer.
3. Select Roast, Super Convection, set temperature to 360°F (182°C), and set time to 4 minutes. Select Start/Stop to begin preheating.
4. Once preheated, place the basket on the roast position.
5. When cooking is complete, the broccoli florets should be crisp-tender. Remove from the oven and serve warm.

Sweet Potato with Lime

Prep time: 5 minutes | Cook time: 22 minutes | Serves 4

5 garnet sweet potatoes, peeled and diced
1½ tablespoons fresh lime juice
1 tablespoon butter, melted
2 teaspoons tamarind paste
1½ teaspoon ground allspice
⅓ teaspoon white pepper
½ teaspoon turmeric powder
A few drops liquid stevia

1. In a large mixing bowl, combine all the ingredients and toss until the sweet potatoes are evenly coated. Place the sweet potatoes in the air fry basket.
2. Select Air Fry, Super Convection, set temperature to 400°F (205°C), and set time to 22 minutes. Select Start/Stop to begin preheating.
3. Once preheated, place the basket on the air fry position. Stir the potatoes twice during cooking.
4. When cooking is complete, the potatoes should be crispy on the outside and soft on the inside. Let the potatoes cool for 5 minutes before serving.

Green Beans with Sesame Seeds

Prep time: 5 minutes | Cook time: 8 minutes | Serves 4

1 tablespoon reduced-sodium soy sauce or tamari
½ tablespoon Sriracha sauce
4 teaspoons toasted sesame oil, divided
12 ounces (340 g) trimmed green beans
½ tablespoon toasted sesame seeds

1. Whisk together the soy sauce, Sriracha sauce, and 1 teaspoon of sesame oil in a small bowl until smooth. Set aside.
2. Toss the green beans with the remaining sesame oil in a large bowl until evenly coated.
3. Place the green beans in the air fry basket in a single layer.
4. Select Air Fry, Super Convection, set temperature to 375°F (190°C), and set time to 8 minutes. Select Start/Stop to begin preheating.
5. Once preheated, place the basket on the air fry position. Stir the green beans halfway through the cooking time.
6. When cooking is complete, the green beans should be lightly charred and tender. Remove from the oven to a platter. Pour the prepared sauce over the top of green beans and toss well. Serve sprinkled with the toasted sesame seeds.

Peppers with Sauce

Prep time: 5 minutes | Cook time: 9 minutes | Serves 3

½ pound (227 g) shishito peppers, rinsed
Cooking spray
Sauce:
1 tablespoon tamari or shoyu
2 teaspoons fresh lime juice
2 large garlic cloves, minced

1. Spritz the air fry basket with cooking spray.
2. Place the shishito peppers in the air fry basket and spritz them with cooking spray.
3. Select Roast, Super Convection, set temperature to 392°F (200°C), and set time to 9 minutes. Select Start/Stop to begin preheating.
4. Once preheated, place the basket on the roast position.
5. Meanwhile, whisk together all the ingredients for the sauce in a large bowl. Set aside.
6. After 3 minutes, remove the basket from the oven. Flip the peppers and spritz them with cooking spray. Return to the oven and continue cooking.
7. After another 3 minutes, remove the basket from the oven. Flip the peppers and spray with cooking spray. Return to the oven and continue roasting for 3 minutes more, or until the peppers are blistered and nicely browned.
8. When cooking is complete, remove the peppers from the oven to the bowl of sauce. Toss to coat well and serve immediately.

Asparagus with Garlic

Prep time: 5 minutes | Cook time: 10 minutes | Serves 4

1 pound (454 g) asparagus, woody ends trimmed
2 tablespoons olive oil
1 tablespoon balsamic vinegar
2 teaspoons minced garlic
Salt and freshly ground black pepper, to taste

1. In a large shallow bowl, toss the asparagus with the olive oil, balsamic vinegar, garlic, salt, and pepper until thoroughly coated. Put the asparagus in the air fry basket.
2. Select Roast, Super Convection, set temperature to 400ºF (205ºC), and set time to 10 minutes. Select Start/Stop to begin preheating.
3. Once preheated, place the basket on the roast position. Flip the asparagus with tongs halfway through the cooking time.
4. When cooking is complete, the asparagus should be crispy. Remove the basket from the oven and serve warm.

Brussels Sprouts with Sauce

Prep time: 10 minutes | Cook time: 11 minutes | Serves 4

2½ cups trimmed Brussels sprouts
Sauce:
1½ teaspoons mellow white miso
1½ tablespoons maple syrup
1 teaspoon toasted sesame oil
1 teaspoons tamari or shoyu
1 teaspoon grated fresh ginger
2 large garlic cloves, finely minced
¼ to ½ teaspoon red chili flakes
Cooking spray

1. Spritz the air fry basket with cooking spray.
2. Arrange the Brussels sprouts in the air fry basket and spray them with cooking spray.
3. Select Air Fry, Super Convection, set temperature to 392ºF (200ºC), and set time to 11 minutes. Select Start/Stop to begin preheating.
4. Once preheated, place the basket on the air fry position.
5. After 6 minutes, remove the basket from the oven. Flip the Brussels sprouts and spritz with cooking spray again. Return to the oven and continue cooking for 5 minutes more.
6. Meanwhile, make the sauce: Stir together the miso and maple syrup in a medium bowl. Add the sesame oil, tamari, ginger, garlic, and red chili flakes and whisk to combine.
7. When cooking is complete, the Brussels sprouts should be crisp-tender. Transfer the Brussels sprouts to the bowl of sauce, tossing to coat well. If you prefer a saltier taste, you can add additional ½ teaspoon tamari to the sauce. Serve immediately.

Butternut Squash Croquettes

Prep time: 5 minutes | Cook time: 17 minutes | Serves 4

⅓ butternut squash, peeled and grated
⅓ cup all-purpose flour
2 eggs, whisked
4 cloves garlic, minced
1½ tablespoons olive oil
1 teaspoon fine sea salt
⅓ teaspoon freshly ground black pepper, or more to taste
⅓ teaspoon dried sage
A pinch of ground allspice

1. Line the air fry basket with parchment paper. Set aside.
2. In a mixing bowl, stir together all the ingredients until well combined.
3. Make the squash croquettes: Use a small cookie scoop to drop tablespoonfuls of the squash mixture onto a lightly floured surface and shape into balls with your hands. Transfer them to the air fry basket.
4. Select Air Fry, Super Convection, set temperature to 345ºF (174ºC), and set time to 17 minutes. Select Start/Stop to begin preheating.
5. Once preheated, place the basket on the air fry position.
6. When cooking is complete, the squash croquettes should be golden brown. Remove from the oven to a plate and serve warm.

Carrot with Glaze

Prep time: 5 minutes | Cook time: 18 minutes | Serves 3

3 medium-size carrots, cut into 2-inch × ½-inch sticks
1 tablespoon orange juice
2 teaspoons balsamic vinegar
1 teaspoon maple syrup
1 teaspoon avocado oil
½ teaspoon dried rosemary
¼ teaspoon sea salt
¼ teaspoon lemon zest

1. Put the carrots in a baking pan and sprinkle with the orange juice, balsamic vinegar, maple syrup, avocado oil, rosemary, sea salt, finished by the lemon zest. Toss well.
2. Select Roast, Super Convection, set temperature to 392ºF (200ºC), and set time to 18 minutes. Select Start/Stop to begin preheating.
3. Once preheated, place the pan on the roast position. Stir the carrots several times during the cooking process.
4. When cooking is complete, the carrots should be nicely glazed and tender. Remove from the oven and serve hot.

Panko Cheese Asparagus

Prep time: 15 minutes | Cook time: 6 minutes | Serves 4

2 egg whites
¼ cup water
¼ cup plus 2 tablespoons grated Parmesan cheese, divided
¾ cup panko bread crumbs
¼ teaspoon salt
12 ounces (340 g) fresh asparagus spears, woody ends trimmed
Cooking spray

1. In a shallow dish, whisk together the egg whites and water until slightly foamy. In a separate shallow dish, thoroughly combine ¼ cup of Parmesan cheese, bread crumbs, and salt.
2. Dip the asparagus in the egg white, then roll in the cheese mixture to coat well.
3. Place the asparagus in the air fry basket in a single layer, leaving space between each spear. Spritz the asparagus with cooking spray.
4. Select Air Fry, Super Convection, set temperature to 390ºF (199ºC), and set time to 6 minutes. Select Start/Stop to begin preheating.
5. Once preheated, place the basket on the air fry position.
6. When cooking is complete, the asparagus should be golden brown and crisp. Remove the basket from the oven. Sprinkle with the remaining 2 tablespoons of cheese and serve hot.

Corn on the Cob

Prep time: 10 minutes | Cook time: 15 minutes | Serves 4

2 tablespoon olive oil, divided
2 tablespoons grated Parmesan cheese
1 teaspoon garlic powder
1 teaspoon chili powder
1 teaspoon ground cumin
1 teaspoon paprika
1 teaspoon salt
¼ teaspoon cayenne pepper (optional)
4 ears fresh corn, shucked

1. Grease the air fry basket with 1 tablespoon of olive oil. Set aside.
2. Combine the Parmesan cheese, garlic powder, chili powder, cumin, paprika, salt, and cayenne pepper (if desired) in a small bowl and stir to mix well.
3. Lightly coat the ears of corn with the remaining 1 tablespoon of olive oil. Rub the cheese mixture all over the ears of corn until completely coated.
4. Arrange the ears of corn in the greased basket in a single layer.
5. Select Air Fry, Super Convection, set temperature to 400ºF (205ºC), and set time to 15 minutes. Select Start/Stop to begin preheating.
6. Once preheated, place the basket on the air fry position. Flip the ears of corn halfway through the cooking time.
7. When cooking is complete, they should be lightly browned. Remove from the oven and let them cool for 5 minutes before serving.

Broccoli with Hot Sauce

Prep time: 5 minutes | Cook time: 14 minutes | Serves 6

Broccoli:
1 medium-sized head broccoli, cut into florets
1½ tablespoons olive oil
1 teaspoon shallot powder
1 teaspoon porcini powder
½ teaspoon freshly grated lemon zest
½ teaspoon hot paprika
½ teaspoon granulated garlic
⅓ teaspoon fine sea salt
⅓ teaspoon celery seeds

Hot Sauce:
½ cup tomato sauce
1 tablespoon balsamic vinegar
½ teaspoon ground allspice

1. In a mixing bowl, combine all the ingredients for the broccoli and toss to coat. Transfer the broccoli to the air fry basket.
2. Select Air Fry, Super Convection, set temperature to 360ºF (182ºC), and set time to 14 minutes. Select Start/Stop to begin preheating.
3. Once preheated, place the basket on the air fry position.
4. Meanwhile, make the hot sauce by whisking together the tomato sauce, balsamic vinegar, and allspice in a small bowl.
5. When cooking is complete, remove the broccoli from the oven and serve with the hot sauce.

Cabbage with Red Pepper

Prep time: 5 minutes | Cook time: 7 minutes | Serves 4

1 head cabbage, sliced into 1-inch-thick ribbons
1 tablespoon olive oil
1 teaspoon garlic powder
1 teaspoon red pepper flakes
1 teaspoon salt
1 teaspoon freshly ground black pepper

1. Toss the cabbage with the olive oil, garlic powder, red pepper flakes, salt, and pepper in a large mixing bowl until well coated.
2. Transfer the cabbage to the air fry basket.
3. Select Roast, Super Convection, set temperature to 350ºF (180ºC), and set time to 7 minutes. Select Start/Stop to begin preheating.
4. Once preheated, place the basket on the roast position. Flip the cabbage with tongs halfway through the cooking time.
5. When cooking is complete, the cabbage should be crisp. Remove from the oven to a plate and serve warm.

Cheesy Broccoli Gratin

Prep time: 5 minutes | Cook time: 14 minutes | Serves 2

⅓ cup fat-free milk
1 tablespoon all-purpose or gluten-free flour
½ tablespoon olive oil
½ teaspoon ground sage
¼ teaspoon kosher salt
⅛ teaspoon freshly ground black pepper
2 cups roughly chopped broccoli florets
6 tablespoons shredded Cheddar cheese
2 tablespoons panko bread crumbs
1 tablespoon grated Parmesan cheese
Olive oil spray

1. Spritz a baking dish with olive oil spray.
2. Mix the milk, flour, olive oil, sage, salt, and pepper in a medium bowl and whisk to combine. Stir in the broccoli florets, Cheddar cheese, bread crumbs, and Parmesan cheese and toss to coat.
3. Pour the broccoli mixture into the prepared baking dish.
4. Select Bake, Super Convection, set temperature to 330ºF (166ºC), and set time to 14 minutes. Select Start/Stop to begin preheating.
5. Once preheated, place the baking dish on the bake position.
6. When cooking is complete, the top should be golden brown and the broccoli should be tender. Remove from the oven and serve immediately.

Squash with Cinnamon

Prep time: 5 minutes | Cook time: 15 minutes | Serves 2

1 medium acorn squash, halved crosswise and deseeded	1 teaspoon light brown sugar
1 teaspoon coconut oil	Few dashes of ground cinnamon
	Few dashes of ground nutmeg

1. On a clean work surface, rub the cut sides of the acorn squash with coconut oil. Scatter with the brown sugar, cinnamon, and nutmeg.
2. Put the squash halves in the air fry basket, cut-side up.
3. Select Air Fry, Super Convection, set temperature to 325°F (163°C), and set time to 15 minutes. Select Start/Stop to begin preheating.
4. Once preheated, place the basket on the air fry position.
5. When cooking is complete, the squash halves should be just tender when pierced in the center with a paring knife. Remove the basket from the oven. Rest for 5 to 10 minutes and serve warm.

Corn Cheese Casserole

Prep time: 5 minutes | Cook time: 15 minutes | Serves 4

2 cups frozen yellow corn	Pinch salt
1 egg, beaten	Freshly ground black pepper, to taste
3 tablespoons flour	2 tablespoons butter, cut into cubes
½ cup grated Swiss or Havarti cheese	Nonstick cooking spray
½ cup light cream	
¼ cup milk	

1. Spritz a baking pan with nonstick cooking spray.
2. Stir together the remaining ingredients except the butter in a medium bowl until well incorporated. Transfer the mixture to the prepared baking pan and scatter with the butter cubes.
3. Select Bake, Super Convection, set temperature to 320°F (160°C), and set time to 15 minutes. Select Start/Stop to begin preheating.
4. Once preheated, place the pan on the bake position.
5. When cooking is complete, the top should be golden brown and a toothpick inserted in the center should come out clean. Remove the pan from the oven. Let the casserole cool for 5 minutes before slicing into wedges and serving.

Potato with Yogurt

Prep time: 5 minutes | Cook time: 35 minutes | Serves 4

4 (7-ounce / 198-g) russet potatoes, rinsed	½ cup 2% plain Greek yogurt
Olive oil spray	¼ cup minced fresh chives
½ teaspoon kosher salt, divided	Freshly ground black pepper, to taste

1. Pat the potatoes dry and pierce them all over with a fork. Spritz the potatoes with olive oil spray. Sprinkle with ¼ teaspoon of the salt.
2. Transfer the potatoes to the air fry basket.
3. Select Bake, Super Convection, set temperature to 400°F (205°C), and set time to 35 minutes. Select Start/Stop to begin preheating.
4. Once preheated, place the basket on the bake position.
5. When cooking is complete, the potatoes should be fork-tender. Remove from the oven and split open the potatoes. Top with the yogurt, chives, the remaining ¼ teaspoon of salt, and finish with the black pepper. Serve immediately.

Zucchini Crisps

Prep time: 5 minutes | Cook time: 14 minutes | Serves 4

2 zucchini, sliced into ¼- to ½-inch-thick rounds (about 2 cups)
¼ teaspoon garlic granules
⅛ teaspoon sea salt
Freshly ground black pepper, to taste (optional)
Cooking spray

1. Spritz the air fry basket with cooking spray.
2. Put the zucchini rounds in the air fry basket, spreading them out as much as possible. Top with a sprinkle of garlic granules, sea salt, and black pepper (if desired). Spritz the zucchini rounds with cooking spray.
3. Select Roast, Super Convection, set temperature to 392ºF (200ºC), and set time to 14 minutes. Select Start/Stop to begin preheating.
4. Once preheated, place the basket on the roast position. Flip the zucchini rounds halfway through.
5. When cooking is complete, the zucchini rounds should be crisp-tender. Remove from the oven. Let them rest for 5 minutes and serve.

Rosemary Potato

Prep time: 5 minutes | Cook time: 20 minutes | Serves 4

1½ pounds (680 g) small red potatoes, cut into 1-inch cubes
2 tablespoons olive oil
2 tablespoons minced fresh rosemary
1 tablespoon minced garlic
1 teaspoon salt, plus additional as needed
½ teaspoon freshly ground black pepper, plus additional as needed

1. Toss the potato cubes with the olive oil, rosemary, garlic, salt, and pepper in a large bowl until thoroughly coated.
2. Arrange the potato cubes in the air fry basket in a single layer.
3. Select Roast, Super Convection, set temperature to 400ºF (205ºC), and set time to 20 minutes. Select Start/Stop to begin preheating.
4. Once preheated, place the basket on the roast position. Stir the potatoes a few times during cooking for even cooking.
5. When cooking is complete, the potatoes should be tender. Remove from the oven to a plate. Taste and add additional salt and pepper as needed.

Creamy Potato

Prep time: 5 minutes | Cook time: 15 to 20 minutes | Serves 4

2 cup sliced frozen potatoes, thawed
3 cloves garlic, minced
Pinch salt
Freshly ground black pepper, to taste
¾ cup heavy cream

1. Toss the potatoes with the garlic, salt, and black pepper in a baking pan until evenly coated. Pour the heavy cream over the top.
2. Select Bake, Super Convection, set temperature to 380ºF (193ºC), and set time to 15 minutes. Select Start/Stop to begin preheating.
3. Once preheated, place the pan on the bake position.
4. When cooking is complete, the potatoes should be tender and the top golden brown. Check for doneness and bake for another 5 minutes if needed. Remove from the oven and serve hot.

Chapter 5 Fish and Seafood

Salmon Spring Rolls with Carrot

Prep time: 20 minutes | Cook time: 18 minutes | Serves 4

½ pound (227 g) salmon fillet
1 teaspoon toasted sesame oil
1 onion, sliced
1 carrot, shredded
1 yellow bell pepper, thinly sliced
1/3 cup chopped fresh flat-leaf parsley
¼ cup chopped fresh basil
8 rice paper wrappers

1. Arrange the salmon in the air fry basket. Drizzle the sesame oil all over the salmon and scatter the onion on top.
2. Select Air Fry, Super Convection, set temperature to 370ºF (188ºC), and set time to 10 minutes. Select Start/Stop to begin preheating.
3. Once preheated, place the basket on the air fry position.
4. Meanwhile, fill a small shallow bowl with warm water. One by one, dip the rice paper wrappers into the water for a few seconds or just until moistened, then put them on a work surface.
5. When cooking is complete, the fish should flake apart with a fork. Remove from the oven to a plate.
6. Make the spring rolls: Place ⅛ of the salmon and onion mixture, carrot, bell pepper, parsley, and basil into the center of the rice wrapper and fold the sides over the filling. Roll up the wrapper carefully and tightly like you would a burrito. Repeat with the remaining wrappers and filling.
7. Transfer the rolls to the air fry basket.
8. Select Bake, Super Convection, set temperature to 380ºF (193ºC), and set time to 8 minutes. Select Start/Stop to begin preheating.
9. Once preheated, place the basket on the bake position.
10. When cooking is complete, the rolls should be crispy and lightly browned. Remove from the oven and cut each roll in half and serve warm.

Snapper with Tomato and Olives

Prep time: 9 minutes | Cook time: 18 minutes | Serves 4

2 tablespoons extra-virgin olive oil
2 large garlic cloves, minced
½ onion, finely chopped
1 (14.5-ounce / 411-g) can diced tomatoes, drained
¼ cup sliced green olives
3 tablespoons capers, divided
2 tablespoons chopped fresh parsley, divided
½ teaspoon dried oregano
4 (6-ounce / 170-g) snapper fillets
½ teaspoon kosher salt

1. Grease the sheet pan generously with olive oil, then place the pan on the roast position.
2. Select Roast, Super Convection, set temperature to 375ºF (190ºC), and set time to 18 minutes. Select Start/Stop to begin preheating.
3. When the oven has preheated, remove the pan and add the garlic and onion to the olive oil in the pan, stirring to coat. Return the pan to the oven and continue cooking.
4. After 2 minutes, remove the pan from the oven. Stir in the tomatoes, olives, 1½ tablespoons of capers, 1 tablespoon of parsley, and oregano. Return the pan to the oven and continue cooking for 6 minutes until heated through.
5. Meanwhile, rub the fillets with the salt on both sides.
6. After another 6 minutes, remove the pan. Put the fillets in the center of the sheet pan and spoon some of the sauce over them. Return the pan to the oven and continue cooking, or until the fish is flaky.
7. When cooked, remove the pan from the oven. Scatter the remaining 1½ tablespoons of capers and 1 tablespoon of parsley on top of the fillets, then serve.

Panko Fish Fillets

Prep time: 20 minutes | Cook time: 7 minutes | Serves 4

1 pound (454 g) fish fillets
1 tablespoon coarse brown mustard
1 teaspoon Worcestershire sauce
½ teaspoon hot sauce
Salt, to taste
Cooking spray

Crumb Coating:
¾ cup panko bread crumbs
¼ cup stone-ground cornmeal
¼ teaspoon salt

1. On your cutting board, cut the fish fillets crosswise into slices, about 1 inch wide.
2. In a small bowl, stir together the mustard, Worcestershire sauce, and hot sauce to make a paste and rub this paste on all sides of the fillets. Season with salt to taste.
3. In a shallow bowl, thoroughly combine all the ingredients for the crumb coating and spread them on a sheet of wax paper.
4. Roll the fish fillets in the crumb mixture until thickly coated. Spritz all sides of the fish with cooking spray, then arrange them in the air fry basket in a single layer.
5. Select Air Fry, Super Convection, set temperature to 400ºF (205ºC), and set time to 7 minutes. Select Start/Stop to begin preheating.
6. Once preheated, place the air fry basket into the oven.
7. When cooking is complete, the fish should flake apart with a fork. Remove from the oven and serve warm.

Cod Fillets with Parsley

Prep time: 15 minutes | Cook time: 12 minutes | Serves 4

4 cod fillets
¼ teaspoon fine sea salt
1 teaspoon cayenne pepper
¼ teaspoon ground black pepper, or more to taste
½ cup fresh Italian parsley, coarsely chopped
½ cup non-dairy milk
4 garlic cloves, minced
1 Italian pepper, chopped
1 teaspoon dried basil
½ teaspoon dried oregano
Cooking spray

1. Lightly spritz a baking dish with cooking spray.
2. Season the fillets with salt, cayenne pepper, and black pepper.
3. Pulse the remaining ingredients in a food processor, then transfer the mixture to a shallow bowl. Coat the fillets with the mixture.
4. Select Air Fry, Super Convection, set temperature to 375ºF (190ºC), and set time to 12 minutes. Select Start/Stop to begin preheating.
5. Once preheated, place the baking dish into the oven.
6. When cooking is complete, the fish will be flaky. Remove from the oven and serve on a plate.

Salmon with Teriyaki Sauce

Prep time: 15 minutes | Cook time: 15 minutes | Serves 4

¾ cup Teriyaki sauce, divided
4 (6-ounce / 170-g) skinless salmon fillets
4 heads baby bok choy, root ends trimmed off and cut in half lengthwise through the root
1 teaspoon sesame oil
1 tablespoon vegetable oil
1 tablespoon toasted sesame seeds

1. Set aside ¼ cup of Teriyaki sauce and pour the remaining sauce into a resealable plastic bag. Put the salmon into the bag and seal, squeezing as much air out as possible. Allow the salmon to marinate for at least 10 minutes.
2. Arrange the bok choy halves on the sheet pan. Drizzle the oils over the vegetables, tossing to coat. Drizzle about 1 tablespoon of the reserved Teriyaki sauce over the bok choy, then push them to the sides of the sheet pan.
3. Put the salmon fillets in the middle of the sheet pan.
4. Select Roast, Super Convection, set temperature to 375ºF (190ºC), and set time to 15 minutes. Select Start/Stop to begin preheating.
5. Once the oven has preheated, place the pan on the roast position.
6. When done, remove the pan and brush the salmon with the remaining Teriyaki sauce. Serve garnished with the sesame seeds.

Mustard Sole Fillets

Prep time: 5 minutes | Cook time: 10 minutes | Serves 4

5 teaspoons low-sodium yellow mustard
1 tablespoon freshly squeezed lemon juice
4 (3.5-ounce / 99-g) sole fillets
2 teaspoons olive oil
½ teaspoon dried marjoram
½ teaspoon dried thyme
⅛ teaspoon freshly ground black pepper
1 slice low-sodium whole-wheat bread, crumbled

1. Whisk together the mustard and lemon juice in a small bowl until thoroughly mixed and smooth. Spread the mixture evenly over the sole fillets, then transfer the fillets to the air fry basket.
2. In a separate bowl, combine the olive oil, marjoram, thyme, black pepper, and bread crumbs and stir to mix well. Gently but firmly press the mixture onto the top of fillets, coating them completely.
3. Select Bake, Super Convection, set temperature to 320ºF (160ºC), and set time to 10 minutes. Select Start/Stop to begin preheating.
4. Once preheated, place the basket on the bake position.
5. When cooking is complete, the fish should reach an internal temperature of 145ºF (63ºC) on a meat thermometer. Remove the basket from the oven and serve on a plate.

Breaded Fish Strips

Prep time: 10 minutes | Cook time: 6 minutes | Serves 8

8 ounces (227 g) fish fillets (pollock or cod), cut into ½ × 3 inches strips
Salt, to taste
(optional)
½ cup plain bread crumbs
Cooking spray

1. Season the fish strips with salt to taste, if desired.
2. Place the bread crumbs on a plate, then roll the fish in the bread crumbs until well coated. Spray all sides of the fish with cooking spray. Transfer to the air fry basket in a single layer.
3. Select Air Fry, Super Convection, set temperature to 400ºF (205ºC), and set time to 6 minutes. Select Start/Stop to begin preheating.
4. Once preheated, place the basket on the air fry position.
5. When cooked, the fish sticks should be golden brown and crispy. Remove from the oven to a plate and serve hot.

Tuna and Pineapple Kebabs

Prep time: 15 minutes | Cook time: 10 minutes | Serves 4

Kebabs:
1 pound (454 g) tuna steaks, cut into 1-inch cubes
½ cup canned pineapple chunks, drained, juice reserved
½ cup large red grapes

Marinade:
1 tablespoon honey
1 teaspoon olive oil
2 teaspoons grated fresh ginger
Pinch cayenne pepper

Special Equipment:
4 metal skewers

1. Make the kebabs: Thread, alternating tuna cubes, pineapple chunks, and red grapes, onto the metal skewers.
2. Make the marinade: Whisk together the honey, olive oil, ginger, and cayenne pepper in a small bowl. Brush generously the marinade over the kebabs and allow to sit for 10 minutes.
3. When ready, transfer the kebabs to the air fry basket.
4. Select Air Fry, Super Convection, set temperature to 370ºF (188ºC), and set time to 10 minutes. Select Start/Stop to begin preheating.
5. Once preheated, place the basket on the air fry position.
6. After 5 minutes, remove from the oven and flip the kebabs and brush with the remaining marinade. Return the basket to the oven and continue cooking for an additional 5 minutes.
7. When cooking is complete, the kebabs should reach an internal temperature of 145ºF (63ºC) on a meat thermometer. Remove from the oven and discard any remaining marinade. Serve hot.

Chapter 3 Vegan and Vegetarian|53

Tuna and Lettuce Wraps with Mayo

Prep time: 10 minutes | Cook time: 4 to 7 minutes | Serves 4

1 pound (454 g) fresh tuna steak, cut into 1-inch cubes
2 garlic cloves, minced
1 tablespoon grated fresh ginger
½ teaspoon toasted sesame oil
4 low-sodium whole-wheat tortillas
2 cups shredded romaine lettuce
1 red bell pepper, thinly sliced
¼ cup low-fat mayonnaise

1. Combine the tuna cubes, garlic, ginger, and sesame oil in a medium bowl and toss until well coated. Allow to sit for 10 minutes.
2. When ready, place the tuna cubes in the air fry basket.
3. Select Air Fry, Super Convection, set temperature to 390°F (199°C), and set time to 6 minutes. Select Start/Stop to begin preheating.
4. Once preheated, place the basket on the air fry position.
5. When cooking is complete, the tuna cubes should be cooked through and golden brown. Remove the tuna cubes from the oven to a plate.
6. Make the wraps: Place the tortillas on a flat work surface and top each tortilla evenly with the cooked tuna, lettuce, bell pepper, and finish with the mayonnaise. Roll them up and serve immediately.

Tilapia and Coleslaw Tacos

Prep time: 10 minutes | Cook time: 10 to 15 minutes | Serves 6

1 tablespoon avocado oil
1 tablespoon Cajun seasoning
4 (5 to 6 ounce / 142 to 170 g) tilapia fillets
1 (14-ounce / 397-g) package coleslaw mix
12 corn tortillas
2 limes, cut into wedges

1. Line a baking pan with parchment paper.
2. In a shallow bowl, stir together the avocado oil and Cajun seasoning to make a marinade. Place the tilapia fillets into the bowl, turning to coat evenly.
3. Put the fillets in the baking pan in a single layer.
4. Select Air Fry, Super Convection, set temperature to 375°F (190°C), and set time to 10 minutes. Select Start/Stop to begin preheating.
5. Once preheated, slide the pan into the oven.
6. When cooked, the fish should be flaky. If necessary, continue cooking for 5 minutes more. Remove the fish from the oven to a plate.
7. Assemble the tacos: Spoon some of the coleslaw mix into each tortilla and top each with ⅓ of a tilapia fillet. Squeeze some lime juice over the top of each taco and serve immediately.

Salmon Patties

Prep time: 10 minutes | Cook time: 13 minutes | Serves 4

1 pound (454 g) salmon, chopped into ½-inch pieces
2 tablespoons coconut flour
2 tablespoons grated Parmesan cheese
1½ tablespoons milk
½ white onion, peeled and finely chopped
½ teaspoon butter, at room temperature
½ teaspoon chipotle powder
½ teaspoon dried parsley flakes
⅓ teaspoon ground black pepper
⅓ teaspoon smoked cayenne pepper
1 teaspoon fine sea salt

1. Put all the ingredients for the salmon patties in a bowl and stir to combine well.
2. Scoop out 2 tablespoons of the salmon mixture and shape into a patty with your palm, about ½ inch thick. Repeat until all the mixture is used. Transfer to the refrigerator for about 2 hours until firm.
3. When ready, arrange the salmon patties in the air fry basket.
4. Select Bake, Super Convection, set temperature to 395°F (202°C), and set time to 13 minutes. Select Start/Stop to begin preheating.
5. Once preheated, place the basket on the bake position. Flip the patties halfway through the cooking time.
6. When cooking is complete, the patties should be golden brown. Remove from the oven and cool for 5 minutes before serving.

Chapter 3 Vegan and Vegetarian

Tuna Cubes over Rice

Prep time: 15 minutes | Cook time: 5 minutes | Serves 4

½ cup hoisin sauce
2 tablespoons rice wine vinegar
2 teaspoons sesame oil
2 teaspoons dried lemongrass
1 teaspoon garlic powder
¼ teaspoon red pepper flakes
½ small onion, quartered and thinly sliced
8 ounces (227 g) fresh tuna, cut into 1-inch cubes
Cooking spray
3 cups cooked jasmine rice

1. In a small bowl, whisk together the hoisin sauce, vinegar, sesame oil, lemongrass, garlic powder, and red pepper flakes.
2. Add the sliced onion and tuna cubes and gently toss until the fish is evenly coated.
3. Arrange the coated tuna cubes in the air fry basket in a single layer.
4. Select Air Fry, Super Convection, set temperature to 390ºF (199ºC), and set time to 5 minutes. Select Start/Stop to begin preheating.
5. Once preheated, place the basket on the air fry position. Flip the fish halfway through the cooking time.
6. When cooking is complete, the fish should begin to flake. Continue cooking for 1 minute, if necessary. Remove from the oven and serve over hot jasmine rice.

Tuna Casserole

Prep time: 10 minutes | Cook time: 16 minutes | Serves 4

½ tablespoon sesame oil
⅓ cup yellow onions, chopped
½ bell pepper, deveined and chopped
2 cups canned tuna, chopped
Cooking spray
5 eggs, beaten
½ chili pepper, deveined and finely minced
1½ tablespoons sour cream
⅓ teaspoon dried basil
⅓ teaspoon dried oregano
Fine sea salt and ground black pepper, to taste

1. Heat the sesame oil in a nonstick skillet over medium heat until it shimmers.
2. Add the onions and bell pepper and sauté for 4 minutes, stirring occasionally, or until tender.
3. Add the canned tuna and keep stirring until the tuna is heated through.
4. Meanwhile, coat a baking dish lightly with cooking spray.
5. Transfer the tuna mixture to the baking dish, along with the beaten eggs, chili pepper, sour cream, basil, and oregano. Stir to combine well. Season with sea salt and black pepper.
6. Select Bake, Super Convection, set temperature to 325ºF (160ºC), and set time to 12 minutes. Select Start/Stop to begin preheating.
7. Once preheated, place the baking dish on the bake position.
8. When cooking is complete, the eggs should be completely set and the top lightly browned. Remove from the oven and serve on a plate.

Snapper with Plums

Prep time: 15 minutes | Cook time: 12 minutes | Serves 4

4 (4-ounce / 113-g) red snapper fillets
2 teaspoons olive oil
3 plums, halved and pitted
3 nectarines, halved and pitted
1 cup red grapes
1 tablespoon freshly squeezed lemon juice
1 tablespoon honey
½ teaspoon dried thyme

1. Arrange the red snapper fillets in the air fry basket and drizzle the olive oil over the top.
2. Select Air Fry, Super Convection, set temperature to 390ºF (199ºC), and set time to 12 minutes. Select Start/Stop to begin preheating.
3. Once preheated, place the basket on the air fry position.
4. After 4 minutes, remove the basket from the oven. Top the fillets with the plums and nectarines. Scatter the red grapes all over the fillets. Drizzle with the lemon juice and honey and sprinkle the thyme on top. Return the basket to the oven and continue cooking for 8 minutes, or until the fish is flaky.
5. When cooking is complete, remove from the oven and serve warm.

Salmon Patties

Prep time: 5 minutes | Cook time: 11 minutes | Makes 6 patties

1 (14.75-ounce / 418-g) can Alaskan pink salmon, drained and bones removed
½ cup bread crumbs
1 egg, whisked
2 scallions, diced
1 teaspoon garlic powder
Salt and pepper, to taste
Cooking spray

1. Stir together the salmon, bread crumbs, whisked egg, scallions, garlic powder, salt, and pepper in a large bowl until well incorporated.
2. Divide the salmon mixture into six equal portions and form each into a patty with your hands.
3. Arrange the salmon patties in the air fry basket and spritz them with cooking spray.
4. Select Air Fry, Super Convection, set temperature to 400°F (205°C), and set time to 10 minutes. Select Start/Stop to begin preheating.
5. Once preheated, place the basket on the air fry position. Flip the patties once halfway through.
6. When cooking is complete, the patties should be golden brown and cooked through. Remove the patties from the oven and serve on a plate.

Beer Cod Fillets

Prep time: 5 minutes | Cook time: 15 minutes | Serves 4

2 eggs
1 cup malty beer
1 cup all-purpose flour
½ cup cornstarch
1 teaspoon garlic powder
Salt and pepper, to taste
4 (4-ounce / 113-g) cod fillets
Cooking spray

1. In a shallow bowl, beat together the eggs with the beer. In another shallow bowl, thoroughly combine the flour and cornstarch. Sprinkle with the garlic powder, salt, and pepper.
2. Dredge each cod fillet in the flour mixture, then in the egg mixture. Dip each piece of fish in the flour mixture a second time.
3. Spritz the air fry basket with cooking spray. Arrange the cod fillets in the basket in a single layer.
4. Select Air Fry, Super Convection, set temperature to 400°F (205°C), and set time to 15 minutes. Select Start/Stop to begin preheating.
5. Once preheated, place the basket on the air fry position. Flip the fillets halfway through the cooking time.
6. When cooking is complete, the cod should reach an internal temperature of 145°F (63°C) on a meat thermometer and the outside should be crispy. Let the fish cool for 5 minutes and serve.

Basil Salmon with Tomato

Prep time: 10 minutes | Cook time: 15 minutes | Serves 4

4 (6-ounce / 170-g) salmon fillets, patted dry
1 teaspoon kosher salt, divided
2 pints cherry or grape tomatoes, halved if large, divided
3 tablespoons extra-virgin olive oil, divided
2 garlic cloves, minced
1 small red bell pepper, deseeded and chopped
2 tablespoons chopped fresh basil, divided

1. Season both sides of the salmon with ½ teaspoon of kosher salt.
2. Put about half of the tomatoes in a large bowl, along with the remaining ½ teaspoon of kosher salt, 2 tablespoons of olive oil, garlic, bell pepper, and 1 tablespoon of basil. Toss to coat and then transfer to the sheet pan.
3. Arrange the salmon fillets on the sheet pan, skin-side down. Brush them with the remaining 1 tablespoon of olive oil.
4. Select Roast, Super Convection, set temperature to 375°F (190°C), and set time to 15 minutes. Select Start/Stop to begin preheating.
5. Once preheated, place the pan on the roast position.
6. After 7 minutes, remove the pan and fold in the remaining tomatoes. Return the pan to the oven and continue cooking.
7. When cooked, remove the pan from the oven. Serve sprinkled with the remaining 1 tablespoon of basil.

Salmon and Asparagus

Prep time: 10 minutes | Cook time: 15 minutes | Serves 4

4 (6-ounce / 170 g) salmon fillets, patted dry
1 teaspoon kosher salt, divided
1 tablespoon honey
2 tablespoons unsalted butter, melted
2 teaspoons Dijon mustard
2 pounds (907 g) asparagus, trimmed
Lemon wedges, for serving

1. Season both sides of the salmon fillets with ½ teaspoon of kosher salt.
2. Whisk together the honey, 1 tablespoon of butter, and mustard in a small bowl. Set aside.
3. Arrange the asparagus on a sheet pan. Drizzle the remaining 1 tablespoon of butter all over and season with the remaining ½ teaspoon of salt, tossing to coat. Move the asparagus to the outside of the sheet pan.
4. Put the salmon fillets on the sheet pan, skin-side down. Brush the fillets generously with the honey mixture.
5. Select Roast, Super Convection, set temperature to 375ºF (190ºC), and set time to 15 minutes. Select Start/Stop to begin preheating.
6. Once the oven has preheated, place the pan on the roast position. Toss the asparagus once halfway through the cooking time.
7. When done, transfer the salmon fillets and asparagus to a plate. Serve warm with a squeeze of lemon juice.

Salmon Steaks with Butter

Prep time: 5 minutes | Cook time: 10 minutes | Serves 4

4 tablespoons butter, melted
2 cloves garlic, minced
Sea salt and ground black pepper, to taste
¼ cup dry white wine
1 tablespoon lime juice
1 teaspoon smoked paprika
½ teaspoon onion powder
4 salmon steaks
Cooking spray

1. Place all the ingredients except the salmon and oil in a shallow dish and stir to mix well.
2. Add the salmon steaks, turning to coat well on both sides. Transfer the salmon to the refrigerator to marinate for 30 minutes.
3. When ready, put the salmon steaks in the air fry basket, discarding any excess marinade. Spray the salmon steaks with cooking spray.
4. Select Air Fry, Super Convection, set temperature to 360ºF (182ºC), and set time to 10 minutes. Select Start/Stop to begin preheating.
5. Once preheated, place the basket on the air fry position. Flip the salmon steaks halfway through.
6. When cooking is complete, remove from the oven and divide the salmon steaks among four plates. Serve warm.

Swordfish Steaks with Lemon

Prep time: 10 minutes | Cook time: 8 minutes | Serves 4

4 (4-ounce / 113-g) swordfish steaks
½ teaspoon toasted sesame oil
1 jalapeño pepper, finely minced
2 garlic cloves, grated
2 tablespoons freshly squeezed lemon juice
1 tablespoon grated fresh ginger
½ teaspoon Chinese five-spice powder
⅛ teaspoon freshly ground black pepper

1. On a clean work surface, place the swordfish steaks and brush both sides of the fish with the sesame oil.
2. Combine the jalapeño, garlic, lemon juice, ginger, five-spice powder, and black pepper in a small bowl and stir to mix well. Rub the mixture all over the fish until completely coated. Allow to sit for 10 minutes.
3. When ready, arrange the swordfish steaks in the air fry basket.
4. Select Air Fry, Super Convection, set temperature to 380ºF (193ºC), and set time to 8 minutes. Select Start/Stop to begin preheating.
5. Once preheated, place the basket on the air fry position. Flip the steaks halfway through.
6. When cooking is complete, remove from the oven and cool for 5 minutes before serving.

Chapter 3 Vegan and Vegetarian|57

Garlicky Cod Fillets

Prep time: 10 minutes | Cook time: 12 minutes | Serves 4

1 teaspoon olive oil
4 cod fillets
¼ teaspoon fine sea salt
¼ teaspoon ground black pepper, or more to taste
1 teaspoon cayenne pepper
½ cup fresh Italian parsley, coarsely chopped
½ cup nondairy milk
1 Italian pepper, chopped
4 garlic cloves, minced
1 teaspoon dried basil
½ teaspoon dried oregano

1. Lightly coat the sides and bottom of a baking dish with the olive oil. Set aside.
2. In a large bowl, sprinkle the fillets with salt, black pepper, and cayenne pepper.
3. In a food processor, pulse the remaining ingredients until smoothly puréed.
4. Add the purée to the bowl of fillets and toss to coat, then transfer to the prepared baking dish.
5. Select Bake, Super Convection, set temperature to 380ºF (193ºC), and set time to 12 minutes. Select Start/Stop to begin preheating.
6. Once preheated, place the baking dish on the bake position.
7. When cooking is complete, the fish should flake when pressed lightly with a fork. Remove from the oven and serve warm.

Salmon with Asparagus

Prep time: 5 minutes | Cook time: 12 minutes | Serves 2

2 teaspoons olive oil, plus additional for drizzling
2 (5-ounce / 142-g) salmon fillets, with skin
Salt and freshly ground black pepper, to taste
1 bunch asparagus, trimmed
1 teaspoon dried tarragon
1 teaspoon dried chives
Fresh lemon wedges, for serving

1. Rub the olive oil all over the salmon fillets. Sprinkle with salt and pepper to taste.
2. Put the asparagus on a foil-lined baking sheet and place the salmon fillets on top, skin-side down.
3. Select Roast, Super Convection, set temperature to 425ºF (220ºC), and set time to 12 minutes. Select Start/Stop to begin preheating.
4. Once preheated, place the pan on the roast position.
5. When cooked, the fillets should register 145ºF (63ºC) on an instant-read thermometer. Remove from the oven and cut the salmon fillets in half crosswise, then use a metal spatula to lift flesh from skin and transfer to a serving plate. Discard the skin and drizzle the salmon fillets with additional olive oil. Scatter with the herbs.
6. Serve the salmon fillets with roasted asparagus spears and lemon wedges on the side.

Catfish Fillets with Pecan

Prep time: 5 minutes | Cook time: 12 minutes | Serves 4

½ cup pecan meal
1 teaspoon fine sea salt
¼ teaspoon ground black pepper
4 (4-ounce / 113-g) catfish fillets
Avocado oil spray

For Garnish (Optional):
Fresh oregano
Pecan halves

1. Spray the air fry basket with avocado oil spray.
2. Combine the pecan meal, sea salt, and black pepper in a large bowl. Dredge each catfish fillet in the meal mixture, turning until well coated. Spritz the fillets with avocado oil spray, then transfer to the air fry basket.
3. Select Air Fry, Super Convection, set temperature to 375ºF (190ºC), and set time to 12 minutes. Select Start/Stop to begin preheating.
4. Once preheated, place the basket on the air fry position. Flip the fillets halfway through the cooking time.
5. When cooking is complete, the fish should be cooked through and no longer translucent. Remove from the oven and sprinkle the oregano sprigs and pecan halves on top for garnish, if desired. Serve immediately.

Salmon Bowl with Salsa

Prep time: 115 minutes | Cook time: 12 minutes | Serves 4

12 ounces (340 g) salmon fillets, cut into 1½-inch cubes	¼ cup low-sodium salsa
1 red onion, chopped	2 teaspoons peanut oil or safflower oil
1 jalapeño pepper, minced	2 tablespoons low-sodium tomato juice
1 red bell pepper, chopped	1 teaspoon chili powder

1. Mix together the salmon cubes, red onion, jalapeño, red bell pepper, salsa, peanut oil, tomato juice, chili powder in a medium metal bowl and stir until well incorporated.
2. Select Bake, Super Convection, set temperature to 370ºF (188ºC), and set time to 12 minutes. Select Start/Stop to begin preheating.
3. Once preheated, place the metal bowl on the bake position. Stir the ingredients once halfway through the cooking time.
4. When cooking is complete, the salmon should be cooked through and the veggies should be fork-tender. Serve warm.

Breaded Catfish Nuggets

Prep time: 10 minutes | Cook time: 7 to 8 minutes | Serves 4

2 medium catfish fillets, cut into chunks (approximately 1 × 2 inch)	2 tablespoons skim milk
Salt and pepper, to taste	½ cup cornstarch
2 eggs	1 cup panko bread crumbs
	Cooking spray

1. In a medium bowl, season the fish chunks with salt and pepper to taste.
2. In a small bowl, beat together the eggs with milk until well combined.
3. Place the cornstarch and bread crumbs into separate shallow dishes.
4. Dredge the fish chunks one at a time in the cornstarch, coating well on both sides, then dip in the egg mixture, shaking off any excess, finally press well into the bread crumbs. Spritz the fish chunks with cooking spray.
5. Arrange the fish chunks in the air fry basket in a single layer.
6. Select Air Fry, Super Convection, set temperature to 390ºF (199ºC), and set time to 8 minutes. Select Start/Stop to begin preheating.
7. Once preheated, place the basket on the air fry position. Flip the fish chunks halfway through the cooking time.
8. When cooking is complete, they should be no longer translucent in the center and golden brown. Remove the fish chunks from the oven to a plate. Serve warm.

Halibut Fillets with Cheese

Prep time: 5 minutes | Cook time: 10 minutes | Serves 4

2 medium-sized halibut fillets	paprika
Dash of tabasco sauce	Kosher salt and freshly cracked mixed peppercorns, to taste
1 teaspoon curry powder	2 eggs
½ teaspoon ground coriander	1½ tablespoons olive oil
½ teaspoon hot	½ cup grated Parmesan cheese

1. On a clean work surface, drizzle the halibut fillets with the tabasco sauce. Sprinkle with the curry powder, coriander, hot paprika, salt, and cracked mixed peppercorns. Set aside.
2. In a shallow bowl, beat the eggs until frothy. In another shallow bowl, combine the olive oil and Parmesan cheese.
3. One at a time, dredge the halibut fillets in the beaten eggs, shaking off any excess, then roll them over the Parmesan cheese until evenly coated.
4. Arrange the halibut fillets in the air fry basket in a single layer.
5. Select Roast, Super Convection, set temperature to 365ºF (185ºC), and set time to 10 minutes. Select Start/Stop to begin preheating.
6. Once preheated, place the basket on the roast position.
7. When cooking is complete, the fish should be golden brown and crisp. Cool for 5 minutes before serving.

Halibut Steaks with Vermouth

Prep time: 5 minutes | Cook time: 10 minutes | Serves 4

1 pound (454 g) halibut steaks
¼ cup vegetable oil
2½ tablespoons Worcester sauce
2 tablespoons honey
2 tablespoons vermouth
1 tablespoon freshly squeezed lemon juice
1 tablespoon fresh parsley leaves, coarsely chopped
Salt and pepper, to taste
1 teaspoon dried basil

1. Put all the ingredients in a large mixing dish and gently stir until the fish is coated evenly. Transfer the fish to the air fry basket.
2. Select Roast, Super Convection, set temperature to 390ºF (199ºC), and set time to 10 minutes. Select Start/Stop to begin preheating.
3. Once preheated, place the basket on the roast position. Flip the fish halfway through cooking time.
4. When cooking is complete, the fish should reach an internal temperature of at least 145ºF (63ºC) on a meat thermometer. Remove from the oven and let the fish cool for 5 minutes before serving.

Lemony Cod Fillets

Prep time: 5 minutes | Cook time: 12 minutes | Makes 2 cod fillets

1 tablespoon Cajun seasoning
1 teaspoon salt
½ teaspoon lemon pepper
½ teaspoon freshly ground black pepper
2 (8-ounce / 227-g) cod fillets, cut to fit into the air fry basket
Cooking spray
2 tablespoons unsalted butter, melted
1 lemon, cut into 4 wedges

1. Spritz the air fry basket with cooking spray.
2. Thoroughly combine the Cajun seasoning, salt, lemon pepper, and black pepper in a small bowl. Rub this mixture all over the cod fillets until completely coated.
3. Put the fillets in the air fry basket and brush the melted butter over both sides of each fillet.
4. Select Bake, Super Convection, set temperature to 360ºF (182ºC), and set time to 12 minutes. Select Start/Stop to begin preheating.
5. Once preheated, place the basket on the bake position. Flip the fillets halfway through the cooking time.
6. When cooking is complete, the fish should flake apart with a fork. Remove the fillets from the oven and serve with fresh lemon wedges.

Red Snapper with Lemon

Prep time: 13 minutes | Cook time: 10 minutes | Serves 4

1 teaspoon olive oil
1½ teaspoons black pepper
¼ teaspoon garlic powder
¼ teaspoon thyme
⅛ teaspoon cayenne pepper
4 (4-ounce / 113-g) red snapper fillets, skin on
4 thin slices lemon
Nonstick cooking spray

1. Spritz the air fry basket with nonstick cooking spray.
2. In a small bowl, stir together the olive oil, black pepper, garlic powder, thyme, and cayenne pepper. Rub the mixture all over the fillets until completely coated.
3. Lay the fillets, skin-side down, in the air fry basket and top each fillet with a slice of lemon.
4. Select Bake, Super Convection, set temperature to 390ºF (199ºC), and set time to 10 minutes. Select Start/Stop to begin preheating.
5. Once preheated, place the basket on the bake position. Flip the fillets halfway through.
6. When cooking is complete, the fish should be cooked through. Let the fish cool for 5 minutes and serve.

Sole and Cauliflower Fritters

Prep time: 5 minutes | Cook time: 24 minutes | Serves 2

½ pound (227 g) sole fillets
½ pound (227 g) mashed cauliflower
½ cup red onion, chopped
1 bell pepper, finely chopped
1 egg, beaten
2 garlic cloves, minced
2 tablespoons fresh parsley, chopped
1 tablespoon olive oil
1 tablespoon coconut aminos
½ teaspoon scotch bonnet pepper, minced
½ teaspoon paprika
Salt and white pepper, to taste
Cooking spray

1. Spray the air fry basket with cooking spray. Place the sole fillets in the basket.
2. Select Air Fry, Super Convection, set temperature to 395°F (202°C), and set time to 10 minutes. Select Start/Stop to begin preheating.
3. Once preheated, place the basket on the air fry position. Flip the fillets halfway through.
4. When cooking is complete, transfer the fish fillets to a large bowl. Mash the fillets into flakes. Add the remaining ingredients and stir to combine.
5. Make the fritters: Scoop out 2 tablespoons of the fish mixture and shape into a patty about ½ inch thick with your hands. Repeat with the remaining fish mixture. Place the patties in the air fry basket.
6. Select Bake, Super Convection, set temperature to 380°F (193°C), and set time to 14 minutes. Select Start/Stop to begin preheating.
7. Once preheated, place the basket on the bake position. Flip the patties halfway through.
8. When cooking is complete, they should be golden brown and cooked through. Remove the basket from the oven and cool for 5 minutes before serving.

Tuna Patties with Cheese Sauce

Prep time: 5 minutes | Cook time: 17 to 18 minutes | Serves 4

Tuna Patties:
1 pound (454 g) canned tuna, drained
1 egg, whisked
2 tablespoons shallots, minced
1 garlic clove, minced
1 cup grated Romano cheese
Sea salt and ground black pepper, to taste
1 tablespoon sesame oil

Cheese Sauce:
1 tablespoon butter
1 cup beer
2 tablespoons grated Colby cheese

1. Mix together the canned tuna, whisked egg, shallots, garlic, cheese, salt, and pepper in a large bowl and stir to incorporate.
2. Divide the tuna mixture into four equal portions and form each portion into a patty with your hands. Refrigerate the patties for 2 hours.
3. When ready, brush both sides of each patty with sesame oil, then place in the air fry basket.
4. Select Bake, Super Convection, set temperature to 360°F (182°C), and set time to 14 minutes. Select Start/Stop to begin preheating.
5. Once preheated, place the basket on the bake position. Flip the patties halfway through the cooking time.
6. Meanwhile, melt the butter in a saucepan over medium heat.
7. Pour in the beer and whisk constantly, or until it begins to bubble. Add the grated Colby cheese and mix well. Continue cooking for 3 to 4 minutes, or until the cheese melts. Remove from the heat.
8. When cooking is complete, the patties should be lightly browned and cooked through. Remove the patties from the oven to a plate. Drizzle them with the cheese sauce and serve immediately.

Tilapia Meunière with Potato

Prep time: 10 minutes | Cook time: 20 minutes | Serves 4

10 ounces (283 g) Yukon Gold potatoes, sliced ¼-inch thick
5 tablespoons unsalted butter, melted, divided
1 teaspoon kosher salt, divided
4 (8-ounce / 227-g) tilapia fillets
½ pound (227 g) green beans, trimmed
Juice of 1 lemon
2 tablespoons chopped fresh parsley, for garnish

1. In a large bowl, drizzle the potatoes with 2 tablespoons of melted butter and ¼ teaspoon of kosher salt. Transfer the potatoes to the sheet pan.
2. Select Roast, Super Convection, set temperature to 375°F (190°C), and set time to 20 minutes. Select Start/Stop to begin preheating.
3. Once the oven has preheated, place the pan on the roast position.
4. Meanwhile, season both sides of the fillets with ½ teaspoon of kosher salt. Put the green beans in the medium bowl and sprinkle with the remaining ¼ teaspoon of kosher salt and 1 tablespoon of butter, tossing to coat.
5. After 10 minutes, remove the pan and push the potatoes to one side. Put the fillets in the middle of the pan and add the green beans on the other side. Drizzle the remaining 2 tablespoons of butter over the fillets. Return the pan to the oven and continue cooking, or until the fish flakes easily with a fork and the green beans are crisp-tender.
6. When cooked, remove the pan from the oven. Drizzle the lemon juice over the fillets and sprinkle the parsley on top for garnish. Serve hot.

Potato and Tuna Nicoise Salad

Prep time: 10 minutes | Cook time: 15 minutes | Serves 4

10 ounces (283 g) small red potatoes, quartered
8 tablespoons extra-virgin olive oil, divided
1 teaspoon kosher salt, divided
½ pound (227 g) green beans, trimmed
1 pint cherry tomatoes
1 teaspoon Dijon mustard
3 tablespoons red wine vinegar
Freshly ground black pepper, to taste
1 (9-ounce / 255-g) bag spring greens, washed and dried if needed
2 (5-ounce / 142-g) cans oil-packed tuna, drained
2 hard-cooked eggs, peeled and quartered
⅓ cup kalamata olives, pitted

1. In a large bowl, drizzle the potatoes with 1 tablespoon of olive oil and season with ¼ teaspoon of kosher salt. Transfer to a sheet pan.
2. Select Roast, Super Convection, set temperature to 375°F (190°C), and set time to 15 minutes. Select Start/Stop to begin preheating.
3. Once the oven has preheated, place the pan on the roast position.
4. Meanwhile, in a mixing bowl, toss the green beans and cherry tomatoes with 1 tablespoon of olive oil and ¼ teaspoon of kosher salt until evenly coated.
5. After 10 minutes, remove the pan and fold in the green beans and cherry tomatoes. Return the pan to the oven and continue cooking.
6. Meanwhile, make the vinaigrette by whisking together the remaining 6 tablespoons of olive oil, mustard, vinegar, the remaining ½ teaspoon of kosher salt, and black pepper in a small bowl. Set aside.
7. When done, remove the pan from the oven. Allow the vegetables to cool for 5 minutes.
8. Spread out the spring greens on a plate and spoon the tuna into the center of the greens. Arrange the potatoes, green beans, cheery tomatoes, and eggs around the tuna. Serve drizzled with the vinaigrette and scattered with the olives.

Chapter 6 Poultry

Italian Herby Chicken with Tomatoes

Prep time: 10 minutes | Cook time: 35 minutes | Serves 8

3 pounds (1.4 kg) chicken breasts, bone-in
1 teaspoon minced fresh basil
1 teaspoon minced fresh rosemary
2 tablespoons minced fresh parsley
1 teaspoon cayenne pepper
½ teaspoon salt
½ teaspoon freshly ground black pepper
4 medium Roma tomatoes, halved
Cooking spray

1. Spritz the air fry basket with cooking spray.
2. Combine all the ingredients, except for the chicken breasts and tomatoes, in a large bowl. Stir to mix well.
3. Dunk the chicken breasts in the mixture and press to coat well.
4. Transfer the chicken breasts to the air fry basket.
5. Select Air Fry, Super Convection. Set temperature to 370ºF (188ºC) and set time to 20 minutes. Press Start/Stop to begin preheating.
6. Once preheated, place the basket on the air fry position. Flip the breasts halfway through the cooking time.
7. When cooking is complete, the internal temperature of the thickest part of the breasts should reach at least 165ºF (74ºC).
8. Remove the cooked chicken breasts from the oven and adjust the temperature to 350ºF (180ºC).
9. Place the tomatoes in the air fry basket and spritz with cooking spray. Sprinkle with a touch of salt.
10. Set time to 10 minutes. Stir the tomatoes halfway through the cooking time.
11. When cooking is complete, the tomatoes should be tender.
12. Serve the tomatoes with chicken breasts on a large serving plate.

Crispy Chili Chicken Skin

Prep time: 5 minutes | Cook time: 6 minutes | Serves 4

1 pound (454 g) chicken skin, cut into slices
1 teaspoon melted butter
½ teaspoon crushed chili flakes
1 teaspoon dried dill
Salt and ground black pepper, to taste

1. Combine all the ingredients in a large bowl. Toss to coat the chicken skin well.
2. Transfer the skin in the air fry basket.
3. Select Air Fry, Super Convection. Set temperature to 360ºF (182ºC) and set time to 6 minutes. Press Start/Stop to begin preheating.
4. Once preheated, place the basket on the air fry position. Stir the skin halfway through.
5. When cooking is complete, the skin should be crispy.
6. Serve immediately.

Cajun Chicken Drumsticks

Prep time: 5 minutes | Cook time: 18 minutes | Serves 5

1 tablespoon olive oil
10 chicken drumsticks
1½ tablespoons Cajun seasoning
Salt and ground black pepper, to taste

1. Grease the air fry basket with olive oil.
2. On a clean work surface, rub the chicken drumsticks with Cajun seasoning, salt, and ground black pepper.
3. Arrange the seasoned chicken drumsticks in the air fry basket.
4. Select Air Fry, Super Convection. Set temperature to 390ºF (199ºC) and set time to 18 minutes. Press Start/Stop to begin preheating.
5. Once preheated, place the basket on the air fry position. Flip the drumsticks halfway through.
6. When cooking is complete, the drumsticks should be lightly browned.
7. Remove the chicken drumsticks from the oven. Serve immediately.

Mozzarella Pepperoni and Chicken Pizza

Prep time: 15 minutes | Cook time: 15 minutes | Serves 6

2 cups cooked chicken, cubed
1 cup pizza sauce
20 slices pepperoni
¼ cup grated Parmesan cheese
1 cup shredded Mozzarella cheese
Cooking spray

1. Spritz a baking pan with cooking spray.
2. Arrange the chicken cubes in the prepared baking pan, then top the cubes with pizza sauce and pepperoni. Stir to coat the cubes and pepperoni with sauce. Scatter the cheeses on top.
3. Select Air Fry, Super Convection. Set temperature to 375ºF (190ºC) and set time to 15 minutes. Press Start/Stop to begin preheating.
4. Once preheated, place the pan into the oven.
5. When cooking is complete, the pizza should be frothy and the cheeses should be melted.
6. Serve immediately.

Barbecue Chicken Drumsticks

Prep time: 5 minutes | Cook time: 18 minutes | Serves 5

1 tablespoon olive oil
10 chicken drumsticks
Chicken seasoning or rub, to taste
Salt and ground black pepper, to taste
1 cup barbecue sauce
¼ cup honey

1. Grease the air fry basket with olive oil.
2. Rub the chicken drumsticks with chicken seasoning or rub, salt and ground black pepper on a clean work surface.
3. Arrange the chicken drumsticks in the air fry basket.
4. Select Air Fry, Super Convection. Set temperature to 390ºF (199ºC) and set time to 18 minutes. Press Start/Stop to begin preheating.
5. Once preheated, place the basket on the air fry position. Flip the drumsticks halfway through.
6. When cooking is complete, the drumsticks should be lightly browned.
7. Meanwhile, combine the barbecue sauce and honey in a small bowl. Stir to mix well.
8. Remove the drumsticks from the oven and baste with the sauce mixture to serve.

Bacon-Wrapped Spiced Chicken Rolls

Prep time: 10 minutes | Cook time: 15 minutes | Serves 4

¼ cup chopped fresh chives
2 tablespoons lemon juice
1 teaspoon dried sage
1 teaspoon fresh rosemary leaves
½ cup fresh parsley leaves
4 cloves garlic, peeled
1 teaspoon ground fennel
3 teaspoons sea salt
½ teaspoon red pepper flakes
4 (4-ounce / 113-g) boneless, skinless chicken breasts, pounded to ¼ inch thick
8 slices bacon
Sprigs of fresh rosemary, for garnish
Cooking spray

1. Spritz the air fry basket with cooking spray.
2. Put the chives, lemon juice, sage, rosemary, parsley, garlic, fennel, salt, and red pepper flakes in a food processor, then pulse to purée until smooth.
3. Unfold the chicken breasts on a clean work surface, then brush the top side of the chicken breasts with the sauce.
4. Roll the chicken breasts up from the shorter side, then wrap each chicken rolls with 2 bacon slices to cover. Secure with toothpicks.
5. Arrange the rolls in the air fry basket.
6. Select Air Fry, Super Convection. Set temperature to 340ºF (171ºC) and set time to 10 minutes. Press Start/Stop to begin preheating.
7. Once preheated, place the basket on the air fry position. Flip the rolls halfway through.
8. After 10 minutes, increase temperature to 390ºF (199ºC) and set time to 5 minutes.
9. When cooking is complete, the bacon should be browned and crispy.
10. Transfer the rolls to a large plate. Discard the toothpicks and spread with rosemary sprigs before serving.

Chicken Drumettes with Buffalo Sauce

Prep time: 10 minutes | Cook time: 20 minutes | Serves 6

16 chicken drumettes (party wings)
Chicken seasoning or rub, to taste
1 teaspoon garlic powder
Ground black pepper, to taste
¼ cup buffalo wings sauce
Cooking spray

1. Spritz the air fry basket with cooking spray.
2. Rub the chicken wings with chicken seasoning, garlic powder, and ground black pepper on a clean work surface.
3. Arrange the chicken wings in the air fry basket. Spritz with cooking spray.
4. Select Air Fry, Super Convection. Set temperature to 400ºF (205ºC) and set time to 10 minutes. Press Start/Stop to begin preheating.
5. Once preheated, place the basket on the air fry position. Flip the chicken wings halfway through.
6. When cooking is complete, the chicken wings should be lightly browned.
7. Transfer the chicken wings in a large bowl, then pour in the buffalo wings sauce and toss to coat well.
8. Put the wings back to the oven and set time to 7 minutes. Flip the wings halfway through.
9. When cooking is complete, the wings should be heated through. Serve immediately.

Bacon-Wrapped Cheesy Chicken Breast

Prep time: 10 minutes | Cook time: 20 minutes | Serves 4

4 (5-ounce / 142-g) boneless, skinless chicken breasts, pounded to ¼ inch thick
1 cup cream cheese
2 tablespoons chopped fresh chives
8 slices thin-cut bacon
Sprig of fresh cilantro, for garnish
Cooking spray

1. Spritz the air fry basket with cooking spray.
2. On a clean work surface, slice the chicken horizontally to make a 1-inch incision on top of each chicken breast with a knife, then cut into the chicken to make a pocket. Leave a ½-inch border along the sides and bottom.
3. Combine the cream cheese and chives in a bowl. Stir to mix well, then gently pour the mixture into the chicken pockets.
4. Wrap each stuffed chicken breast with 2 bacon slices, then secure the ends with toothpicks.
5. Arrange them in the air fry basket.
6. Select Air Fry, Super Convection. Set temperature to 400ºF (205ºC) and set time to 20 minutes. Press Start/Stop to begin preheating.
7. Once preheated, place the basket on the air fry position. Flip the bacon-wrapped chicken halfway through the cooking time.
8. When cooking is complete, the bacon should be browned and crispy.
9. Transfer them on a large plate and serve with cilantro on top.

Baked Garlicky Whole Chicken

Prep time: 10 minutes | Cook time: 1 hour | Serves 2 to 4

½ cup melted butter
3 tablespoons garlic, minced
Salt, to taste
1 teaspoon ground black pepper
1 (1-pound / 454-g) whole chicken

1. Combine the butter with garlic, salt, and ground black pepper in a small bowl.
2. Brush the butter mixture over the whole chicken, then place the chicken in the air fry basket, skin side down.
3. Select Bake, Super Convection, set temperature to 350ºF (180ºC) and set time to 60 minutes. Press Start/Stop to begin preheating.
4. Once preheated, place the basket on the bake position. Flip the chicken halfway through.
5. When cooking is complete, an instant-read thermometer inserted in the thickest part of the chicken should register at least 165ºF (74ºC).
6. Remove the chicken from the oven and allow to cool for 15 minutes before serving.

Hawaiian Glazed Chicken Bites

Prep time: 15 minutes | Cook time: 15 minutes | Serves 4

½ cup pineapple juice
2 tablespoons apple cider vinegar
½ tablespoon minced ginger
½ cup ketchup
2 garlic cloves, minced
½ cup brown sugar
2 tablespoons sherry
½ cup soy sauce
4 chicken breasts, cubed
Cooking spray

1. Combine the pineapple juice, cider vinegar, ginger, ketchup, garlic, and sugar in a saucepan. Stir to mix well. Heat over low heat for 5 minutes or until thickened. Fold in the sherry and soy sauce.
2. Dunk the chicken cubes in the mixture. Press to submerge. Wrap the bowl in plastic and refrigerate to marinate for at least an hour.
3. Spritz the air fry basket with cooking spray.
4. Remove the chicken cubes from the marinade. Shake the excess off and put in the air fry basket. Spritz with cooking spray.
5. Select Air Fry, Super Convection. Set temperature to 360ºF (182ºC) and set time to 15 minutes. Press Start/Stop to begin preheating.
6. Once preheated, place the basket on the air fry position. Flip the chicken cubes at least three times during the air frying.
7. When cooking is complete, the chicken cubes should be glazed and well browned.
8. Serve immediately.

Parmesan Breaded Chicken Cutlets

Prep time: 15 minutes | Cook time: 15 minutes | Serves 4

2 tablespoons panko bread crumbs
¼ cup grated Parmesan cheese
⅛ tablespoon paprika
½ tablespoon garlic powder
2 large eggs
4 chicken cutlets
1 tablespoon parsley
Salt and ground black pepper, to taste
Cooking spray

1. Spritz the air fry basket with cooking spray.
2. Combine the bread crumbs, Parmesan, paprika, garlic powder, salt, and ground black pepper in a large bowl. Stir to mix well. Beat the eggs in a separate bowl.
3. Dredge the chicken cutlets in the beaten eggs, then roll over the bread crumbs mixture to coat well. Shake the excess off.
4. Transfer the chicken cutlets in the air fry basket and spritz with cooking spray.
5. Select Air Fry, Super Convection. Set temperature to 400ºF (205ºC) and set time to 15 minutes. Press Start/Stop to begin preheating.
6. Once preheated, place the basket on the air fry position. Flip the cutlets halfway through.
7. When cooking is complete, the cutlets should be crispy and golden brown.
8. Serve with parsley on top.

Panko-Crusted Chicken Livers

Prep time: 10 minutes | Cook time: 10 minutes | Serves 4

2 eggs
2 tablespoons water
¾ cup flour
2 cups panko bread crumbs
1 teaspoon salt
½ teaspoon ground black pepper
20 ounces (567 g) chicken livers
Cooking spray

1. Spritz the air fry basket with cooking spray.
2. Whisk the eggs with water in a large bowl. Pour the flour in a separate bowl. Pour the panko on a shallow dish and sprinkle with salt and pepper.
3. Dredge the chicken livers in the flour. Shake the excess off, then dunk the livers in the whisked eggs, and then roll the livers over the panko to coat well.
4. Arrange the livers in the air fry basket and spritz with cooking spray.
5. Select Air Fry, Super Convection. Set temperature to 390ºF (199ºC) and set time to 10 minutes. Press Start/Stop to begin preheating.
6. Once preheated, place the basket on the air fry position. Flip the livers halfway through.
7. When cooking is complete, the livers should be golden and crispy.
8. Serve immediately.

Bruschetta Stuffed Chicken

Prep time: 10 minutes | Cook time: 10 minutes | Serves 4

Bruschetta Stuffing:
1 tomato, diced
3 tablespoons balsamic vinegar
1 teaspoon Italian seasoning
2 tablespoons chopped fresh basil
3 garlic cloves, minced
2 tablespoons extra-virgin olive oil

Chicken:
4 (4-ounce / 113-g) boneless, skinless chicken breasts, cut 4 slits each
1 teaspoon Italian seasoning
Chicken seasoning or rub, to taste
Cooking spray

1. Spritz the air fry basket with cooking spray.
2. Combine the ingredients for the bruschetta stuffing in a bowl. Stir to mix well. Set aside.
3. Rub the chicken breasts with Italian seasoning and chicken seasoning on a clean work surface.
4. Arrange the chicken breasts, slits side up, in the air fry basket and spritz with cooking spray.
5. Select Air Fry, Super Convection. Set temperature to 370ºF (188ºC) and set time to 10 minutes. Press Start/Stop to begin preheating.
6. Once preheated, place the basket on the air fry position. Flip the breast and fill the slits with the bruschetta stuffing halfway through.
7. When cooking is complete, the chicken should be well browned.
8. Serve immediately.

Stuffed Chicken Rolls with Bell Peppers

Prep time: 10 minutes | Cook time: 12 minutes | Serves 4

2 (4-ounce / 113-g) boneless, skinless chicken breasts, slice in half horizontally
1 tablespoon olive oil
Juice of ½ lime
2 tablespoons taco seasoning
½ green bell pepper, cut into strips
½ red bell pepper, cut into strips
¼ onion, sliced

1. Unfold the chicken breast slices on a clean work surface. Rub with olive oil, then drizzle with lime juice and sprinkle with taco seasoning.
2. Top the chicken slices with equal amount of bell peppers and onion. Roll them up and secure with toothpicks.
3. Arrange the chicken roll-ups in the air fry basket.
4. Select Air Fry, Super Convection. Set temperature to 400ºF (205ºC) and set time to 12 minutes. Press Start/Stop to begin preheating.
5. Once preheated, place the basket on the air fry position. Flip the chicken roll-ups halfway through.
6. When cooking is complete, the internal temperature of the chicken should reach at least 165ºF (74ºC).
7. Remove the chicken from the oven. Discard the toothpicks and serve immediately.

Chicken Goulash

Prep time: 5 minutes | Cook time: 17 minutes | Serves 2

2 red bell peppers, chopped
1 pound (454 g) ground chicken
2 medium tomatoes, diced
½ cup chicken broth
Salt and ground black pepper, to taste
Cooking spray

1. Spritz a baking pan with cooking spray.
2. Set the bell pepper in the baking pan.
3. Select Broil, Super Convection, set temperature to 365ºF (185ºC) and set time to 5 minutes. Press Start/Stop to begin preheating.
4. Once preheated, place the pan on the broil position. Stir the bell pepper halfway through.
5. When broiling is complete, the bell pepper should be tender.
6. Add the ground chicken and diced tomatoes in the baking pan and stir to mix well.
7. Set the time of oven to 12 minutes. Press Start/Stop. Stir the mixture and mix in the chicken broth, salt and ground black pepper halfway through.
8. When cooking is complete, the chicken should be well browned.
9. Serve immediately.

Baked Turkey and Cauliflower Meatloaf

Prep time: 10 minutes | Cook time: 50 minutes | Serves 6

2 pounds (907 g) lean ground turkey
1 1/3 cups riced cauliflower
2 large eggs, lightly beaten
¼ cup almond flour
2/3 cup chopped yellow or white onion
1 teaspoon ground dried turmeric
1 teaspoon ground cumin
1 teaspoon ground coriander
1 tablespoon minced garlic
1 teaspoon salt
1 teaspoon ground black pepper
Cooking spray

1. Spritz a loaf pan with cooking spray.
2. Combine all the ingredients in a large bowl. Stir to mix well. Pour half of the mixture in the prepared loaf pan and press with a spatula to coat the bottom evenly. Spritz the mixture with cooking spray.
3. Select Bake, Super Convection, set temperature to 350ºF (180ºC) and set time to 25 minutes. Press Start/Stop to begin preheating.
4. Once preheated, place the pan on the bake position.
5. When cooking is complete, the meat should be well browned and the internal temperature should reach at least 165ºF (74ºC).
6. Remove the loaf pan from the oven and serve immediately.

Air-Fried Duck Leg

Prep time: 5 minutes | Cook time: 45 minutes | Serves 4

4 (½-pound / 227-g) skin-on duck leg quarters
2 medium garlic cloves, minced
½ teaspoon salt
½ teaspoon ground black pepper

1. Spritz the air fry basket with cooking spray.
2. On a clean work surface, rub the duck leg quarters with garlic, salt, and black pepper.
3. Arrange the leg quarters in the air fry basket and spritz with cooking spray.
4. Select Air Fry, Super Convection. Set temperature to 300ºF (150ºC) and set time to 30 minutes. Press Start/Stop to begin preheating.
5. Once preheated, place the basket on the air fry position.
6. After 30 minutes, remove the basket from the oven. Flip the leg quarters. Increase temperature to 375ºF (190ºC) and set time to 15 minutes. Return the basket to the oven and continue cooking.
7. When cooking is complete, the leg quarters should be well browned and crispy.
8. Remove the duck leg quarters from the oven and allow to cool for 10 minutes before serving.

Turkey Scotch Eggs

Prep time: 15 minutes | Cook time: 12 minutes | Serves 4

1 egg
1 cup panko bread crumbs
½ teaspoon rosemary
1 pound (454 g) ground turkey
4 hard-boiled eggs, peeled
Salt and ground black pepper, to taste
Cooking spray

1. Spritz the air fry basket with cooking spray.
2. Whisk the egg with salt in a bowl. Combine the bread crumbs with rosemary in a shallow dish.
3. Stir the ground turkey with salt and ground black pepper in a separate large bowl, then divide the ground turkey into four portions.
4. Wrap each hard-boiled egg with a portion of ground turkey. Dredge in the whisked egg, then roll over the bread crumb mixture.
5. Place the wrapped eggs in the air fry basket and spritz with cooking spray.
6. Select Air Fry, Super Convection. Set temperature to 400ºF (205ºC) and set time to 12 minutes. Press Start/Stop to begin preheating.
7. Once preheated, place the basket on the air fry position. Flip the eggs halfway through.
8. When cooking is complete, the scotch eggs should be golden brown and crunchy.
9. Serve immediately.

Chapter 3 Vegan and Vegetarian

Chicken Breast Nuggets

Prep time: 10 minutes | Cook time: 8 minutes | Serves 4

1 pound (454 g) boneless, skinless chicken breasts, cut into 1-inch pieces
2 tablespoons panko bread crumbs
6 tablespoons bread crumbs
Chicken seasoning or rub, to taste
Salt and ground black pepper, to taste
2 eggs
Cooking spray

1. Spritz the air fry basket with cooking spray.
2. Combine the bread crumbs, chicken seasoning, salt, and black pepper in a large bowl. Stir to mix well. Whisk the eggs in a separate bowl.
3. Dunk the chicken pieces in the egg mixture, then in the bread crumb mixture. Shake the excess off.
4. Arrange the well-coated chicken pieces in the air fry basket. Spritz with cooking spray.
5. Select Air Fry, Super Convection. Set temperature to 400°F (205°C) and set time to 8 minutes. Press Start/Stop to begin preheating.
6. Once preheated, place the basket on the air fry position. Flip the chicken halfway through.
7. When cooking is complete, the chicken should be crispy and golden brown.
8. Serve immediately.

Air-Fried Chicken Wings

Prep time: 10 minutes | Cook time: 15 minutes | Serves 4

1 tablespoon olive oil
8 whole chicken wings
Chicken seasoning or rub, to taste
1 teaspoon garlic powder
Freshly ground black pepper, to taste

1. Grease the air fry basket with olive oil.
2. On a clean work surface, rub the chicken wings with chicken seasoning and rub, garlic powder, and ground black pepper.
3. Arrange the well-coated chicken wings in the air fry basket.
4. Select Air Fry, Super Convection. Set temperature to 400°F (205°C) and set time to 15 minutes. Press Start/Stop to begin preheating.
5. Once preheated, place the basket on the air fry position. Flip the chicken wings halfway through.
6. When cooking is complete, the internal temperature of the chicken wings should reach at least 165°F (74°C).
7. Remove the chicken wings from the oven. Serve immediately.

Maple-Mustard Turkey Breast

Prep time: 15 minutes | Cook time: 30 minutes | Serves 6

½ teaspoon dried rosemary
2 minced garlic cloves
2 teaspoons salt
1 teaspoon ground black pepper
¼ cup olive oil
2½ pounds (1.1 kg) turkey breast
¼ cup pure maple syrup
1 tablespoon stone-ground brown mustard
1 tablespoon melted vegan butter

1. Combine the rosemary, garlic, salt, ground black pepper, and olive oil in a large bowl. Stir to mix well.
2. Dunk the turkey breast in the mixture and wrap the bowl in plastic. Refrigerate for 2 hours to marinate.
3. Remove the bowl from the refrigerator and let sit for half an hour before cooking.
4. Spritz the air fry basket with cooking spray.
5. Remove the turkey from the marinade and place in the air fry basket.
6. Select Air Fry, Super Convection. Set temperature to 400°F (205°C) and set time to 20 minutes. Press Start/Stop to begin preheating.
7. Once preheated, place the basket on the air fry position. Flip the breast halfway through.
8. When cooking is complete, the breast should be well browned.
9. Meanwhile, combine the remaining ingredients in a small bowl. Stir to mix well.
10. Pour half of the butter mixture over the turkey breast in the oven and air fry for 10 more minutes. Flip the breast and pour the remaining half of butter mixture over halfway through.
11. Transfer the turkey on a plate and slice to serve.

Tangy Chicken Breast with Cilantro

Prep time: 10 minutes | Cook time: 10 minutes | Serves 4

4 (4-ounce / 113-g) boneless, skinless chicken breasts
½ cup chopped fresh cilantro
Juice of 1 lime
Chicken seasoning or rub, to taste
Salt and ground black pepper, to taste
Cooking spray

1. Put the chicken breasts in the large bowl, then add the cilantro, lime juice, chicken seasoning, salt, and black pepper. Toss to coat well.
2. Wrap the bowl in plastic and refrigerate to marinate for at least 30 minutes.
3. Spritz the air fry basket with cooking spray.
4. Remove the marinated chicken breasts from the bowl and place in the air fry basket. Spritz with cooking spray.
5. Select Air Fry, Super Convection. Set temperature to 400°F (205°C) and set time to 10 minutes. Press Start/Stop to begin preheating.
6. Once preheated, place the basket on the air fry position. Flip the breasts halfway through.
7. When cooking is complete, the internal temperature of the chicken should reach at least 165°F (74°C).
8. Serve immediately.

Chinese Spiced Turkey Thighs

Prep time: 10 minutes | Cook time: 25 minutes | Serves 6

2 pounds (907 g) turkey thighs
1 teaspoon Chinese five-spice powder
¼ teaspoon Sichuan pepper
1 teaspoon pink Himalayan salt
1 tablespoon Chinese rice vinegar
1 tablespoon mustard
1 tablespoon chili sauce
2 tablespoons soy sauce
Cooking spray

1. Spritz the air fry basket with cooking spray.
2. Rub the turkey thighs with five-spice powder, Sichuan pepper, and salt on a clean work surface.
3. Put the turkey thighs in the air fry basket and spritz with cooking spray.
4. Select Air Fry, Super Convection. Set temperature to 360°F (182°C) and set time to 22 minutes. Press Start/Stop to begin preheating.
5. Once preheated, place the basket on the air fry position. Flip the thighs at least three times during the cooking.
6. When cooking is complete, the thighs should be well browned.
7. Meanwhile, heat the remaining ingredients in a saucepan over medium-high heat. Cook for 3 minutes or until the sauce is thickened and reduces to two thirds.
8. Transfer the thighs onto a plate and baste with sauce before serving.

Sweet-Sour Chicken Nuggets

Prep time: 10 minutes | Cook time: 15 minutes | Serves 4

1 cup cornstarch
Chicken seasoning or rub, to taste
Salt and ground black pepper, to taste
2 eggs
2 (4-ounce/ 113-g) boneless, skinless chicken breasts, cut into 1-inch pieces
1½ cups sweet-and-sour sauce
Cooking spray

1. Spritz the air fry basket with cooking spray.
2. Combine the cornstarch, chicken seasoning, salt, and pepper in a large bowl. Stir to mix well. Whisk the eggs in a separate bowl.
3. Dredge the chicken pieces in the bowl of cornstarch mixture first, then in the bowl of whisked eggs, and then in the cornstarch mixture again.
4. Arrange the well-coated chicken pieces in the air fry basket. Spritz with cooking spray.
5. Select Air Fry, Super Convection. Set temperature to 360°F (182°C) and set time to 15 minutes. Press Start/Stop to begin preheating.
6. Once preheated, place the basket on the air fry position. Flip the chicken halfway through.
7. When cooking is complete, the chicken should be golden brown and crispy.
8. Transfer the chicken pieces on a large serving plate, then baste with sweet-and-sour sauce before serving.

Strawberry Puréed-Glazed Turkey Breast

Prep time: 5 minutes | Cook time: 37 minutes | Serves 2

2 pounds (907 g) turkey breast
1 tablespoon olive oil
Salt and ground black pepper, to taste
1 cup fresh strawberries

1. Rub the turkey bread with olive oil on a clean work surface, then sprinkle with salt and ground black pepper.
2. Transfer the turkey in the air fry basket and spritz with cooking spray.
3. Select Air Fry, Super Convection. Set temperature to 375ºF (190ºC) and set time to 30 minutes. Press Start/Stop to begin preheating.
4. Once preheated, place the basket on the air fry position. Flip the turkey breast halfway through.
5. Meanwhile, put the strawberries in a food processor and pulse until smooth.
6. When cooking is complete, spread the puréed strawberries over the turkey and fry for 7 more minutes.
7. Serve immediately.

Orange-Balsamic Glazed Duck Breasts

Prep time: 5 minutes | Cook time: 13 minutes | Serves 4

4 (6-ounce / 170-g) skin-on duck breasts
1 teaspoon salt
¼ cup orange marmalade
1 tablespoon white balsamic vinegar
¾ teaspoon ground black pepper

1. Cut 10 slits into the skin of the duck breasts, then sprinkle with salt on both sides.
2. Place the breasts in the air fry basket, skin side up.
3. Select Air Fry, Super Convection. Set temperature to 400ºF (205ºC) and set time to 10 minutes. Press Start/Stop to begin preheating.
4. Once preheated, place the basket on the air fry position.
5. Meanwhile, combine the remaining ingredients in a small bowl. Stir to mix well.
6. When cooking is complete, brush the duck skin with the marmalade mixture. Flip the breast and air fry for 3 more minutes or until the skin is crispy and the breast is well browned.
7. Serve immediately.

Bacon-Wrapped Balsamic Turkey with Carrots

Prep time: 10 minutes | Cook time: 25 minutes | Serves 4

2 (12-ounce / 340-g) turkey tenderloins
1 teaspoon kosher salt, divided
6 slices bacon
3 tablespoons balsamic vinegar
2 tablespoons honey
1 tablespoon Dijon mustard
½ teaspoon dried thyme
6 large carrots, peeled and cut into ¼-inch rounds
1 tablespoon olive oil

1. Sprinkle the turkey with ¾ teaspoon of the salt. Wrap each tenderloin with 3 strips of bacon, securing the bacon with toothpicks. Place the turkey in a baking pan.
2. In a small bowl, mix the balsamic vinegar, honey, mustard, and thyme.
3. Place the carrots in a medium bowl and drizzle with the oil. Add 1 tablespoon of the balsamic mixture and ¼ teaspoon of kosher salt and toss to coat. Place these on the pan around the turkey tenderloins. Baste the tenderloins with about one-half of the remaining balsamic mixture.
4. Select Roast, Super Convection, set temperature to 375ºF (190ºC), and set time to 25 minutes. Press Start/Stop to begin preheating.
5. Once preheated, place the pan on the roast position.
6. After 13 minutes, remove the pan from the oven. Gently stir the carrots. Flip the tenderloins and baste with the remaining balsamic mixture. Return the pan to the oven and continue cooking.
7. When cooking is complete, the carrots should tender and the center of the tenderloins should register 165ºF (74ºC) on a meat thermometer. Remove the pan from the oven. Slice the turkey and serve with the carrots.

Panko-Crusted Chicken Fingers

Prep time: 20 minutes | Cook time: 10 minutes | Makes 12 chicken fingers

½ cup all-purpose flour
2 cups panko bread crumbs
2 tablespoons canola oil
1 large egg
3 boneless and skinless chicken breasts, each cut into 4 strips
Kosher salt and freshly ground black pepper, to taste
Cooking spray

1. Spritz the air fry basket with cooking spray.
2. Pour the flour in a large bowl. Combine the panko and canola oil on a shallow dish. Whisk the egg in a separate bowl.
3. Rub the chicken strips with salt and ground black pepper on a clean work surface, then dip the chicken in the bowl of flour. Shake the excess off and dunk the chicken strips in the bowl of whisked egg, then roll the strips over the panko to coat well.
4. Arrange the strips in the air fry basket.
5. Select Air Fry, Super Convection. Set temperature to 360ºF (182ºC) and set time to 10 minutes. Press Start/Stop to begin preheating.
6. Once preheated, place the basket on the air fry position. Flip the strips halfway through.
7. When cooking is complete, the strips should be crunchy and lightly browned.
8. Serve immediately.

Parmesan Chicken with Roasted Peanuts

Prep time: 10 minutes | Cook time: 12 minutes | Serves 4

½ cup grated Parmesan cheese
½ teaspoon garlic powder
1 teaspoon red pepper flakes
Sea salt and ground black pepper, to taste
2 tablespoons peanut oil
1½ pounds (680 g) chicken tenderloins
2 tablespoons peanuts, roasted and roughly chopped
Cooking spray

1. Spritz the air fry basket with cooking spray.
2. Combine the Parmesan cheese, garlic powder, red pepper flakes, salt, black pepper, and peanut oil in a large bow. Stir to mix well.
3. Dip the chicken tenderloins in the cheese mixture, then press to coat well. Shake the excess off.
4. Transfer the chicken tenderloins in the air fry basket.
5. Select Air Fry, Super Convection. Set temperature to 360ºF (182ºC) and set time to 12 minutes. Press Start/Stop to begin preheating.
6. Once preheated, place the basket on the air fry position. Flip the tenderloin halfway through.
7. When cooking is complete, the tenderloin should be well browned.
8. Transfer the chicken tenderloins on a large plate and top with roasted peanuts before serving.

Honey-Glazed Chicken

Prep time: 5 minutes | Cook time: 10 minutes | Serves 4

4 (4-ounce / 113-g) boneless, skinless chicken breasts
Chicken seasoning or rub, to taste
Salt and ground black pepper, to taste
¼ cup honey
2 tablespoons soy sauce
2 teaspoons grated fresh ginger
2 garlic cloves, minced
Cooking spray

1. Spritz the air fry basket with cooking spray.
2. Rub the chicken breasts with chicken seasoning, salt, and black pepper on a clean work surface.
3. Arrange the chicken breasts in the air fry basket and spritz with cooking spray.
4. Select Air Fry, Super Convection. Set temperature to 400ºF (205ºC) and set time to 10 minutes. Press Start/Stop to begin preheating.
5. Once preheated, place the basket on the air fry position. Flip the chicken breasts halfway through.
6. When cooking is complete, the internal temperature of the thickest part of the chicken should reach at least 165ºF (74ºC).
7. Meanwhile, combine the honey, soy sauce, ginger, and garlic in a saucepan and heat over medium-high heat for 3 minutes or until thickened. Stir constantly.
8. Remove the chicken from the oven and serve with the honey glaze.

Chapter 3 Vegan and Vegetarian | 73

Chicken Breast with Veggies and Beans

Prep time: 20 minutes | Cook time: 25 minutes | Serves 2

1 cup canned cannellini beans, rinsed
1½ tablespoons red wine vinegar
1 garlic clove, minced
2 tablespoons extra-virgin olive oil, divided
Salt and ground black pepper, to taste
½ red onion, sliced thinly
8 ounces (227 g) asparagus, trimmed and cut into 1-inch lengths
2 (8-ounce / 227-g) boneless, skinless chicken breasts, trimmed
¼ teaspoon paprika
½ teaspoon ground coriander
2 ounces (57 g) baby arugula, rinsed and drained

1. Warm the beans in microwave for 1 minutes and combine with red wine vinegar, garlic, 1 tablespoon of olive oil, ¼ teaspoon of salt, and ¼ teaspoon of ground black pepper in a bowl. Stir to mix well.
2. Combine the onion with ⅛ teaspoon of salt, ⅛ teaspoon of ground black pepper, and 2 teaspoons of olive oil in a separate bowl. Toss to coat well.
3. Place the onion in the air fry basket.
4. Select Air Fry, Super Convection. Set temperature to 400ºF (205ºC) and set time to 2 minutes. Press Start/Stop to begin preheating.
5. Once preheated, place the basket on the air fry position.
6. After 2 minutes, add the asparagus and set time to 8 minutes. Stir the vegetable halfway through.
7. When cooking is complete, the asparagus should be tender.
8. Transfer the onion and asparagus to the bowl with beans. Set aside.
9. Toss the chicken breasts with remaining ingredients, except for the baby arugula, in a large bowl.
10. Put the chicken breasts in the air fry basket.
11. Select Air Fry, Super Convection. Set time to 14 minutes. Place the basket on the air fry position. Flip the breasts halfway through.
12. When cooking is complete, the internal temperature of the chicken reaches at least 165ºF (74ºC).
13. Remove the chicken from the oven and serve on an aluminum foil with asparagus, beans, onion, and arugula. Sprinkle with salt and ground black pepper. Toss to serve.

Air-Fried Apricot-Glazed Drumsticks

Prep time: 15 minutes | Cook time: 30 minutes | Makes 6 drumsticks

For the Glaze:
½ cup apricot preserves
½ teaspoon tamari
¼ teaspoon chili powder
2 teaspoons Dijon mustard

For the Chicken:
6 chicken drumsticks
½ teaspoon seasoning salt
1 teaspoon salt
½ teaspoon ground black pepper
Cooking spray

Make the glaze:
1. Combine the ingredients for the glaze in a saucepan, then heat over low heat for 10 minutes or until thickened.
2. Turn off the heat and sit until ready to use.

Make the Chicken:
3. Spritz the air fry basket with cooking spray.
4. Combine the seasoning salt, salt, and pepper in a small bowl. Stir to mix well.
5. Place the chicken drumsticks in the air fry basket. Spritz with cooking spray and sprinkle with the salt mixture on both sides.
6. Select Air Fry, Super Convection. Set temperature to 370ºF (188ºC) and set time to 20 minutes. Press Start/Stop to begin preheating.
7. Once preheated, place the basket on the air fry position. Flip the chicken halfway through.
8. When cooking is complete, the chicken should be well browned.
9. Baste the chicken with the glaze and air fry for 2 more minutes or until the chicken tenderloin is glossy.
10. Serve immediately.

Cherry Sauce-Glazed Duck

Prep time: 10 minutes | Cook time: 32 minutes | Serves 12

1 whole duck (about 5 pounds / 2.3 kg in total), split in half, back and rib bones removed, fat trimmed
1 teaspoon olive oil
Salt and freshly ground black pepper, to taste

Cherry Sauce:
1 tablespoon butter
1 shallot, minced
½ cup sherry
1 cup chicken stock
1 teaspoon white wine vinegar
¾ cup cherry preserves
1 teaspoon fresh thyme leaves
Salt and freshly ground black pepper, to taste

1. On a clean work surface, rub the duck with olive oil, then sprinkle with salt and ground black pepper to season.
2. Place the duck in the air fry basket, breast side up.
3. Select Air Fry, Super Convection. Set temperature to 400ºF (205ºC) and set time to 25 minutes. Press Start/Stop to begin preheating.
4. Once preheated, place the basket on the air fry position. Flip the ducks halfway through the cooking time.
5. Meanwhile, make the cherry sauce: Heat the butter in a skillet over medium-high heat or until melted.
6. Add the shallot and sauté for 5 minutes or until lightly browned.
7. Add the sherry and simmer for 6 minutes or until it reduces in half.
8. Add the chicken stick, white wine vinegar, and cherry preserves. Stir to combine well. Simmer for 6 more minutes or until thickened.
9. Fold in the thyme leaves and sprinkle with salt and ground black pepper. Stir to mix well.
10. When the cooking of the duck is complete, glaze the duck with a quarter of the cherry sauce, then air fry for another 4 minutes.
11. Flip the duck and glaze with another quarter of the cherry sauce. Air fry for an additional 3 minutes.
12. Transfer the duck on a large plate and serve with remaining cherry sauce.

Pomegranate-Glazed Chicken with Couscous Salad

Prep time: 15 minutes | Cook time: 20 minutes | Serves 4

3 tablespoons plus 2 teaspoons pomegranate molasses
½ teaspoon ground cinnamon
1 teaspoon minced fresh thyme
Salt and ground black pepper, to taste
2 (12-ounce / 340-g) bone-in split chicken breasts, trimmed
¼ cup chicken broth
¼ cup water
½ cup couscous
1 tablespoon minced fresh parsley
2 ounces (57 g) cherry tomatoes, quartered
1 scallion, white part minced, green part sliced thin on bias
1 tablespoon extra-virgin olive oil
1 ounce (28 g) feta cheese, crumbled
Cooking spray

1. Spritz the air fry basket with cooking spray.
2. Combine 3 tablespoons of pomegranate molasses, cinnamon, thyme, and ⅛ teaspoon of salt in a small bowl. Stir to mix well. Set aside.
3. Place the chicken breasts in the air fry basket, skin side down, and spritz with cooking spray. Sprinkle with salt and ground black pepper.
4. Select Air Fry, Super Convection. Set temperature to 350ºF (180ºC) and set time to 20 minutes. Press Start/Stop to begin preheating.
5. Once preheated, place the basket on the air fry position. Flip the chicken and brush with pomegranate molasses mixture halfway through.
6. Meanwhile, pour the broth and water in a pot and bring to a boil over medium-high heat. Add the couscous and sprinkle with salt. Cover and simmer for 7 minutes or until the liquid is almost absorbed.
7. Combine the remaining ingredients, except for the cheese, with cooked couscous in a large bowl. Toss to mix well. Scatter with the feta cheese.
8. When cooking is complete, remove the chicken from the oven and allow to cool for 10 minutes. Serve with vegetable and couscous salad.

Chapter 3 Vegan and Vegetarian

Hearty Chicken Rochambeau with Mushroom Sauce

Prep time: 25 minutes | Cook time: 30 minutes | Serves 4

1 tablespoon melted butter	to cover an English muffin
¼ cup all-purpose flour	2 English muffins, split in halves
4 chicken tenders, cut in half crosswise	Salt and ground black pepper, to taste
4 slices ham, ¼-inch thick, large enough	Cooking spray

Mushroom Sauce:

2 tablespoons butter	1 cup chicken broth
½ cup chopped mushrooms	1½ teaspoons Worcestershire sauce
½ cup chopped green onions	¼ teaspoon garlic powder
2 tablespoons flour	

1. Put the butter in a baking pan. Combine the flour, salt, and ground black pepper in a shallow dish. Roll the chicken tenders over to coat well.
2. Arrange the chicken in the baking pan and flip to coat with the melted butter.
3. Select Broil, Super Convection, set temperature to 390ºF (199ºC) and set time to 10 minutes. Press Start/Stop to begin preheating.
4. Once preheated, place the pan on the broil position. Flip the tenders halfway through.
5. When cooking is complete, the juices of chicken tenders should run clear.
6. Meanwhile, make the mushroom sauce: melt 2 tablespoons of butter in a saucepan over medium-high heat.
7. Add the mushrooms and onions to the saucepan and sauté for 3 minutes or until the onions are translucent.
8. Gently mix in the flour, broth, Worcestershire sauce, and garlic powder until smooth.
9. Reduce the heat to low and simmer for 5 minutes or until it has a thick consistency. Set the sauce aside until ready to serve.
10. When broiling is complete, remove the baking pan from the oven and set the ham slices into the air fry basket.
11. Select Air Fry, Super Convection. Set time to 5 minutes. Press Start/Stop. Flip the ham slices halfway through.
12. When cooking is complete, the ham slices should be heated through.
13. Remove the ham slices from the oven and set in the English muffin halves and warm for 1 minute.
14. Arrange each ham slice on top of each muffin half, then place each chicken tender over the ham slice.
15. Transfer to the oven and set time to 2 minutes on Air Fry, Super Convection.
16. Serve with the sauce on top.

Chicken Tostadas with Coleslaw Topping

Prep time: 15 minutes | Cook time: 10 minutes | Makes 4 tostadas

Coleslaw:

¼ cup sour cream	½ teaspoon garlic powder
¼ small green cabbage, finely chopped	½ teaspoon salt
½ tablespoon white vinegar	¼ teaspoon ground black pepper

Tostadas:

2 cups pulled rotisserie chicken	4 corn tortillas
½ cup barbecue sauce	½ cup shredded Mozzarella cheese
	Cooking spray

Make the Coleslaw:
1. Combine the ingredients for the coleslaw in a large bowl. Toss to mix well.
2. Refrigerate until ready to serve.

Make the Tostadas:
1. Spritz the air fry basket with cooking spray.
2. Toss the chicken with barbecue sauce in a separate large bowl to combine well. Set aside.
3. Place one tortilla in the air fry basket and spritz with cooking spray.
4. Select Air Fry, Super Convection. Set temperature to 370ºF (188ºC) and set time to 10 minutes. Press Start/Stop to begin preheating.
5. Once preheated, place the basket on the air fry position. Flip the tortilla and spread the barbecue chicken and cheese over halfway through.
6. When cooking is complete, the tortilla should be browned and the cheese should be melted.
7. Serve the tostadas with coleslaw on top.

Honey Chicken Thighs on Waffles

Prep time: 20 minutes | Cook time: 20 minutes | Serves 4

For the chicken:
4 chicken thighs, skin on
1 cup low-fat buttermilk
½ cup all-purpose flour
½ teaspoon garlic powder
½ teaspoon mustard powder
1 teaspoon kosher salt
½ teaspoon freshly ground black pepper
¼ cup honey, for serving
Cooking spray

For the waffles:
½ cup all-purpose flour
½ cup whole wheat pastry flour
1 large egg, beaten
1 cup low-fat buttermilk
1 teaspoon baking powder
2 tablespoons canola oil
½ teaspoon kosher salt
1 tablespoon granulated sugar

1. Combine the chicken thighs with buttermilk in a large bowl. Wrap the bowl in plastic and refrigerate to marinate for at least an hour.
2. Spritz the air fry basket with cooking spray.
3. Combine the flour, mustard powder, garlic powder, salt, and black pepper in a shallow dish. Stir to mix well.
4. Remove the thighs from the buttermilk and pat dry with paper towels. Sit the bowl of buttermilk aside.
5. Dip the thighs in the flour mixture first, then into the buttermilk, and then into the flour mixture. Shake the excess off.
6. Arrange the thighs in the air fry basket and spritz with cooking spray.
7. Select Air Fry, Super Convection. Set temperature to 360ºF (182ºC) and set time to 20 minutes. Press Start/Stop to begin preheating.
8. Once preheated, place the basket on the air fry position. Flip the thighs halfway through.
9. When cooking is complete, an instant-read thermometer inserted in the thickest part of the chicken thighs should register at least 165ºF (74ºC).
10. Meanwhile, make the waffles: combine the ingredients for the waffles in a large bowl. Stir to mix well, then arrange the mixture in a waffle iron and cook until a golden and fragrant waffle forms.
11. Remove the waffles from the waffle iron and slice into 4 pieces. Remove the chicken thighs from the oven and allow to cool for 5 minutes.
12. Arrange each chicken thigh on each waffle piece and drizzle with 1 tablespoon of honey. Serve warm.

Lettuce-Wrapped Chicken with Peanut Sauce

Prep time: 15 minutes | Cook time: 6 minutes | Serves 4

1 pound (454 g) ground chicken
2 cloves garlic, minced
¼ cup diced onions
¼ teaspoon sea salt
Cooking spray

Peanut Sauce:
¼ cup creamy peanut butter, at room temperature
2 tablespoons tamari
1½ teaspoons hot sauce
2 tablespoons lime juice
2 tablespoons grated fresh ginger
2 tablespoons chicken broth
2 teaspoons sugar

For Serving:
2 small heads butter lettuce, leaves separated
Lime slices (optional)

1. Spritz a baking pan with cooking spray.
2. Combine the ground chicken, garlic, and onions in the baking pan, then sprinkle with salt. Use a fork to break the ground chicken and combine them well.
3. Select Bake, Super Convection, set temperature to 350ºF (180ºC) and set time to 5 minutes. Press Start/Stop to begin preheating.
4. Once preheated, place the pan on the bake position. Stir them halfway through the cooking time.
5. When cooking is complete, the chicken should be lightly browned.
6. Meanwhile, combine the ingredients for the sauce in a small bowl. Stir to mix well.
7. Pour the sauce in the pan of chicken, then bake for 1 more minute or until heated through.
8. Unfold the lettuce leaves on a large serving plate, then divide the chicken mixture on the lettuce leaves. Drizzle with lime juice and serve immediately.

Chapter 3 Vegan and Vegetarian|77

Teriyaki Chicken with Lemony Snow Peas

Prep time: 20 minutes | Cook time: 34 minutes | Serves 4

¼ cup chicken broth
½ teaspoon grated fresh ginger
⅛ teaspoon red pepper flakes
1½ tablespoons soy sauce
4 (5-ounce / 142-g) bone-in chicken thighs, trimmed
1 tablespoon mirin
½ teaspoon cornstarch
1 tablespoon sugar
6 ounces (170 g) snow peas, strings removed
⅛ teaspoon lemon zest
1 garlic clove, minced
¼ teaspoon salt
Ground black pepper, to taste
½ teaspoon lemon juice

1. Combine the broth, ginger, pepper flakes, and soy sauce in a large bowl. Stir to mix well.
2. Pierce 10 to 15 holes into the chicken skin. Put the chicken in the broth mixture and toss to coat well. Let sit for 10 minutes to marinate.
3. Transfer the marinated chicken on a plate and pat dry with paper towels.
4. Scoop 2 tablespoons of marinade in a microwave-safe bowl and combine with mirin, cornstarch and sugar. Stir to mix well. Microwave for 1 minute or until frothy and has a thick consistency. Set aside.
5. Arrange the chicken in the air fry basket, skin side up.
6. Select Air Fry, Super Convection. Set temperature to 400ºF (205ºC) and set time to 25 minutes. Press Start/Stop to begin preheating.
7. Once preheated, place the basket on the air fry position. Flip the chicken halfway through.
8. When cooking is complete, brush the chicken skin with marinade mixture. Air fry the chicken for 5 more minutes or until glazed.
9. Remove the chicken from the oven. Allow the chicken to cool for 10 minutes.
10. Meanwhile, combine the snow peas, lemon zest, garlic, salt, and ground black pepper in a small bowl. Toss to coat well.
11. Transfer the snow peas in the air fry basket.
12. Select Air Fry, Super Convection. Set temperature to 400ºF (205ºC) and set time to 3 minutes. Place the basket on the air fry position.
13. When cooking is complete, the peas should be soft.
14. Remove the peas from the oven and toss with lemon juice.
15. Serve the chicken with lemony snow peas.

Herby Turkey with Dijon Sauce

Prep time: 10 minutes | Cook time: 30 minutes | Serves 4

1 teaspoon chopped fresh sage
1 teaspoon chopped fresh tarragon
1 teaspoon chopped fresh thyme leaves
1 teaspoon chopped fresh rosemary leaves
1½ teaspoons sea salt
1 teaspoon ground black pepper
1 (2-pound / 907-g) turkey breast
3 tablespoons Dijon mustard
3 tablespoons butter, melted
Cooking spray

1. Spritz the air fry basket with cooking spray.
2. Combine the herbs, salt, and black pepper in a small bowl. Stir to mix well. Set aside.
3. Combine the Dijon mustard and butter in a separate bowl. Stir to mix well.
4. Rub the turkey with the herb mixture on a clean work surface, then brush the turkey with Dijon mixture.
5. Arrange the turkey in the air fry basket.
6. Select Air Fry, Super Convection. Set temperature to 390ºF (199ºC) and set time to 30 minutes. Press Start/Stop to begin preheating.
7. Once preheated, place the basket on the air fry position. Flip the turkey breast halfway through.
8. When cooking is complete, an instant-read thermometer inserted in the thickest part of the turkey breast should reach at least 165ºF (74ºC).
9. Transfer the cooked turkey breast on a large plate and slice to serve.

Cheddar Turkey Burgers

Prep time: 10 minutes | Cook time: 25 minutes | Serves 4

2 medium yellow onions
1 tablespoon olive oil
1½ teaspoons kosher salt, divided
1¼ pound (567 g) ground turkey
⅓ cup mayonnaise
1 tablespoon Dijon mustard
2 teaspoons Worcestershire sauce
4 slices sharp Cheddar cheese (about 4 ounces / 113 g in total)
4 hamburger buns, sliced

1. Trim the onions and cut them in half through the root. Cut one of the halves in half. Grate one quarter. Place the grated onion in a large bowl. Thinly slice the remaining onions and place in a medium bowl with the oil and ½ teaspoon of kosher salt. Toss to coat. Place the onions in a single layer on a baking pan.
2. Select Roast, Super Convection, set temperature to 350ºF (180ºC), and set time to 10 minutes. Press Start/Stop to begin preheating.
3. Once preheated, place the pan on the roast position.
4. While the onions are cooking, add the turkey to the grated onion. Add the remaining kosher salt, mayonnaise, mustard, and Worcestershire sauce. Mix just until combined, being careful not to overwork the turkey. Divide the mixture into 4 patties, each about ¾-inch thick.
5. When cooking is complete, remove the pan from the oven. Move the onions to one side of the pan and place the burgers on the pan. Poke your finger into the center of each burger to make a deep indentation.
6. Select Broil, Super Convection, set temperature to High, and set time to 12 minutes. Press Start/Stop to begin preheating.
7. Once preheated, place the pan on the broil position. After 6 minutes, remove the pan. Turn the burgers and stir the onions. Return the pan to the oven and continue cooking. After about 4 minutes, remove the pan and place the cheese slices on the burgers. Return the pan to the oven and continue cooking for about 1 minute, or until the cheese is melted and the center of the burgers has reached at least 165ºF (74ºC) on a meat thermometer.
8. When cooking is complete, remove the pan from the oven. Loosely cover the burgers with foil.
9. Lay out the buns, cut-side up, on the oven rack. Select Broil, Super Convection, set temperature to High, and set time to 3 minutes. Place the pan on the broil position. Check the buns after 2 minutes; they should be lightly browned.
10. Remove the buns from the oven. Assemble the burgers and serve.

Curried Chicken and Sweet Potato

Prep time: 10 minutes | Cook time: 20 minutes | Serves 4

1 pound (454 g) boneless, skinless chicken thighs
1 teaspoon kosher salt, divided
¼ cup unsalted butter, melted
1 tablespoon curry powder
2 medium sweet potatoes, peeled and cut in 1-inch cubes
12 ounces (340 g) Brussels sprouts, halved

1. Sprinkle the chicken thighs with ½ teaspoon of kosher salt. Place them in the single layer on a baking pan.
2. In a small bowl, stir together the butter and curry powder.
3. Place the sweet potatoes and Brussels sprouts in a large bowl. Drizzle half the curry butter over the vegetables and add the remaining kosher salt. Toss to coat. Transfer the vegetables to the baking pan and place in a single layer around the chicken. Brush half of the remaining curry butter over the chicken.
4. Select Roast, Super Convection, set temperature to 400ºF (205ºC), and set time to 20 minutes. Press Start/Stop to begin preheating.
5. Once preheated, place the pan on the roast position.
6. After 10 minutes, remove the pan from the oven and turn over the chicken thighs. Baste them with the remaining curry butter. Return the pan to the oven and continue cooking.
7. Cooking is complete when the sweet potatoes are tender and the chicken is cooked through and reads 165ºF (74ºC) on a meat thermometer.

Korean-Inspired Chicken Wings

Prep time: 10 minutes | Cook time: 25 minutes | Serves 4

Wings:
2 pounds (907 g) chicken wings
1 teaspoon salt
1 teaspoon ground black pepper

Sauce:
2 tablespoons gochujang
1 tablespoon mayonnaise
1 tablespoon minced ginger
1 tablespoon minced garlic
1 teaspoon agave nectar
2 packets splenda
1 tablespoon sesame oil

For Garnish:
2 teaspoons sesame seeds
¼ cup chopped green onions

1. Line a baking pan with aluminum foil, then arrange the rack on the pan.
2. On a clean work surface, rub the chicken wings with salt and ground black pepper, then arrange the seasoned wings on the rack.
3. Select Air Fry, Super Convection. Set temperature to 400°F (205°C) and set time to 20 minutes. Press Start/Stop to begin preheating.
4. Once preheated, place the pan into the oven. Flip the wings halfway through.
5. When cooking is complete, the wings should be well browned.
6. Meanwhile, combine the ingredients for the sauce in a small bowl. Stir to mix well. Reserve half of the sauce in a separate bowl until ready to serve.
7. Remove the air fried chicken wings from the oven and toss with remaining half of the sauce to coat well.
8. Place the wings back to the oven. Select Air Fry, Super Convection. Set time to 5 minutes.
9. When cooking is complete, the internal temperature of the wings should reach at least 165°F (74°C).
10. Remove the wings from the oven and place on a large plate. Sprinkle with sesame seeds and green onions. Serve with reserved sauce.

Paprika Chicken Skewers with Satay Sauce

Prep time: 15 minutes | Cook time: 10 minutes | Serves 4

4 (6-ounce / 170-g) boneless, skinless chicken breasts, sliced into strips
1 teaspoon sea salt
1 teaspoon paprika
Cooking spray

Satay Sauce:
¼ cup creamy almond butter
½ teaspoon hot sauce
1½ tablespoons coconut vinegar
2 tablespoons chicken broth
1 teaspoon peeled and minced fresh ginger
1 clove garlic, minced
1 teaspoon sugar

For Serving:
¼ cup chopped cilantro leaves
Red pepper flakes, to taste
Thinly sliced red, orange, or / and yellow bell peppers

Special Equipment:
16 wooden or bamboo skewers, soaked in water for 15 minutes

1. Spritz the air fry basket with cooking spray.
2. Run the bamboo skewers through the chicken strips, then arrange the chicken skewers in the air fry basket and sprinkle with salt and paprika.
3. Select Air Fry, Super Convection. Set temperature to 400°F (205°C) and set time to 10 minutes. Press Start/Stop to begin preheating.
4. Once preheated, place the basket on the air fry position. Flip the chicken skewers halfway during the cooking.
5. When cooking is complete, the chicken should be lightly browned.
6. Meanwhile, combine the ingredients for the sauce in a small bowl. Stir to mix well.
7. Transfer the cooked chicken skewers on a large plate, then top with cilantro, sliced bell peppers, red pepper flakes. Serve with the sauce or just baste the sauce over before serving.

Oregano-Balsamic Chicken Breast

Prep time: 10 minutes | Cook time: 40 minutes | Serves 2

¼ cup balsamic vinegar
2 teaspoons dried oregano
2 garlic cloves, minced
1 tablespoon olive oil
⅛ teaspoon salt
½ teaspoon freshly ground black pepper
2 (4-ounce / 113-g) boneless, skinless, chicken-breast halves
Cooking spray

1. In a small bowl, add the vinegar, oregano, garlic, olive oil, salt, and pepper. Mix to combine.
2. Put the chicken in a resealable plastic bag. Pour the vinegar mixture in the bag with the chicken, seal the bag, and shake to coat the chicken. Refrigerate for 30 minutes to marinate.
3. Spritz a baking pan with cooking spray. Put the chicken in the prepared baking pan and pour the marinade over the chicken.
4. Select Bake, Super Convection, set temperature to 400ºF (205ºC) and set time to 40 minutes. Press Start/Stop to begin preheating.
5. Once preheated, place the pan on the bake position.
6. After 20 minutes, remove the pan from the oven. Flip the chicken. Return the pan to the oven and continue cooking.
7. When cooking is complete, the internal temperature of the chicken should registers at least 165ºF (74ºC).
8. Let sit for 5 minutes, then serve.

Parmesan Chicken Ciabatta Sandwiches

Prep time: 10 minutes | Cook time: 13 minutes | Serves 4

2 (8-ounce / 227-g) boneless, skinless chicken breasts
1 teaspoon kosher salt, divided
1 cup all-purpose flour
1 teaspoon Italian seasoning
2 large eggs
2 tablespoons plain yogurt
2 cups panko bread crumbs
1⅓ cups grated Parmesan cheese, divided
2 tablespoons olive oil
4 ciabatta rolls, split in half
½ cup marinara sauce
½ cup shredded Mozzarella cheese

1. Lay the chicken breasts on a cutting board and cut each one in half parallel to the board so you have 4 fairly even, flat fillets. Place a piece of plastic wrap over the chicken pieces and use a rolling pin to gently pound them to an even thickness, about ½-inch thick. Season the chicken on both sides with ½ teaspoon of kosher salt.
2. Place the flour on a plate and add the remaining kosher salt and the Italian seasoning. Mix with a fork to distribute evenly. In a wide bowl, whisk together the eggs with the yogurt. In a small bowl combine the panko, 1 cup of Parmesan cheese, and olive oil. Place this in a shallow bowl.
3. Lightly dredge both sides of the chicken pieces in the seasoned flour, and then dip them in the egg wash to coat completely, letting the excess drip off. Finally, dredge the chicken in the bread crumbs. Carefully place the breaded chicken pieces in the air fry basket.
4. Select Air Fry, Super Convection, set temperature to 375ºF (190ºC), and set time to 10 minutes. Press Start/Stop to begin preheating.
5. Once preheated, place the air fry basket into the oven.
6. After 5 minutes, remove the air fry basket from the oven. Carefully turn the chicken over. Return the air fry basket to the oven and continue cooking. When cooking is complete, remove the air fry basket from the oven.
7. Unfold the rolls on the air fry basket and spread each half with 1 tablespoon of marinara sauce. Place a chicken breast piece on the bottoms of the buns and sprinkle the remaining Parmesan cheese over the chicken pieces. Divide the Mozzarella among the top halves of the buns.
8. Select Broil, Super Convection, set temperature to High, and set time to 3 minutes. Press Start/Stop to begin preheating.
9. Once preheated, place the basket on the broil position. Check the sandwiches halfway through. When cooking is complete, the Mozzarella cheese should be melted and bubbly.
10. Remove the air fry basket from the oven. Close the sandwiches and serve.

Lettuce Turkey and Mushroom Taco

Prep time: 20 minutes | Cook time: 15 minutes | Serves 6

Sauce:
2 tablespoons tamari
2 tablespoons tomato sauce
1 tablespoon lime juice
¼ teaspoon peeled and grated fresh ginger
1 clove garlic, smashed to a paste
½ cup chicken broth
⅓ cup sugar
2 tablespoons toasted sesame oil
Cooking spray

Meatballs:
2 pounds (907 g) ground turkey
¾ cup finely chopped button mushrooms
2 large eggs, beaten
1½ teaspoons tamari
¼ cup finely chopped green onions, plus more for garnish
2 teaspoons peeled and grated fresh ginger
1 clove garlic, smashed
2 teaspoons toasted sesame oil
2 tablespoons sugar

For Serving:
Lettuce leaves, for serving
Sliced red chiles, for garnish (optional)
Toasted sesame seeds, for garnish (optional)

1. Spritz the air fry basket with cooking spray.
2. Combine the ingredients for the sauce in a small bowl. Stir to mix well. Set aside.
3. Combine the ingredients for the meatballs in a large bowl. Stir to mix well, then shape the mixture in twelve 1½-inch meatballs.
4. Arrange the meatballs in the air fry basket, then baste with the sauce.
5. Select Air Fry, Super Convection. Set temperature to 350ºF (180ºC) and set time to 15 minutes. Press Start/Stop to begin preheating.
6. Once preheated, place the basket on the air fry position. Flip the balls halfway through.
7. When cooking is complete, the meatballs should be golden brown.
8. Unfold the lettuce leaves on a large serving plate, then transfer the cooked meatballs on the leaves. Spread the red chiles and sesame seeds over the balls, then serve.

Roasted Chicken and Sausage with Peppers

Prep time: 10 minutes | Cook time: 27 minutes | Serves 4

4 bone-in, skin-on chicken thighs (about 1½ pounds / 680 g)
1½ teaspoon kosher salt, divided
1 link sweet Italian sausage (about 4 ounces / 113 g), whole
8 ounces (227 g) miniature bell peppers, halved and deseeded
1 small onion, thinly sliced
2 garlic cloves, minced
1 tablespoon olive oil
4 hot pickled cherry peppers, deseeded and quartered, along with 2 tablespoons pickling liquid from the jar
¼ cup chicken stock
Cooking spray

1. Salt the chicken thighs on both sides with 1 teaspoon of kosher salt. Spritz a baking pan with cooking spray and place the thighs skin-side down on the pan. Add the sausage.
2. Select Roast, Super Convection, set temperature to 375ºF (190ºC), and set time to 27 minutes. Press Start/Stop to begin preheating.
3. Once preheated, place the pan on the roast position.
4. While the chicken and sausage cook, place the bell peppers, onion, and garlic in a large bowl. Sprinkle with the remaining kosher salt and add the olive oil. Toss to coat.
5. After 10 minutes, remove the pan from the oven and flip the chicken thighs and sausage. Add the pepper mixture to the pan. Return the pan to the oven and continue cooking.
6. After another 10 minutes, remove the pan from the oven and add the pickled peppers, pickling liquid, and stock. Stir the pickled peppers into the peppers and onion. Return the pan to the oven and continue cooking.
7. When cooking is complete, the peppers and onion should be soft and the chicken should read 165ºF (74ºC) on a meat thermometer. Remove the pan from the oven. Slice the sausage into thin pieces and stir it into the pepper mixture. Spoon the peppers over four plates. Top with a chicken thigh.

Fried Thai Hens with Vegetable Salad

Prep time: 15 minutes | Cook time: 25 minutes | Serves 6

2 (1¼-pound / 567-g) Cornish game hens, giblets discarded
1 tablespoon fish sauce
6 tablespoons chopped fresh cilantro
2 teaspoons lime zest
1 teaspoon ground coriander
2 garlic cloves, minced
2 tablespoons packed light brown sugar
2 teaspoons vegetable oil
Salt and ground black pepper, to taste
1 English cucumber, halved lengthwise and sliced thin
1 Thai chile, stemmed, deseeded, and minced
2 tablespoons chopped dry-roasted peanuts
1 small shallot, sliced thinly
1 tablespoon lime juice
Lime wedges, for serving
Cooking spray

1. Arrange a game hen on a clean work surface, remove the backbone with kitchen shears, then pound the hen breast to flat. Cut the breast in half. Repeat with the remaining game hen.
2. Loose the breast and thigh skin with your fingers, then pat the game hens dry and pierce about 10 holes into the fat deposits of the hens. Tuck the wings under the hens.
3. Combine 2 teaspoons of fish sauce, ¼ cup of cilantro, lime zest, coriander, garlic, 4 teaspoons of sugar, 1 teaspoon of vegetable oil, ½ teaspoon of salt, and ⅛ teaspoon of ground black pepper in a small bowl. Stir to mix well.
4. Rub the fish sauce mixture under the breast and thigh skin of the game hens, then let sit for 10 minutes to marinate.
5. Spritz the air fry basket with cooking spray.
6. Arrange the marinated game hens in the basket, skin side down.
7. Select Air Fry, Super Convection. Set temperature to 400ºF (205ºC) and set time to 25 minutes. Press Start/Stop to begin preheating.
8. Once preheated, place the basket on the air fry position. Flip the game hens halfway through the cooking time.
9. When cooking is complete, the hen skin should be golden brown and the internal temperature of the hens should read at least 165ºF (74ºC).
10. Meanwhile, combine all the remaining ingredients, except for the lime wedges, in a large bowl and sprinkle with salt and black pepper. Toss to mix well.
11. Transfer the fried hens on a large plate, then sit the salad aside and squeeze the lime wedges over before serving.

Breaded Chicken Schnitzel

Prep time: 15 minutes | Cook time: 5 minutes | Serves 4

½ cup all-purpose flour
1 teaspoon marjoram
½ teaspoon thyme
1 teaspoon dried parsley flakes
½ teaspoon salt
1 egg
1 teaspoon lemon juice
1 teaspoon water
1 cup bread crumbs
4 chicken tenders, pounded thin, cut in half lengthwise
Cooking spray

1. Spritz the air fry basket with cooking spray.
2. Combine the flour, marjoram, thyme, parsley, and salt in a shallow dish. Stir to mix well.
3. Whisk the egg with lemon juice and water in a large bowl. Pour the bread crumbs in a separate shallow dish.
4. Roll the chicken halves in the flour mixture first, then in the egg mixture, and then roll over the bread crumbs to coat well. Shake the excess off.
5. Arrange the chicken halves in the air fry basket and spritz with cooking spray on both sides.
6. Select Air Fry, Super Convection. Set temperature to 390ºF (199ºC) and set time to 5 minutes. Press Start/Stop to begin preheating.
7. Once preheated, place the basket on the air fry position. Flip the halves halfway through.
8. When cooking is complete, the chicken halves should be golden brown and crispy.
9. Serve immediately.

Chicken and Peppers Skewers with Corn

Prep time: 15 minutes | Cook time: 10 minutes | Serves 4

1 pound (454 g) boneless, skinless chicken breast, cut into 1½-inch chunks
1 green bell pepper, deseeded and cut into 1-inch pieces
1 red bell pepper, deseeded and cut into 1-inch pieces
1 large onion, cut into large chunks
2 tablespoons fajita seasoning
3 tablespoons vegetable oil, divided
2 teaspoons kosher salt, divided
2 cups corn, drained
¼ teaspoon granulated garlic
1 teaspoon freshly squeezed lime juice
1 tablespoon mayonnaise
3 tablespoons grated Parmesan cheese

Special Equipment:
12 wooden skewers, soaked in water for at least 30 minutes

1. Place the chicken, bell peppers, and onion in a large bowl. Add the fajita seasoning, 2 tablespoons of vegetable oil, and 1½ teaspoons of kosher salt. Toss to coat evenly.
2. Alternate the chicken and vegetables on the skewers, making about 12 skewers.
3. Place the corn in a medium bowl and add the remaining vegetable oil. Add the remaining kosher salt and the garlic, and toss to coat. Place the corn in an even layer on a baking pan and place the skewers on top.
4. Select Roast, Super Convection, set temperature to 375°F (190°C), and set time to 10 minutes. Press Start/Stop to begin preheating.
5. Once preheated, place the pan on the roast position.
6. After about 5 minutes, remove the pan from the oven and turn the skewers. Return the pan to the oven and continue cooking.
7. When cooking is complete, remove the pan from the oven. Place the skewers on a platter. Put the corn back to the bowl and combine with the lime juice, mayonnaise, and Parmesan cheese. Stir to mix well. Serve the skewers with the corn.

Air-Fried Chicken and Fingerling Potato

Prep time: 15 minutes | Cook time: 25 minutes | Serves 2

2 teaspoons minced fresh oregano, divided
2 teaspoons minced fresh thyme, divided
2 teaspoons extra-virgin olive oil, plus extra as needed
1 pound (454 g) fingerling potatoes, unpeeled
2 (12-ounce / 340-g) bone-in split chicken breasts, trimmed
1 garlic clove, minced
¼ cup oil-packed sun-dried tomatoes, patted dry and chopped
1½ tablespoons red wine vinegar
1 tablespoon capers, rinsed and minced
1 small shallot, minced
Salt and ground black pepper, to taste

1. Combine 1 teaspoon of oregano, 1 teaspoon of thyme, ¼ teaspoon of salt, ¼ teaspoon of ground black pepper, 1 teaspoons of olive oil in a large bowl. Add the potatoes and toss to coat well.
2. Combine the chicken with remaining thyme, oregano, and olive oil. Sprinkle with garlic, salt, and pepper. Toss to coat well.
3. Place the potatoes in the air fry basket, then arrange the chicken on top of the potatoes.
4. Select Air Fry, Super Convection. Set temperature to 350°F (180°C) and set time to 25 minutes. Press Start/Stop to begin preheating.
5. Once preheated, place the basket on the air fry position. Flip the chicken and potatoes halfway through.
6. When cooking is complete, the internal temperature of the chicken should reach at least 165°F (74°C) and the potatoes should be wilted.
7. Meanwhile, combine the sun-dried tomatoes, vinegar, capers, and shallot in a separate large bowl. Sprinkle with salt and ground black pepper. Toss to mix well.
8. Remove the chicken and potatoes from the oven and allow to cool for 10 minutes. Serve with the sun-dried tomato mix.

Ham-Chicken Meatballs with Lemony Mustard

Prep time: 10 minutes | Cook time: 15 minutes | Serves 4

Meatballs:
½ pound (227 g) ham, diced
½ pound (227 g) ground chicken
½ cup grated Swiss cheese
1 large egg, beaten
3 cloves garlic, minced
¼ cup chopped onions
1½ teaspoons sea salt
1 teaspoon ground black pepper
Cooking spray

Dijon Sauce:
3 tablespoons Dijon mustard
2 tablespoons lemon juice
¼ cup chicken broth, warmed
¾ teaspoon sea salt
¼ teaspoon ground black pepper
Chopped fresh thyme leaves, for garnish

1. Spritz the air fry basket with cooking spray.
2. Combine the ingredients for the meatballs in a large bowl. Stir to mix well, then shape the mixture in twelve 1½-inch meatballs.
3. Arrange the meatballs in the air fry basket.
4. Select Air Fry, Super Convection. Set temperature to 390ºF (199ºC) and set time to 15 minutes. Press Start/Stop to begin preheating.
5. Once preheated, place the basket on the air fry position. Flip the balls halfway through.
6. When cooking is complete, the balls should be lightly browned.
7. Meanwhile, combine the ingredients, except for the thyme leaves, for the sauce in a small bowl. Stir to mix well.
8. Transfer the cooked meatballs on a large plate, then baste the sauce over. Garnish with thyme leaves and serve.

Tandoori Drumsticks

Prep time: 10 minutes | Cook time: 14 minutes | Serves 4

8 (4- to 5-ounce / 113- to 142-g) skinless bone-in chicken drumsticks
½ cup plain full-fat or low-fat yogurt
¼ cup buttermilk
2 teaspoons minced garlic
2 teaspoons minced fresh ginger
2 teaspoons ground cinnamon
2 teaspoons ground coriander
2 teaspoons mild paprika
1 teaspoon salt
1 teaspoon Tabasco hot red pepper sauce

1. In a large bowl, stir together all the ingredients except for chicken drumsticks until well combined. Add the chicken drumsticks to the bowl and toss until well coated. Cover in plastic and set in the refrigerator to marinate for 1 hour, tossing once.
2. Arrange the marinated drumsticks in the air fry basket, leaving enough space between them.
3. Select Air Fry, Super Convection. Set temperature to 375ºF (190ºC) and set time to 14 minutes. Press Start/Stop to begin preheating.
4. Once preheated, place the basket on the air fry position. Flip the drumsticks once halfway through to ensure even cooking.
5. When cooking is complete, the internal temperature of the chicken drumsticks should reach 160ºF (71ºC) on a meat thermometer.
6. Transfer the drumsticks to plates. Rest for 5 minutes before serving.

Spanish Chicken and Sweet Pepper

Prep time: 10 minutes | Cook time: 20 minutes | Serves 2

1¼ pounds (567 g) assorted small chicken parts, breasts cut into halves
¼ teaspoon salt
¼ teaspoon ground black pepper
2 teaspoons olive oil
½ pound (227 g) mini sweet peppers
¼ cup light mayonnaise
¼ teaspoon smoked paprika
½ clove garlic, crushed
Baguette, for serving
Cooking spray

1. Spritz the air fry basket with cooking spray.
2. Toss the chicken with salt, ground black pepper, and olive oil in a large bowl.
3. Arrange the sweet peppers and chicken in the air fry basket.
4. Select Air Fry, Super Convection. Set temperature to 375ºF (190ºC) and set time to 20 minutes. Press Start/Stop to begin preheating.
5. Once preheated, place the basket on the air fry position. Flip the chicken and transfer the peppers on a plate halfway through.
6. When cooking is complete, the chicken should be well browned.
7. Meanwhile, combine the mayo, paprika, and garlic in a small bowl. Stir to mix well.
8. Assemble the baguette with chicken and sweet pepper, then spread with mayo mixture and serve.

Japanese Skewered Chicken (Yakitori)

Prep time: 10 minutes | Cook time: 15 minutes | Serves 4

½ cup mirin
¼ cup dry white wine
½ cup soy sauce
1 tablespoon light brown sugar
1½ pounds (680 g) boneless, skinless chicken thighs, cut into 1½-inch pieces, fat trimmed
4 medium scallions, trimmed, cut into 1½-inch pieces
Cooking spray

Special Equipment:
4 (4-inch) bamboo skewers, soaked in water for at least 30 minutes

1. Combine the mirin, dry white wine, soy sauce, and brown sugar in a saucepan. Bring to a boil over medium heat. Keep stirring.
2. Boil for another 2 minutes or until it has a thick consistency. Turn off the heat.
3. Spritz the air fry basket with cooking spray.
4. Run the bamboo skewers through the chicken pieces and scallions alternatively.
5. Arrange the skewers in the air fry basket, then brush with mirin mixture on both sides. Spritz with cooking spray.
6. Select Air Fry, Super Convection. Set temperature to 400ºF (205ºC) and set time to 10 minutes. Press Start/Stop to begin preheating.
7. Once preheated, place the basket on the air fry position. Flip the skewers halfway through.
8. When cooking is complete, the chicken and scallions should be glossy.
9. Serve immediately.

Chapter 7 Appetizers and Snacks

Parmesan Ranch Snack Mix

Prep time: 5 minutes | Cook time: 6 minutes | Makes 6 cups

2 cups oyster crackers
2 cups Chex rice
1 cup sesame sticks
⅔ cup finely grated Parmesan cheese
8 tablespoons unsalted butter, melted
1½ teaspoons granulated garlic
½ teaspoon kosher salt

1. Toss together all the ingredients in a large bowl until well coated. Spread the mixture on the sheet pan in an even layer.
2. Select Roast, Super Convection, set temperature to 350ºF (180ºC) and set time to 6 minutes. Select Start/Stop to begin preheating.
3. When the unit has preheated, place the pan on the roast position.
4. After 3 minutes, remove the pan and stir the mixture. Return the pan to the oven and continue cooking.
5. When cooking is complete, the mixture should be lightly browned and fragrant. Let cool before serving.

Fish Sticks

Prep time: 5 minutes | Cook time: 12 minutes | Serves 4

2 eggs
2 tablespoons milk
2 cups flour
1 cup cornmeal
1 teaspoon seafood seasoning
Salt and black pepper, to taste
1 cup bread crumbs
1 pound (454 g) cod fillets, cut into 1-inch strips

1. Beat the eggs with the milk in a shallow bowl. In another shallow bowl, combine the flour, cornmeal, seafood seasoning, salt, and pepper. On a plate, place the bread crumbs.
2. Dredge the cod strips, one at a time, in the flour mixture, then in the egg mixture, finally roll in the bread crumb to coat evenly.
3. Transfer the cod strips to the air fry basket.
4. Select Air Fry, Super Convection, set temperature to 400ºF (205ºC), and set time to 12 minutes. Select Start/Stop to begin preheating.
5. Once preheated, place the basket on the air fry position.
6. When cooking is complete, the cod strips should be crispy. Remove from the oven to a paper towel-lined plate and serve warm.

Buttermilk Fried Chicken Wings

Prep time: 10 minutes | Cook time: 18 minutes | Serves 4

2 pounds (907 g) chicken wings
Marinade:
1 cup buttermilk
½ teaspoon salt
Coating:
1 cup flour
1 cup panko bread crumbs
Cooking spray
½ teaspoon black pepper
2 tablespoons poultry seasoning
2 teaspoons salt

1. Whisk together all the ingredients for the marinade in a large bowl.
2. Add the chicken wings to the marinade and toss well. Transfer to the refrigerator to marinate for at least an hour.
3. Spritz the air fry basket with cooking spray. Set aside.
4. Thoroughly combine all the ingredients for the coating in a shallow bowl.
5. Remove the chicken wings from the marinade and shake off any excess. Roll them in the coating mixture.
6. Place the chicken wings in the air fry basket in a single layer. Mist the wings with cooking spray.
7. Select Air Fry, Super Convection, set temperature to 360ºF (182ºC), and set time to 18 minutes. Select Start/Stop to begin preheating.
8. Once preheated, place the basket on the air fry position. Flip the wings halfway through the cooking time.
9. When cooking is complete, the wings should be crisp and golden brown on the outside. Remove from the oven to a plate and serve hot.

Sweet and Spicy Roasted Walnuts

Prep time: 5 minutes | Cook time: 15 minutes | Makes 4 cups

1 pound (454 g) walnut halves and pieces
½ cup granulated sugar
3 tablespoons vegetable oil
1 teaspoon cayenne pepper
½ teaspoon fine salt

1. Soak the walnuts in a large bowl with boiling water for a minute or two. Drain the walnuts. Stir in the sugar, oil and cayenne pepper to coat well. Spread the walnuts in a single layer on the sheet pan.
2. Select Roast, Super Convection, set temperature to 325°F (163°C) and set time to 15 minutes. Select Start/Stop to begin preheating.
3. When the unit has preheated, place the pan on the roast position.
4. After 7 or 8 minutes, remove the pan from the oven. Stir the nuts. Return the pan to the oven and continue cooking, check frequently.
5. When cooking is complete, the walnuts should be dark golden brown. Remove the pan from the oven. Sprinkle the nuts with the salt and let cool. Serve.

Polenta Fries with Tangy Chili Mayonnaise

Prep time: 10 minutes | Cook time: 28 minutes | Serves 4

Polenta Fries:
2 teaspoons vegetable or olive oil
¼ teaspoon paprika
1 pound (454 g) prepared polenta, cut into 3-inch × ½-inch strips
Salt and freshly ground black pepper, to taste

Chili-Lime Mayo:
½ cup mayonnaise
1 teaspoon chili powder
1 teaspoon chopped fresh cilantro
¼ teaspoon ground cumin
Juice of ½ lime
Salt and freshly ground black pepper, to taste

1. Mix the oil and paprika in a bowl. Add the polenta strips and toss until evenly coated. Transfer the polenta strips to the air fry basket.
2. Select Air Fry, Super Convection, set temperature to 400°F (205°C), and set time to 28 minutes. Select Start/Stop to begin preheating.
3. Once preheated, place the basket on the air fry position. Stir the polenta strips halfway through the cooking time.
4. Meanwhile, whisk together all the ingredients for the chili-lime mayo in a small bowl.
5. When cooking is complete, remove the polenta fries from the oven to a plate. Season as desired with salt and pepper. Serve alongside the chili-lime mayo as a dipping sauce.

Coated Pickle Spears

Prep time: 10 minutes | Cook time: 15 minutes | Serves 6

2 jars sweet and sour pickle spears, patted dry
2 medium-sized eggs
⅓ cup milk
1 teaspoon garlic powder
1 teaspoon sea salt
½ teaspoon shallot powder
⅓ teaspoon chili powder
⅓ cup all-purpose flour
Cooking spray

1. Spritz the air fry basket with cooking spray.
2. In a bowl, beat together the eggs with milk. In another bowl, combine garlic powder, sea salt, shallot powder, chili powder and all-purpose flour until well blended.
3. One by one, roll the pickle spears in the powder mixture, then dredge them in the egg mixture. Dip them in the powder mixture a second time for additional coating.
4. Place the coated pickles in the air fry basket.
5. Select Air Fry, Super Convection, set temperature to 385°F (196°C), and set time to 15 minutes. Select Start/Stop to begin preheating.
6. Once preheated, place the basket on the air fry position. Stir the pickles halfway through the cooking time.
7. When cooking is complete, they should be golden and crispy. Transfer to a plate and let cool for 5 minutes before serving.

Parma Prosciutto-Wrapped Pears

Prep time: 5 minutes | Cook time: 6 minutes | Serves 8

2 large, ripe Anjou pears
4 thin slices Parma prosciutto
2 teaspoons aged balsamic vinegar

1. Peel the pears. Slice into 8 wedges and cut out the core from each wedge.
2. Cut the prosciutto into 8 long strips. Wrap each pear wedge with a strip of prosciutto. Place the wrapped pears in the sheet pan.
3. Select Broil, Super Convection, set temperature to High and set time to 6 minutes. Select Start/Stop to begin preheating.
4. When the unit has preheated, place the pan on the broil position.
5. After 2 or 3 minutes, check the pears. The pears should be turned over if the prosciutto is beginning to crisp up and brown. Return the pan to the oven and continue cooking.
6. When cooking is complete, remove the pan from the oven. Drizzle the pears with the balsamic vinegar and serve warm.

Small Hush Puppies

Prep time: 15 minutes | Cook time: 10 minutes | Serves 12

1 cup self-rising yellow cornmeal
½ cup all-purpose flour
1 teaspoon sugar
1 teaspoon salt
1 teaspoon freshly ground black pepper
1 large egg
⅓ cup canned creamed corn
1 cup minced onion
2 teaspoons minced jalapeño pepper
2 tablespoons olive oil, divided

1. Thoroughly combine the cornmeal, flour, sugar, salt, and pepper in a large bowl.
2. Whisk together the egg and corn in a small bowl. Pour the egg mixture into the bowl of cornmeal mixture and stir to combine. Stir in the minced onion and jalapeño. Cover the bowl with plastic wrap and place in the refrigerator for 30 minutes.
3. Line the air fry basket with parchment paper and lightly brush it with 1 tablespoon of olive oil.
4. Scoop out the cornmeal mixture and form into 24 balls, about 1 inch.
5. Arrange the balls on the parchment, leaving space between each ball.
6. Select Air Fry, Super Convection, set temperature to 375°F (190°C), and set time to 10 minutes. Select Start/Stop to begin preheating.
7. Once preheated, place the basket on the air fry position.
8. After 5 minutes, remove the basket from the oven. Flip the balls and brush them with the remaining 1 tablespoon of olive oil. Return to the oven and continue cooking for 5 minutes until golden brown.
9. When cooking is complete, remove the balls (hush puppies) from the oven and serve on a plate.

Buttery Snack Mix

Prep time: 10 minutes | Cook time: 10 minutes | Makes about 10 cups

3 tablespoons butter, melted
½ cup honey
1 teaspoon salt
2 cups granola
2 cups sesame sticks
2 cups crispy corn puff cereal
2 cups mini pretzel crisps
1 cup cashews
1 cup pepitas
1 cup dried cherries

1. In a small mixing bowl, mix together the butter, honey, and salt until well incorporated.
2. In a large bowl, combine the granola, sesame sticks, corn puff cereal and pretzel crisps, cashews, and pepitas. Drizzle with the butter mixture and toss until evenly coated. Transfer the snack mix to a sheet pan.
3. Select Air Fry, Super Convection, set temperature to 370°F (188°C), and set time to 10 minutes. Select Start/Stop to begin preheating.
4. Once preheated, slide the pan into the oven. Stir the snack mix halfway through the cooking time.
5. When cooking is complete, they should be lightly toasted. Remove from the oven and allow to cool completely. Scatter with the dried cherries and mix well. Serve immediately.

Breaded Green Tomatoes with Horseradish

Prep time: 15 minutes | Cook time: 13 minutes | Serves 4

2 eggs
¼ cup buttermilk
½ cup bread crumbs
½ cup cornmeal
¼ teaspoon salt
1½ pounds (680 g) firm green tomatoes, cut into ¼-inch slices
Cooking spray
Horseradish Sauce:
¼ cup sour cream
¼ cup mayonnaise
2 teaspoons prepared horseradish
½ teaspoon lemon juice
½ teaspoon Worcestershire sauce
⅛ teaspoon black pepper

1. Spritz the air fry basket with cooking spray. Set aside.
2. In a small bowl, whisk together all the ingredients for the horseradish sauce until smooth. Set aside.
3. In a shallow dish, beat the eggs and buttermilk.
4. In a separate shallow dish, thoroughly combine the bread crumbs, cornmeal, and salt.
5. Dredge the tomato slices, one at a time, in the egg mixture, then roll in the bread crumb mixture until evenly coated.
6. Place the tomato slices in the air fry basket in a single layer. Spray them with cooking spray.
7. Select Air Fry, Super Convection, set temperature to 390ºF (199ºC), and set time to 13 minutes. Select Start/Stop to begin preheating.
8. Once preheated, place the basket on the air fry position. Flip the tomato slices halfway through the cooking time.
9. When cooking is complete, the tomato slices should be nicely browned and crisp. Remove from the oven to a platter and serve drizzled with the prepared horseradish sauce.

Double Cheese Sausage Balls

Prep time: 10 minutes | Cook time: 10 minutes | Serves 8

12 ounces (340 g) mild ground sausage
1½ cups baking mix
1 cup shredded mild Cheddar cheese
3 ounces (85 g) cream cheese, at room temperature
1 to 2 tablespoons olive oil

1. Line the air fry basket with parchment paper. Set aside.
2. Mix together the ground sausage, baking mix, Cheddar cheese, and cream cheese in a large bowl and stir to incorporate.
3. Divide the sausage mixture into 16 equal portions and roll them into 1-inch balls with your hands. Arrange the sausage balls on the parchment, leaving space between each ball. Brush the sausage balls with the olive oil.
4. Select Air Fry, Super Convection, set temperature to 325ºF (163ºC), and set time to 10 minutes. Select Start/Stop to begin preheating.
5. Once preheated, place the basket on the air fry position. Flip the balls halfway through the cooking time.
6. When cooking is complete, the balls should be firm and lightly browned on both sides. Remove from the oven to a plate and serve warm.

Breaded Zucchini Tots

Prep time: 10 minutes | Cook time: 6 minutes | Serves 8

2 medium zucchini (about 12 ounces / 340 g), shredded
1 large egg, whisked
½ cup grated Pecorino Romano cheese
½ cup panko bread crumbs
¼ teaspoon black pepper
1 clove garlic, minced
Cooking spray

1. Using your hands, squeeze out as much liquid from the zucchini as possible. In a large bowl, mix the zucchini with the remaining ingredients except the oil until well incorporated.
2. Make the zucchini tots: Use a spoon or cookie scoop to place tablespoonfuls of the zucchini mixture onto a lightly floured cutting board and form into 1-inch logs.
3. Spritz the air fry basket with cooking spray. Place the zucchini tots in the pan.
4. Select Air Fry, Super Convection, set temperature to 375ºF (190ºC), and set time to 6 minutes. Select Start/Stop to begin preheating.
5. Once preheated, place the basket on the air fry position.
6. When cooking is complete, the tots should be golden brown. Remove from the oven to a serving plate and serve warm.

Homemade Potato Chips

Prep time: 5 minutes | Cook time: 22 minutes | Serves 3

2 medium potatoes, preferably Yukon Gold, scrubbed
Cooking spray
2 teaspoons olive oil
½ teaspoon garlic granules
¼ teaspoon paprika
¼ teaspoon plus ⅛ teaspoon sea salt
¼ teaspoon freshly ground black pepper
Ketchup or hot sauce, for serving

1. Spritz the air fry basket with cooking spray.
2. On a flat work surface, cut the potatoes into ¼-inch-thick slices. Transfer the potato slices to a medium bowl, along with the olive oil, garlic granules, paprika, salt, and pepper and toss to coat well. Transfer the potato slices to the air fry basket.
3. Select Air Fry, Super Convection, set temperature to 392ºF (200ºC), and set time to 22 minutes. Select Start/Stop to begin preheating.
4. Once preheated, place the basket on the air fry position. Stir the potato slices twice during the cooking process.
5. When cooking is complete, the potato chips should be tender and nicely browned. Remove from the oven and serve alongside the ketchup for dipping.

Deviled Eggs wiih Paprika

Prep time: 10 minutes | Cook time: 16 minutes | Serves 12

3 cups ice
12 large eggs
½ cup mayonnaise
10 hamburger dill pickle chips, diced
¼ cup diced onion
2 teaspoons salt
2 teaspoons yellow mustard
1 teaspoon freshly ground black pepper
½ teaspoon paprika

1. Put the ice in a large bowl and set aside. Carefully place the eggs in the air fry basket.
2. Select Bake, Super Convection, set temperature to 250ºF (121ºC), and set time to 16 minutes. Select Start/Stop to begin preheating.
3. Once preheated, place the basket on the bake position.
4. When cooking is complete, transfer the eggs to the large bowl of ice to cool.
5. When cool enough to handle, peel the eggs. Slice them in half lengthwise and scoop out yolks into a small bowl. Stir in the mayonnaise, pickles, onion, salt, mustard, and pepper. Mash the mixture with a fork until well combined.
6. Fill each egg white half with 1 to 2 teaspoons of the egg yolk mixture.
7. Sprinkle the paprika on top and serve immediately.

Smoky Sausage and Mushroom Empanadas

Prep time: 5 minutes | Cook time: 12 minutes | Serves 4

½ pound (227 g) Kielbasa smoked sausage, chopped
4 chopped canned mushrooms
2 tablespoons chopped onion
½ teaspoon ground cumin
¼ teaspoon paprika
Salt and black pepper, to taste
½ package puff pastry dough, at room temperature
1 egg, beaten
Cooking spray

1. Combine the sausage, mushrooms, onion, cumin, paprika, salt, and pepper in a bowl and stir to mix well.
2. Make the empanadas: Place the puff pastry dough on a lightly floured surface. Cut circles into the dough with a glass. Place 1 tablespoon of the sausage mixture into the center of each pastry circle. Fold each in half and pinch the edges to seal. Using a fork, crimp the edges. Brush them with the beaten egg and mist with cooking spray.
3. Spritz the air fry basket with cooking spray. Place the empanadas in the air fry basket.
4. Select Air Fry, Super Convection, set temperature to 360ºF (182ºC), and set time to 12 minutes. Select Start/Stop to begin preheating.
5. Once preheated, place the basket on the air fry position. Flip the empanadas halfway through the cooking time.
6. When cooking is complete, the empanadas should be golden brown. Remove the basket from the oven. Allow them to cool for 5 minutes and serve hot.

Roasted Walnuts, Pecans, and Almonds

Prep time: 5 minutes | Cook time: 20 minutes | Serves 6

2 cups mixed nuts (walnuts, pecans, and almonds)
2 tablespoons egg white
2 tablespoons sugar
1 teaspoon paprika
1 teaspoon ground cinnamon
Cooking spray

1. Line the air fry basket with parchment paper and spray with cooking spray.
2. Stir together the mixed nuts, egg white, sugar, paprika, and cinnamon in a small bowl until the nuts are fully coated. Place the nuts in the air fry basket.
3. Select Roast, Super Convection, set temperature to 300ºF (150ºC), and set time to 20 minutes. Select Start/Stop to begin preheating.
4. Once preheated, place the basket on the roast position. Stir the nuts halfway through the cooking time.
5. When cooking is complete, remove the basket from the oven. Transfer the nuts to a bowl and serve warm.

Apple Chips

Prep time: 10 minutes | Cook time: 10 minutes | Serves 4

4 medium apples (any type will work), cored and thinly sliced
¼ teaspoon nutmeg
¼ teaspoon cinnamon
Cooking spray

1. Place the apple slices in a large bowl and sprinkle the spices on top. Toss to coat.
2. Put the apple slices in the air fry basket in a single layer and spray them with cooking spray.
3. Select Air Fry, Super Convection, set temperature to 360ºF (182ºC), and set time to 10 minutes. Select Start/Stop to begin preheating.
4. Once preheated, place the basket on the air fry position. Stir the apple slices halfway through.
5. When cooking is complete, the apple chips should be crispy. Transfer the apple chips to a paper towel-lined plate and rest for 5 minutes before serving.

Sesame Kale Chips

Prep time: 15 minutes | Cook time: 8 minutes | Serves 5

8 cups deribbed kale leaves, torn into 2-inch pieces
1½ tablespoons olive oil
¾ teaspoon chili powder
¼ teaspoon garlic powder
½ teaspoon paprika
2 teaspoons sesame seeds

1. In a large bowl, toss the kale with the olive oil, chili powder, garlic powder, paprika, and sesame seeds until well coated.
2. Transfer the kale to the air fry basket.
3. Select Air Fry, Super Convection, set temperature to 350ºF (180ºC), and set time to 8 minutes. Select Start/Stop to begin preheating.
4. Once preheated, place the basket on the air fry position. Flip the kale twice during cooking.
5. When cooking is complete, the kale should be crispy. Remove from the oven and serve warm.

Brie Pear Sandwiches

Prep time: 5 minutes | Cook time: 6 minutes | Serves 4 to 8

8 ounces (227 g) Brie
8 slices oat nut bread
1 large ripe pear, cored and cut into ½-inch-thick slices
2 tablespoons butter, melted

1. Make the sandwiches: Spread each of 4 slices of bread with ¼ of the Brie. Top the Brie with the pear slices and remaining 4 bread slices.
2. Brush the melted butter lightly on both sides of each sandwich.
3. Arrange the sandwiches in the air fry basket.
4. Select Bake, Super Convection, set temperature to 360ºF (182ºC), and set time to 6 minutes. Select Start/Stop to begin preheating.
5. Once preheated, place the basket on the bake position.
6. When cooking is complete, the cheese should be melted. Remove the basket from the oven and serve warm.

Mozzarella Chicken Sausage Pizza

Prep time: 10 minutes | Cook time: 8 minutes | Serves 1

1 piece naan bread
¼ cup barbecue sauce
¼ cup shredded Monterrey Jack cheese
¼ cup shredded Mozzarella cheese
½ chicken herby sausage, sliced
2 tablespoons red onion, thinly sliced
Chopped cilantro or parsley, for garnish
Cooking spray

1. Spritz the bottom of naan bread with cooking spray, then transfer to the air fry basket.
2. Brush with the Barbecue sauce. Top with the cheeses, sausage, and finish with the red onion.
3. Select Air Fry, Super Convection, set temperature to 400ºF (205ºC), and set time to 8 minutes. Select Start/Stop to begin preheating.
4. Once preheated, place the basket on the air fry position.
5. When cooking is complete, the cheese should be melted. Remove the basket from the oven. Garnish with the chopped cilantro or parsley before slicing to serve.

Panko- Crusted Artichoke Bites

Prep time: 5 minutes | Cook time: 8 minutes | Serves 4

14 whole artichoke hearts packed in water
½ cup all-purpose flour
1 egg
⅓ cup panko bread crumbs
1 teaspoon Italian seasoning
Cooking spray

1. Drain the artichoke hearts and dry thoroughly with paper towels.
2. Place the flour on a plate. Beat the egg in a shallow bowl until frothy. Thoroughly combine the bread crumbs and Italian seasoning in a separate shallow bowl.
3. Dredge the artichoke hearts in the flour, then in the beaten egg, and finally roll in the bread crumb mixture until evenly coated.
4. Place the artichoke hearts in the air fry basket and mist them with cooking spray.
5. Select Air Fry, Super Convection, set temperature to 375ºF (190ºC), and set time to 8 minutes. Select Start/Stop to begin preheating.
6. Once preheated, place the basket on the air fry position. Flip the artichoke hearts halfway through the cooking time.
7. When cooking is complete, the artichoke hearts should start to brown and the edges should be crispy. Remove the basket from the oven. Let the artichoke hearts sit for 5 minutes before serving.

Ham and Cheese Stuffed Mushroom

Prep time: 10 minutes | Cook time: 12 minutes | Serves 8

4 ounces (113 g) Mozzarella cheese, cut into pieces
½ cup diced ham
2 green onions, chopped
2 tablespoons bread crumbs
½ teaspoon garlic powder
¼ teaspoon ground oregano
¼ teaspoon ground black pepper
1 to 2 teaspoons olive oil
16 fresh Baby Bella mushrooms, stemmed removed

1. Process the cheese, ham, green onions, bread crumbs, garlic powder, oregano, and pepper in a food processor until finely chopped.
2. With the food processor running, slowly drizzle in 1 to 2 teaspoons olive oil until a thick paste has formed. Transfer the mixture to a bowl.
3. Evenly divide the mixture into the mushroom caps and lightly press down the mixture.
4. Lay the mushrooms in the air fry basket in a single layer.
5. Select Roast, Super Convection, set temperature to 390ºF (199ºC), and set time to 12 minutes. Select Start/Stop to begin preheating.
6. Once preheated, place the basket on the roast position.
7. When cooking is complete, the mushrooms should be lightly browned and tender. Remove from the oven to a plate. Let the mushrooms cool for 5 minutes and serve warm.

Cuban Pork and Turkey Sandwiches

Prep time: 10 minutes | Cook time: 8 minutes | Makes 4 sandwiches

8 slices ciabatta bread, about ¼-inch thick
Toppings:
6 to 8 ounces (170 to 227 g) thinly sliced leftover roast pork
4 ounces (113 g) thinly sliced deli turkey
Cooking spray
1 tablespoon brown mustard
1/3 cup bread and butter pickle slices
2 to 3 ounces (57 to 85 g) Pepper Jack cheese slices

1. On a clean work surface, spray one side of each slice of bread with cooking spray. Spread the other side of each slice of bread evenly with brown mustard.
2. Top 4 of the bread slices with the roast pork, turkey, pickle slices, cheese, and finish with remaining bread slices. Transfer to the air fry basket.
3. Select Air Fry, Super Convection, set temperature to 390°F (199°C), and set time to 8 minutes. Select Start/Stop to begin preheating.
4. Once preheated, place the basket on the air fry position.
5. When cooking is complete, remove the basket from the oven. Cool for 5 minutes and serve warm.

Hot Chickpeas

Prep time: 5 minutes | Cook time: 18 minutes | Serves 4

½ teaspoon chili powder
½ teaspoon ground cumin
¼ teaspoon cayenne pepper
¼ teaspoon salt
1 (19-ounce / 539-g) can chickpeas, drained and rinsed
Cooking spray

1. Lina the air fry basket with parchment paper and lightly spritz with cooking spray.
2. Mix the chili powder, cumin, cayenne pepper, and salt in a small bowl.
3. Place the chickpeas in a medium bowl and lightly mist with cooking spray.
4. Add the spice mixture to the chickpeas and toss until evenly coated. Transfer the chickpeas to the parchment.
5. Select Air Fry, Super Convection, set temperature to 390°F (199°C), and set time to 18 minutes. Select Start/Stop to begin preheating.
6. Once preheated, place the basket on the air fry position. Stir the chickpeas twice during cooking.
7. When cooking is complete, the chickpeas should be crunchy. Remove the basket from the oven. Let the chickpeas cool for 5 minutes before serving.

Muffuletta with Mozzarella Olives Topping

Prep time: 15 minutes | Cook time: 6 minutes | Makes 8 sliders

¼ pound (113 g) thinly sliced deli ham
¼ pound (113 g) thinly sliced pastrami
4 ounces (113 g) low-fat Mozzarella cheese, grated
8 slider buns, split in half
Cooking spray
1 tablespoon sesame seeds
Olive Mix:
½ cup sliced green olives with pimentos
¼ cup sliced black olives
¼ cup chopped kalamata olives
1 teaspoon red wine vinegar
¼ teaspoon basil
⅛ teaspoon garlic powder

1. Combine all the ingredients for the olive mix in a small bowl and stir well.
2. Stir together the ham, pastrami, and cheese in a medium bowl and divide the mixture into 8 equal portions.
3. Assemble the sliders: Top each bottom bun with 1 portion of meat and cheese, 2 tablespoons of olive mix, finished by the remaining buns. Lightly spritz the tops with cooking spray. Scatter the sesame seeds on top.
4. Arrange the sliders in the air fry basket.
5. Select Bake, Super Convection, set temperature to 360°F (182°C), and set time to 6 minutes. Select Start/Stop to begin preheating.
6. Once preheated, place the basket on the bake position.
7. When cooking is complete, the cheese should be melted. Remove the basket from the oven and serve.

Bruschetta with Parmesan Tomato

Prep time: 5 minutes | Cook time: 3 minutes | Serves 6

4 tomatoes, diced
1/3 cup shredded fresh basil
¼ cup shredded Parmesan cheese
1 tablespoon balsamic vinegar
1 tablespoon minced garlic
1 teaspoon olive oil
1 teaspoon salt
1 teaspoon freshly ground black pepper
1 loaf French bread, cut into 1-inch-thick slices
Cooking spray

1. Mix together the tomatoes and basil in a medium bowl. Add the cheese, vinegar, garlic, olive oil, salt, and pepper and stir until well incorporated. Set aside.
2. Spritz the air fry basket with cooking spray and lay the bread slices in the pan in a single layer. Spray the slices with cooking spray.
3. Select Bake, Super Convection, set temperature to 250ºF (121ºC), and set time to 3 minutes. Select Start/Stop to begin preheating.
4. Once preheated, place the basket on the bake position.
5. When cooking is complete, remove from the oven to a plate. Top each slice with a generous spoonful of the tomato mixture and serve.

Turkey Bacon-Wrapped Almond Stuffed Dates

Prep time: 10 minutes | Cook time: 6 minutes | Makes 16 appetizers

16 whole dates, pitted
16 whole almonds
6 to 8 strips turkey bacon, cut in half

Special Equipment:
16 toothpicks, soaked in water for at least 30 minutes

1. On a flat work surface, stuff each pitted date with a whole almond.
2. Wrap half slice of bacon around each date and secure it with a toothpick.
3. Place the bacon-wrapped dates in the air fry basket.
4. Select Air Fry, Super Convection, set temperature to 390ºF (199ºC), and set time to 6 minutes. Select Start/Stop to begin preheating.
5. Once preheated, place the basket on the air fry position.
6. When cooking is complete, transfer the dates to a paper towel-lined plate to drain. Serve hot.

Tuna Melts Sandwiches

Prep time: 10 minutes | Cook time: 6 minutes | Serves 6

2 (5- to 6-ounce / 142- to 170-g) cans oil-packed tuna, drained
1 large scallion, chopped
1 small stalk celery, chopped
1/3 cup mayonnaise
1 tablespoon chopped fresh dill
1 tablespoon capers, drained
¼ teaspoon celery salt
12 slices cocktail rye bread
2 tablespoons butter, melted
6 slices sharp Cheddar cheese

1. In a medium bowl, stir together the tuna, scallion, celery, mayonnaise, dill, capers and celery salt.
2. Brush one side of the bread slices with the butter. Arrange the bread slices on the sheet pan, buttered-side down. Scoop a heaping tablespoon of the tuna mixture on each slice of bread, spreading it out evenly to the edges.
3. Cut the cheese slices to fit the dimensions of the bread and place a cheese slice on each piece.
4. Select Roast, Super Convection, set temperature to 375ºF (190ºC) and set time to 6 minutes. Select Start/Stop to begin preheating.
5. Once the unit has preheated, place the pan on the roast position.
6. After 4 minutes, remove the pan from the oven and check the tuna melts. The tuna melts are done when the cheese has melted and the tuna is heated through. If needed, continue cooking.
7. When cooking is complete, remove the pan from the oven. Use a spatula to transfer the tuna melts to a clean work surface and slice each one in half diagonally. Serve warm.

Edamame

Prep time: 5 minutes | Cook time: 9 minutes | Serves 4

1 (16-ounce / 454-g) bag frozen edamame in pods
2 tablespoon olive oil, divided
½ teaspoon garlic salt
½ teaspoon salt
¼ teaspoon freshly ground black pepper
½ teaspoon red pepper flakes (optional)

1. Place the edamame in a medium bowl and drizzle with 1 tablespoon of olive oil. Toss to coat well.
2. Stir together the garlic salt, salt, pepper, and red pepper flakes (if desired) in a small bowl. Pour the mixture into the bowl of edamame and toss until the edamame is fully coated.
3. Grease the air fry basket with the remaining 1 tablespoon of olive oil.
4. Place the edamame in the greased basket.
5. Select Air Fry, Super Convection, set temperature to 375ºF (190ºC), and set time to 9 minutes. Select Start/Stop to begin preheating.
6. Once preheated, place the basket on the air fry position. Stir the edamame once halfway through the cooking time.
7. When cooking is complete, the edamame should be crisp. Remove from the oven to a plate and serve warm.

Caramelized Cinnamon Peaches

Prep time: 5 minutes | Cook time: 10 to 13 minutes | Serves 4

2 tablespoons sugar
¼ teaspoon ground cinnamon
4 peaches, cut into wedges
Cooking spray

1. Toss the peaches with the sugar and cinnamon in a medium bowl until evenly coated.
2. Lightly spray the air fry basket with cooking spray. Place the peaches in the air fry basket in a single layer. Lightly mist the peaches with cooking spray.
3. Select Air Fry, Super Convection, set temperature to 350ºF (180ºC), and set time to 10 minutes. Select Start/Stop to begin preheating.
4. Once preheated, place the basket on the air fry position.
5. After 5 minutes, remove from the oven and flip the peaches. Return to the oven and continue cooking for 5 minutes.
6. When cooking is complete, the peaches should be caramelized. If necessary, continue cooking for 3 minutes. Remove the basket from the oven. Let the peaches cool for 5 minutes and serve warm.

Italian Cheesy Rice Balls

Prep time: 10 minutes | Cook time: 10 minutes | Makes 8 rice balls

1½ cups cooked sticky rice
½ teaspoon Italian seasoning blend
¾ teaspoon salt, divided
8 black olives, pitted
1 ounce (28 g) Mozzarella cheese, cut into tiny pieces (small enough to stuff into olives)
2 eggs
⅓ cup Italian bread crumbs
¾ cup panko bread crumbs
Cooking spray

1. Stuff each black olive with a piece of Mozzarella cheese.
2. In a bowl, combine the cooked sticky rice, Italian seasoning blend, and ½ teaspoon of salt and stir to mix well. Form the rice mixture into a log with your hands and divide it into 8 equal portions. Mold each portion around a black olive and roll into a ball.
3. Transfer to the freezer to chill for 10 to 15 minutes until firm.
4. In a shallow dish, place the Italian bread crumbs. In a separate shallow dish, whisk the eggs. In a third shallow dish, combine the panko bread crumbs and remaining salt.
5. One by one, roll the rice balls in the Italian bread crumbs, then dip in the whisked eggs, finally coat them with the panko bread crumbs.
6. Arrange the rice balls in the air fry basket and spritz both sides with cooking spray.
7. Select Air Fry, Super Convection, set temperature to 390ºF (199ºC), and set time to 10 minutes. Select Start/Stop to begin preheating.
8. Once preheated, place the basket on the air fry position. Flip the balls halfway through the cooking time.
9. When cooking is complete, the rice balls should be golden brown. Remove from the oven and serve warm.

Ricotta Capers with Lemon Zest

Prep time: 10 minutes | Cook time: 8 minutes | Serves 4 to 6

1½ cups whole milk ricotta cheese
2 tablespoons extra-virgin olive oil
2 tablespoons capers, rinsed
Zest of 1 lemon, plus more for garnish
1 teaspoon finely chopped fresh rosemary
Pinch crushed red pepper flakes
Salt and freshly ground black pepper, to taste
1 tablespoon grated Parmesan cheese

1. In a mixing bowl, stir together the ricotta cheese, olive oil, capers, lemon zest, rosemary, red pepper flakes, salt, and pepper until well combined.
2. Spread the mixture evenly in a baking dish.
3. Select Air Fry, Super Convection, set temperature to 380ºF (193ºC), and set time to 8 minutes. Select Start/Stop to begin preheating.
4. Once preheated, place the baking dish in the oven.
5. When cooking is complete, the top should be nicely browned. Remove from the oven and top with a sprinkle of grated Parmesan cheese. Garnish with the lemon zest and serve warm.

Shrimp Toasts with Thai Chili Sauce

Prep time: 15 minutes | Cook time: 8 minutes | Serves 4 to 6

½ pound (227 g) raw shrimp, peeled and deveined
1 egg, beaten
2 scallions, chopped, plus more for garnish
2 tablespoons chopped fresh cilantro
2 teaspoons grated fresh ginger
1 to 2 teaspoons sriracha sauce
1 teaspoon soy sauce
½ teaspoon toasted sesame oil
6 slices thinly sliced white sandwich bread
½ cup sesame seeds
Cooking spray
Thai chili sauce, for serving

1. In a food processor, add the shrimp, egg, scallions, cilantro, ginger, sriracha sauce, soy sauce and sesame oil, and pulse until chopped finely. You'll need to stop the food processor occasionally to scrape down the sides. Transfer the shrimp mixture to a bowl.
2. On a clean work surface, cut the crusts off the sandwich bread. Using a brush, generously brush one side of each slice of bread with shrimp mixture.
3. Place the sesame seeds on a plate. Press bread slices, shrimp-side down, into sesame seeds to coat evenly. Cut each slice diagonally into quarters.
4. Spritz the air fry basket with cooking spray. Spread the coated slices in a single layer in the air fry basket.
5. Select Air Fry, Super Convection, set temperature to 400ºF (205ºC), and set time to 8 minutes. Select Start/Stop to begin preheating.
6. Once preheated, place the basket on the air fry position. Flip the bread slices halfway through.
7. When cooking is complete, they should be golden and crispy. Remove from the oven to a plate and let cool for 5 minutes. Top with the chopped scallions and serve warm with Thai chili sauce.

Cinnamon Apple Chips

Prep time: 5 minutes | Cook time: 10 minutes | Serves 4

2 apples, cored and cut into thin slices
2 heaped teaspoons ground cinnamon
Cooking spray

1. Spritz the air fry basket with cooking spray.
2. In a medium bowl, sprinkle the apple slices with the cinnamon. Toss until evenly coated. Spread the coated apple slices on the pan in a single layer.
3. Select Air Fry, Super Convection, set temperature to 350ºF (180ºC) and set time to 10 minutes. Select Start/Stop to begin preheating.
4. Once preheated, place the basket on the air fry position.
5. After 5 minutes, remove the basket from the oven. Stir the apple slices and return the basket to the oven to continue cooking.
6. When cooking is complete, the slices should be until crispy Remove the basket from the oven and let rest for 5 minutes before serving.

Cinnamon Apple Wedges with Yogurt

Prep time: 5 minutes | Cook time: 12 minutes | Serves 4

2 medium apples, cored and sliced into ¼-inch wedges
1 teaspoon canola oil
2 teaspoons peeled and grated fresh ginger
½ teaspoon ground cinnamon
½ cup low-fat Greek vanilla yogurt, for serving

1. In a large bowl, toss the apple wedges with the canola oil, ginger, and cinnamon until evenly coated. Put the apple wedges in the air fry basket.
2. Select Air Fry, Super Convection, set temperature to 360ºF (182ºC), and set time to 12 minutes. Select Start/Stop to begin preheating.
3. Once preheated, place the basket on the air fry position.
4. When cooking is complete, the apple wedges should be crisp-tender. Remove the apple wedges from the oven and serve drizzled with the yogurt.

Spicy Corn Tortilla Chips

Prep time: 5 minutes | Cook time: 5 minutes | Serves 4

½ teaspoon ground cumin
½ teaspoon paprika
½ teaspoon chili powder
½ teaspoon salt
Pinch cayenne pepper
8 (6-inch) corn tortillas, each cut into 6 wedges
Cooking spray

1. Lightly spritz the air fry basket with cooking spray.
2. Stir together the cumin, paprika, chili powder, salt, and pepper in a small bowl.
3. Place the tortilla wedges in the air fry basket in a single layer. Lightly mist them with cooking spray. Sprinkle the seasoning mixture on top of the tortilla wedges.
4. Select Air Fry, Super Convection, set temperature to 375ºF (190ºC), and set time to 5 minutes. Select Start/Stop to begin preheating.
5. Once preheated, place the basket on the air fry position. Stir the tortilla wedges halfway through the cooking time.
6. When cooking is complete, the chips should be lightly browned and crunchy. Remove the basket from the oven. Let the tortilla chips cool for 5 minutes and serve.

Spinach and Mushroom Cheese Calzones

Prep time: 15 minutes | Cook time: 26 to 27 minutes | Serves 4

2 tablespoons olive oil
1 onion, chopped
2 garlic cloves, minced
¼ cup chopped mushrooms
1 pound (454 g) spinach, chopped
1 tablespoon Italian seasoning
½ teaspoon oregano
Salt and black pepper, to taste
1½ cups marinara sauce
1 cup ricotta cheese, crumbled
1 (13-ounce / 369-g) pizza crust
Cooking spray

Make the Filling:
1. Heat the olive oil in a pan over medium heat until shimmering.
2. Add the onion, garlic, and mushrooms and sauté for 4 minutes, or until softened.
3. Stir in the spinach and sauté for 2 to 3 minutes, or until the spinach is wilted. Sprinkle with the Italian seasoning, oregano, salt, and pepper and mix well.
4. Add the marinara sauce and cook for about 5 minutes, stirring occasionally, or until the sauce is thickened.
5. Remove the pan from the heat and stir in the ricotta cheese. Set aside.

Make the Calzones:
1. Spritz the air fry basket with cooking spray. Set aside.
2. Roll the pizza crust out with a rolling pin on a lightly floured work surface, then cut it into 4 rectangles.
3. Spoon ¼ of the filling into each rectangle and fold in half. Crimp the edges with a fork to seal. Mist them with cooking spray. Transfer the calzones to the air fry basket.
4. Select Air Fry, Super Convection, set temperature to 375ºF (190ºC), and set time to 15 minutes. Select Start/Stop to begin preheating.
5. Once preheated, place the basket on the air fry position. Flip the calzones halfway through the cooking time.
6. When cooking is complete, the calzones should be golden brown and crisp. Transfer the calzones to a paper towel-lined plate and serve.

Air-Fried Old Bay Chicken Wings

Prep time: 5 minutes | Cook time: 13 minutes | Serves 4

2 tablespoons Old Bay seasoning
2 teaspoons baking powder
2 teaspoons salt
2 pounds (907 g) chicken wings, patted dry
Cooking spray

1. Combine the Old Bay seasoning, baking powder, and salt in a large zip-top plastic bag. Add the chicken wings, seal, and shake until the wings are thoroughly coated in the seasoning mixture.
2. Lightly spray the air fry basket with cooking spray. Lay the chicken wings in the air fry basket in a single layer and lightly mist them with cooking spray.
3. Select Air Fry, Super Convection, set temperature to 400ºF (205ºC), and set time to 13 minutes. Select Start/Stop to begin preheating.
4. Once preheated, place the basket on the air fry position. Flip the wings halfway through the cooking time.
5. When cooking is complete, the wings should reach an internal temperature of 165ºF (74ºC) on a meat thermometer. Remove from the oven to a plate and serve hot.

Lime Avocado Chips

Prep time: 15 minutes | Cook time: 10 minutes | Serves 4

1 egg
1 tablespoon lime juice
⅛ teaspoon hot sauce
2 tablespoons flour
¾ cup panko bread crumbs
¼ cup cornmeal
¼ teaspoon salt
1 large avocado, pitted, peeled, and cut into ½-inch slices
Cooking spray

1. Whisk together the egg, lime juice, and hot sauce in a small bowl.
2. On a sheet of wax paper, place the flour. In a separate sheet of wax paper, combine the bread crumbs, cornmeal, and salt.
3. Dredge the avocado slices one at a time in the flour, then in the egg mixture, finally roll them in the bread crumb mixture to coat well.
4. Place the breaded avocado slices in the air fry basket and mist them with cooking spray.
5. Select Air Fry, Super Convection, set temperature to 390ºF (199ºC), and set time to 10 minutes. Select Start/Stop to begin preheating.
6. Once preheated, place the basket on the air fry position.
7. When cooking is complete, the slices should be nicely browned and crispy. Transfer the avocado slices to a plate and serve.

Corn and Black Bean Chunky Salsa

Prep time: 10 minutes | Cook time: 10 minutes | Serves 4

½ (15-ounce / 425-g) can corn, drained and rinsed
½ (15-ounce / 425-g) can black beans, drained and rinsed
¼ cup chunky salsa
2 ounces (57 g) reduced-fat cream cheese, softened
¼ cup shredded reduced-fat Cheddar cheese
½ teaspoon paprika
½ teaspoon ground cumin
Salt and freshly ground black pepper, to taste

1. Combine the corn, black beans, salsa, cream cheese, Cheddar cheese, paprika, and cumin in a medium bowl. Sprinkle with salt and pepper and stir until well blended.
2. Pour the mixture into a baking dish.
3. Select Air Fry, Super Convection, set temperature to 325ºF (163ºC), and set time to 10 minutes. Select Start/Stop to begin preheating.
4. Once preheated, place the baking dish in the oven.
5. When cooking is complete, the mixture should be heated through. Rest for 5 minutes and serve warm.

Chapter 8 Desserts

Peach and Blueberry Galette

Prep time: 10 minutes | Cook time: 20 minutes | Serves 6

1 pint blueberries, rinsed and picked through (about 2 cups)
2 large peaches or nectarines, peeled and cut into ½-inch slices (about 2 cups)
⅓ cup plus 2 tablespoons granulated sugar, divided
2 tablespoons unbleached all-purpose flour
½ teaspoon grated lemon zest (optional)
¼ teaspoon ground allspice or cinnamon
Pinch kosher or fine salt
1 (9-inch) refrigerated piecrust (or use homemade)
2 teaspoons unsalted butter, cut into pea-size pieces
1 large egg, beaten

1. Mix together the blueberries, peaches, ⅓ cup of sugar, flour, lemon zest (if desired), allspice, and salt in a medium bowl.
2. Unroll the crust on the sheet pan, patching any tears if needed. Place the fruit in the center of the crust, leaving about 1½ inches of space around the edges. Scatter the butter pieces over the fruit. Fold the outside edge of the crust over the outer circle of the fruit, making pleats as needed.
3. Brush the egg over the crust. Sprinkle the crust and fruit with the remaining 2 tablespoons of sugar.
4. Select Bake, Super Convection, set temperature to 350ºF (180ºC), and set time to 20 minutes. Select Start/Stop to begin preheating.
5. Once the unit has preheated, place the pan on the bake position.
6. After about 15 minutes, check the galette, rotating the pan if the crust is not browning evenly. Continue cooking until the crust is deep golden brown and the fruit is bubbling.
7. When cooking is complete, remove the pan from the oven and allow to cool for 10 minutes before slicing and serving.

Apple-Cinnamon Fritters

Prep time: 10 minutes | Cook time: 7 minutes | Serves 6

1 cup chopped, peeled Granny Smith apple
½ cup granulated sugar
1 teaspoon ground cinnamon
1 cup all-purpose flour
1 teaspoon baking powder
1 teaspoon salt
2 tablespoons milk
2 tablespoons butter, melted
1 large egg, beaten
Cooking spray
¼ cup confectioners' sugar (optional)

1. Mix together the apple, granulated sugar, and cinnamon in a small bowl. Allow to sit for 30 minutes.
2. Combine the flour, baking powder, and salt in a medium bowl. Add the milk, butter, and egg and stir to incorporate.
3. Pour the apple mixture into the bowl of flour mixture and stir with a spatula until a dough forms.
4. On a clean work surface, divide the dough into 12 equal portions and shape into 1-inch balls. Flatten them into patties with your hands.
5. Line the air fry basket with parchment paper and spray it with cooking spray.
6. Transfer the apple fritters onto the parchment paper, evenly spaced but not too close together. Spray the fritters with cooking spray.
7. Select Bake, Super Convection, set temperature to 350ºF (180ºC), and set time to 7 minutes. Select Start/Stop to begin preheating.
8. Once the oven has preheated, place the basket on the bake position. Flip the fritters halfway through the cooking time.
9. When cooking is complete, the fritters should be lightly browned.
10. Remove from the oven to a plate and serve with the confectioners' sugar sprinkled on top, if desired.

Mixed Berry Crisp with Coconut Chips

Prep time: 10 minutes | Cook time: 20 minutes | Serves 6

1 tablespoon butter, melted	½ teaspoon ground cinnamon
12 ounces (340 g) mixed berries	¼ teaspoon ground cloves
1/3 cup granulated Swerve	¼ teaspoon grated nutmeg
1 teaspoon pure vanilla extract	½ cup coconut chips, for garnish

1. Coat a baking pan with melted butter.
2. Put the remaining ingredients except the coconut chips in the prepared baking pan.
3. Select Bake, Super Convection, set temperature to 330ºF (166ºC), and set time to 20 minutes. Select Start/Stop to begin preheating.
4. Once the oven has preheated, place the pan on the bake position.
5. When cooking is complete, remove from the oven. Serve garnished with the coconut chips.

S'mores

Prep time: 5 minutes | Cook time: 3 minutes | Makes 12 s'mores

12 whole cinnamon graham crackers, halved	g) chocolate bars, cut into 12 pieces
2 (1.55-ounce / 44-	12 marshmallows

1. Arrange 12 graham cracker squares in the air fry basket in a single layer.
2. Top each square with a piece of chocolate.
3. Select Bake, Super Convection, set temperature to 350ºF (180ºC), and set time to 3 minutes. Select Start/Stop to begin preheating.
4. Once the oven has preheated, place the basket on the bake position.
5. After 2 minutes, remove the basket and place a marshmallow on each piece of melted chocolate. Return the basket to the oven and continue to cook for another 1 minute.
6. Remove from the oven to a serving plate.
7. Serve topped with the remaining graham cracker squares

Desiccated Coconut-Pineapple Sticks

Prep time: 5 minutes | Cook time: 10 minutes | Serves 4

½ fresh pineapple, cut into sticks	¼ cup desiccated coconut

1. Place the desiccated coconut on a plate and roll the pineapple sticks in the coconut until well coated.
2. Lay the pineapple sticks in the air fry basket.
3. Select Air Fry, Super Convection, set temperature to 400ºF (205ºC), and set time to 10 minutes. Select Start/Stop to begin preheating.
4. Once the oven has preheated, place the basket on the air fry position.
5. When cooking is complete, the pineapple sticks should be crisp-tender.
6. Serve warm.

Chocolate Bread Pudding

Prep time: 10 minutes | Cook time: 10 minutes | Serves 8

1 egg	2 tablespoons cocoa powder
1 egg yolk	1 teaspoon vanilla
¾ cup chocolate milk	5 slices firm white bread, cubed
3 tablespoons brown sugar	Nonstick cooking spray
3 tablespoons peanut butter	

1. Spritz a baking pan with nonstick cooking spray.
2. Whisk together the egg, egg yolk, chocolate milk, brown sugar, peanut butter, cocoa powder, and vanilla until well combined.
3. Fold in the bread cubes and stir to mix well. Allow the bread soak for 10 minutes.
4. When ready, transfer the egg mixture to the prepared baking pan.
5. Select Bake, Super Convection, set temperature to 330ºF (166ºC), and set time to 10 minutes. Select Start/Stop to begin preheating.
6. Once the oven has preheated, place the pan on the bake position.
7. When done, the pudding should be just firm to the touch.
8. Serve at room temperature.

Pistachio and Walnut Baklava

Prep time: 10 minutes | Cook time: 16 minutes | Serves 10

1 cup walnut pieces
1 cup shelled raw pistachios
½ cup unsalted butter, melted
¼ cup plus 2 tablespoons honey, divided
3 tablespoons granulated sugar
1 teaspoon ground cinnamon
2 (1.9-ounce / 54-g) packages frozen miniature phyllo tart shells

1. Place the walnuts and pistachios in the air fry basket in an even layer.
2. Select Air Fry, Super Convection, set the temperature to 350ºF (180ºC), and set the time for 4 minutes. Select Start/Stop to begin preheating.
3. Once the unit has preheated, place the basket on the air fry position.
4. After 2 minutes, remove the basket and stir the nuts. Transfer the basket back to the oven and cook for another 1 to 2 minutes until the nuts are golden brown and fragrant.
5. Meanwhile, stir together the butter, ¼ cup of honey, sugar, and cinnamon in a medium bowl.
6. When done, remove the basket from the oven and place the nuts on a cutting board and allow to cool for 5 minutes. Finely chop the nuts. Add the chopped nuts and all the "nut dust" to the butter mixture and stir well.
7. Arrange the phyllo cups on the basket. Evenly fill the phyllo cups with the nut mixture, mounding it up. As you work, stir the nuts in the bowl frequently so that the syrup is evenly distributed throughout the filling.
8. Select Bake, Super Convection, set temperature to 350ºF (180ºC), and set time to 12 minutes. Select Start/Stop to begin preheating.
9. Once the unit has preheated, place the basket on the bake position. After about 8 minutes, check the cups. Continue cooking until the cups are golden brown and the syrup is bubbling.
10. When cooking is complete, remove the baklava from the oven, drizzle each cup with about ⅛ teaspoon of the remaining honey over the top.
11. Allow to cool for 5 minutes before serving.

Ricotta Cheesecake

Prep time: 5 minutes | Cook time: 25 minutes | Serves 6

17.5 ounces (496 g) ricotta cheese
5.4 ounces (153 g) sugar
3 eggs, beaten
3 tablespoons flour
1 lemon, juiced and zested
2 teaspoons vanilla extract

1. In a large mixing bowl, stir together all the ingredients until the mixture reaches a creamy consistency.
2. Pour the mixture into a baking pan and place in the oven.
3. Select Bake, Super Convection, set temperature to 320ºF (160ºC), and set time to 25 minutes. Select Start/Stop to begin preheating.
4. Once the oven has preheated, place the pan on the bake position.
5. When cooking is complete, a toothpick inserted in the center should come out clean.
6. Allow to cool for 10 minutes on a wire rack before serving.

Cinnamon Candy Covered Apple

Prep time: 15 minutes | Cook time: 12 minutes | Serves 4

1 cup packed light brown sugar
2 teaspoons ground cinnamon
2 medium Granny Smith apples, peeled and diced

1. Thoroughly combine the brown sugar and cinnamon in a medium bowl.
2. Add the apples to the bowl and stir until well coated. Transfer the apples to a baking pan.
3. Select Bake, Super Convection, set temperature to 350ºF (180ºC), and set time to 12 minutes. Select Start/Stop to begin preheating.
4. Once the oven has preheated, place the pan on the bake position.
5. After about 9 minutes, stir the apples and bake for an additional 3 minutes. When cooking is complete, the apples should be softened.
6. Serve warm.

Walnut-Coconut Tart

Prep time: 5 minutes | Cook time: 13 minutes | Serves 6

1 cup coconut milk
½ cup walnuts, ground
½ cup Swerve
½ cup almond flour
½ stick butter, at room temperature
2 eggs
1 teaspoon vanilla essence
¼ teaspoon ground cardamom
¼ teaspoon ground cloves
Cooking spray

1. Coat a baking pan with cooking spray.
2. Combine all the ingredients except the oil in a large bowl and stir until well blended. Spoon the batter mixture into the baking pan.
3. Select Bake, Super Convection, set temperature to 360ºF (182ºC), and set time to 13 minutes. Select Start/Stop to begin preheating.
4. Once the oven has preheated, place the pan on the bake position.
5. When cooking is complete, a toothpick inserted into the center of the tart should come out clean.
6. Remove from the oven and place on a wire rack to cool. Serve immediately.

Butter Shortbread

Prep time: 10 minutes | Cook time: 36 to 40 minutes | Makes 4 dozen cookies

1 tablespoon grated lemon zest
1 cup granulated sugar
1 pound (454 g) unsalted butter, at room temperature
¼ teaspoon fine salt
4 cups all-purpose flour
⅓ cup cornstarch
Cooking spray

1. Add the lemon zest and sugar to a stand mixer fitted with the paddle attachment and beat on medium speed for 1 to 2 minute. Let stand for about 5 minutes. Fold in the butter and salt and blend until fluffy.
2. Mix together the flour and cornstarch in a large bowl. Add to the butter mixture and mix to combine.
3. Spritz the sheet pan with cooking spray and spread a piece of parchment paper onto the pan. Scrape the dough into the pan until even and smooth.
4. Select Bake, Super Convection, set temperature to 325ºF (160ºC), and set time to 36 minutes. Select Start/Stop to begin preheating.
5. Once the unit has preheated, place the pan on the bake position.
6. After 20 minutes, check the shortbread, rotating the pan if it is not browning evenly. Continue cooking for another 16 minutes until lightly browned.
7. When done, remove the pan from the oven. Slice and allow to cool for 5 minutes before serving.

Coffee-Coconut Cake

Prep time: 10 minutes | Cook time: 30 minutes | Serves 8

Dry Ingredients:
1½ cups almond flour
½ cup coconut meal
⅔ cup Swerve
1 teaspoon baking powder
¼ teaspoon salt

Wet Ingredients:
1 egg
1 stick butter, melted
½ cup hot strongly brewed coffee

Topping:
½ cup confectioner's Swerve
¼ cup coconut flour
3 tablespoons coconut oil
1 teaspoon ground cinnamon
½ teaspoon ground cardamom

1. In a medium bowl, combine the almond flour, coconut meal, Swerve, baking powder, and salt.
2. In a large bowl, whisk the egg, melted butter, and coffee until smooth.
3. Add the dry mixture to the wet and stir until well incorporated. Transfer the batter to a greased baking pan.
4. Stir together all the ingredients for the topping in a small bowl. Spread the topping over the batter and smooth the top with a spatula.
5. Select Bake, Super Convection, set temperature to 330ºF (166ºC), and set time to 30 minutes. Select Start/Stop to begin preheating.
6. Once the oven has preheated, place the pan on the bake position.
7. When cooking is complete, the cake should spring back when gently pressed with your fingers.
8. Rest for 10 minutes before serving.

Chapter 3 Vegan and Vegetarian | 105

Vanilla Chocolate and Coconut Cake

Prep time: 5 minutes | Cook time: 15 minutes | Serves 6

½ cup unsweetened chocolate, chopped
½ stick butter, at room temperature
1 tablespoon liquid stevia
1½ cups coconut flour
2 eggs, whisked
½ teaspoon vanilla extract
A pinch of fine sea salt
Cooking spray

1. Place the chocolate, butter, and stevia in a microwave-safe bowl. Microwave for about 30 seconds until melted.
2. Let the chocolate mixture cool for 5 to 10 minutes.
3. Add the remaining ingredients to the bowl of chocolate mixture and whisk to incorporate.
4. Lightly spray a baking pan with cooking spray.
5. Scrape the chocolate mixture into the prepared baking pan.
6. Select Bake, Super Convection, set temperature to 330ºF (166ºC), and set time to 15 minutes. Select Start/Stop to begin preheating.
7. Once the oven has preheated, place the pan on the bake position.
8. When cooking is complete, the top should spring back lightly when gently pressed with your fingers.
9. Let the cake cool for 5 minutes and serve.

Strawberry and Rhubarb Crisp

Prep time: 10 minutes | Cook time: 12 to 17 minutes | Serves 6

1½ cups sliced fresh strawberries
⅓ cup sugar
¾ cup sliced rhubarb
⅔ cup quick-cooking oatmeal
¼ cup packed brown sugar
½ cup whole-wheat pastry flour
½ teaspoon ground cinnamon
3 tablespoons unsalted butter, melted

1. Place the strawberries, sugar, and rhubarb in a baking pan and toss to coat.
2. Combine the oatmeal, brown sugar, pastry flour, and cinnamon in a medium bowl.
3. Add the melted butter to the oatmeal mixture and stir until crumbly. Sprinkle this generously on top of the strawberries and rhubarb.
4. Select Bake, Super Convection, set temperature to 370ºF (188ºC), and set the time to 12 minutes. Select Start/Stop to begin preheating.
5. Once the unit has preheated, place the pan on the bake position.
6. Bake, Super Convection until the fruit is bubbly and the topping is golden brown. Continue cooking for an additional 2 to 5 minutes if needed.
7. When cooking is complete, remove from the oven and serve warm.

Tangy Coconut Cake

Prep time: 10 minutes | Cook time: 17 minutes | Serves 6

1 stick butter, melted
¾ cup granulated Swerve
2 eggs, beaten
¾ cup coconut flour
¼ teaspoon salt
⅓ teaspoon grated nutmeg
⅓ cup coconut milk
1¼ cups almond flour
½ teaspoon baking powder
2 tablespoons unsweetened orange jam
Cooking spray

1. Coat a baking pan with cooking spray. Set aside.
2. In a large mixing bowl, whisk together the melted butter and granulated Swerve until fluffy.
3. Mix in the beaten eggs and whisk again until smooth. Stir in the coconut flour, salt, and nutmeg and gradually pour in the coconut milk. Add the remaining ingredients and stir until well incorporated.
4. Scrape the batter into the baking pan.
5. Select Bake, Super Convection, set temperature to 355ºF (179ºC), and set time to 17 minutes. Select Start/Stop to begin preheating.
6. Once the oven has preheated, place the pan on the bake position.
7. When cooking is complete, the top of the cake should spring back when gently pressed with your fingers.
8. Remove from the oven to a wire rack to cool. Serve chilled.

Raspberry Muffins

Prep time: 10 minutes | Cook time: 15 minutes | Serves 6

2 cups almond flour
¾ cup Swerve
1¼ teaspoons baking powder
⅓ teaspoon ground allspice
⅓ teaspoon ground anise star
½ teaspoon grated lemon zest
¼ teaspoon salt
2 eggs
1 cup sour cream
½ cup coconut oil
½ cup raspberries

1. Line a muffin pan with 6 paper liners.
2. In a mixing bowl, mix the almond flour, Swerve, baking powder, allspice, anise, lemon zest, and salt.
3. In another mixing bowl, beat the eggs, sour cream, and coconut oil until well mixed. Add the egg mixture to the flour mixture and stir to combine. Mix in the raspberries.
4. Scrape the batter into the prepared muffin cups, filling each about three-quarters full.
5. Select Bake, Super Convection, set temperature to 345°F (174°C), and set time to 15 minutes. Select Start/Stop to begin preheating.
6. Once the oven has preheated, place the muffin pan on the bake position.
7. When cooking is complete, the tops should be golden and a toothpick inserted in the middle should come out clean.
8. Allow the muffins to cool for 10 minutes in the muffin pan before removing and serving.

Apple-Peach Crumble with Oatmeal

Prep time: 10 minutes | Cook time: 10 to 12 minutes | Serves 4

2 peaches, peeled, pitted, and chopped
1 apple, peeled and chopped
2 tablespoons honey
3 tablespoons packed brown sugar
2 tablespoons unsalted butter, at room temperature
½ cup quick-cooking oatmeal
⅓ cup whole-wheat pastry flour
½ teaspoon ground cinnamon

1. Place the peaches, apple, and honey in a baking pan and toss until thoroughly combined.
2. Mix together the brown sugar, butter, oatmeal, pastry flour, and cinnamon in a medium bowl and stir until crumbly. Sprinkle this mixture generously on top of the peaches and apples.
3. Select Bake, Super Convection, set temperature to 380°F (193°C), and set the time to 10 minutes. Select Start/Stop to begin preheating.
4. Once the unit has preheated, place the pan on the bake position.
5. Bake, Super Convection until the fruit is bubbling and the topping is golden brown.
6. Once cooking is complete, remove the pan from the oven and allow to cool for 5 minutes before serving.

Mixed Berries with Mixed Nuts Streusel

Prep time: 5 minutes | Cook time: 17 minutes | Serves 3

½ cup mixed berries
Topping:
1 egg, beaten
3 tablespoons almonds, slivered
3 tablespoons chopped pecans
2 tablespoons chopped walnuts
Cooking spray
3 tablespoons granulated Swerve
2 tablespoons cold salted butter, cut into pieces
½ teaspoon ground cinnamon

1. Lightly spray a baking dish with cooking spray.
2. Make the topping: In a medium bowl, stir together the beaten egg, nuts, Swerve, butter, and cinnamon until well blended.
3. Put the mixed berries in the bottom of the baking dish and spread the topping over the top.
4. Select Bake, Super Convection, set temperature to 340°F (171°C), and set time to 17 minutes. Select Start/Stop to begin preheating.
5. Once the oven has preheated, place the baking dish on the bake position.
6. When cooking is complete, the fruit should be bubbly and topping should be golden brown.
7. Allow to cool for 5 to 10 minutes before serving.

Bourbon Chocolate Pecan Pie

Prep time: 20 minutes | Cook time: 25 minutes | Serves 8

1 (9-inch) unbaked pie crust
Filling:
2 large eggs
⅓ cup butter, melted
1 cup sugar
½ cup all-purpose flour
1 cup milk chocolate chips
1½ cups coarsely chopped pecans
2 tablespoons bourbon

1. Whisk the eggs and melted butter in a large bowl until creamy.
2. Add the sugar and flour and stir to incorporate. Mix in the milk chocolate chips, pecans, and bourbon and stir until well combined.
3. Use a fork to prick holes in the bottom and sides of the pie crust. Pour the prepared filling into the pie crust. Place the pie crust in the air fry basket.
4. Select Bake, Super Convection, set temperature to 350ºF (180ºC), and set time to 25 minutes. Select Start/Stop to begin preheating.
5. Once the oven has preheated, place the basket on the bake position.
6. When cooking is complete, a toothpick inserted in the center should come out clean.
7. Allow the pie cool for 10 minutes in the basket before serving.

White Chocolate Cookies

Prep time: 10 minutes | Cook time: 11 minutes | Serves 10

8 ounces (227 g) unsweetened white chocolate
2 eggs, well beaten
¾ cup butter, at room temperature
1⅔ cups almond flour
½ cup coconut flour
¾ cup granulated Swerve
2 tablespoons coconut oil
⅓ teaspoon grated nutmeg
⅓ teaspoon ground allspice
⅓ teaspoon ground anise star
¼ teaspoon fine sea salt

1. Line a baking sheet with parchment paper.
2. Combine all the ingredients in a mixing bowl and knead for about 3 to 4 minutes, or until a soft dough forms. Transfer to the refrigerator to chill for 20 minutes.
3. Make the cookies: Roll the dough into 1-inch balls and transfer to the parchment-lined baking sheet, spacing 2 inches apart. Flatten each with the back of a spoon.
4. Select Bake, Super Convection, set temperature to 350ºF (180ºC), and set time to 11 minutes. Select Start/Stop to begin preheating.
5. Once the oven has preheated, place the baking sheet on the bake position.
6. When cooking is complete, the cookies should be golden and firm to the touch.
7. Transfer to a wire rack and let the cookies cool completely. Serve immediately.

Coconut Flake-Coated Pineapple Rings

Prep time: 10 minutes | Cook time: 7 minutes | Serves 6

1 cup rice milk
⅔ cup flour
½ cup water
¼ cup unsweetened flaked coconut
4 tablespoons sugar
½ teaspoon baking soda
½ teaspoon baking powder
½ teaspoon vanilla essence
½ teaspoon ground cinnamon
¼ teaspoon ground anise star
Pinch of kosher salt
1 medium pineapple, peeled and sliced

1. In a large bowl, stir together all the ingredients except the pineapple.
2. Dip each pineapple slice into the batter until evenly coated.
3. Arrange the pineapple slices in the air fry basket.
4. Select Air Fry, Super Convection, set temperature to 380ºF (193ºC), and set time to 7 minutes. Select Start/Stop to begin preheating.
5. Once the oven has preheated, place the basket on the air fry position.
6. When cooking is complete, the pineapple rings should be golden brown.
7. Remove from the oven to a plate and cool for 5 minutes before serving.

Apple-Peach Crisp

Prep time: 10 minutes | Cook time: 11 minutes | Serves 4

1 apple, peeled and chopped
2 peaches, peeled, pitted, and chopped
2 tablespoons honey
½ cup quick-cooking oatmeal
⅓ cup whole-wheat pastry flour
2 tablespoons unsalted butter, at room temperature
3 tablespoons packed brown sugar
½ teaspoon ground cinnamon

1. Mix together the apple, peaches, and honey in a baking pan until well incorporated.
2. In a bowl, combine the oatmeal, pastry flour, butter, brown sugar, and cinnamon and stir to mix well. Spread this mixture evenly over the fruit.
3. Select Bake, Super Convection, set temperature to 380ºF (193ºC), and set time to 11 minutes. Select Start/Stop to begin preheating.
4. Once the oven has preheated, place the pan on the bake position.
5. When cooking is complete, the fruit should be bubbling around the edges and the topping should be golden brown.
6. Remove from the oven and serve warm.

Pecan-Coconut Cookies

Prep time: 10 minutes | Cook time: 25 minutes | Serves 10

1½ cups coconut flour
1½ cups extra-fine almond flour
½ teaspoon baking powder
⅓ teaspoon baking soda
3 eggs plus an egg yolk, beaten
¾ cup coconut oil, at room temperature
1 cup unsalted pecan nuts, roughly chopped
¾ cup monk fruit
¼ teaspoon freshly grated nutmeg
⅓ teaspoon ground cloves
½ teaspoon pure vanilla extract
½ teaspoon pure coconut extract
⅛ teaspoon fine sea salt

1. Line the air fry basket with parchment paper.
2. Mix the coconut flour, almond flour, baking powder, and baking soda in a large mixing bowl.
3. In another mixing bowl, stir together the eggs and coconut oil. Add the wet mixture to the dry mixture.
4. Mix in the remaining ingredients and stir until a soft dough forms.
5. Drop about 2 tablespoons of dough on the parchment paper for each cookie and flatten each biscuit until it's 1 inch thick.
6. Select Bake, Super Convection, set temperature to 370ºF (188ºC), and set time to 25 minutes. Select Start/Stop to begin preheating.
7. Once the oven has preheated, place the basket on the bake position.
8. When cooking is complete, the cookies should be golden and firm to the touch.
9. Remove from the oven to a plate. Let the cookies cool to room temperature and serve.

Caramelized Fruity Kebabs

Prep time: 10 minutes | Cook time: 4 minutes | Serves 4

2 peaches, peeled, pitted, and thickly sliced
3 plums, halved and pitted
3 nectarines, halved and pitted
1 tablespoon honey
½ teaspoon ground cinnamon
¼ teaspoon ground allspice
Pinch cayenne pepper

Special Equipment:
8 metal skewers

1. Thread, alternating peaches, plums, and nectarines onto the metal skewers that fit into the oven.
2. Thoroughly combine the honey, cinnamon, allspice, and cayenne in a small bowl. Brush generously the glaze over the fruit skewers.
3. Transfer the fruit skewers to the air fry basket.
4. Select Air Fry, Super Convection, set temperature to 400ºF (205ºC), and set time to 4 minutes. Select Start/Stop to begin preheating.
5. Once the oven has preheated, place the basket on the air fry position.
6. When cooking is complete, the fruit should be caramelized.
7. Remove the fruit skewers from the oven and let rest for 5 minutes before serving.

Apple Wedges with Apricots and Cinnamon

Prep time: 5 minutes | Cook time: 15 to 18 minutes | Serves 4

4 large apples, peeled and sliced into 8 wedges
2 tablespoons olive oil
½ cup dried apricots, chopped
1 to 2 tablespoons sugar
½ teaspoon ground cinnamon

1. Toss the apple wedges with the olive oil in a mixing bowl until well coated.
2. Place the apple wedges in the air fry basket.
3. Select Air Fry, Super Convection, set temperature to 350ºF (180ºC), and set time to 15 minutes. Select Start/Stop to begin preheating.
4. Once the oven has preheated, place the basket on the air fry position.
5. After about 12 minutes, remove from the oven. Sprinkle with the dried apricots and air fry for another 3 minutes.
6. Meanwhile, thoroughly combine the sugar and cinnamon in a small bowl.
7. Remove the apple wedges from the oven to a plate. Serve sprinkled with the sugar mixture.

Pound Cake

Prep time: 10 minutes | Cook time: 30 minutes | Serves 8

1 stick butter, at room temperature
1 cup Swerve
4 eggs
1½ cups coconut flour
½ cup buttermilk
½ teaspoon baking soda
½ teaspoon baking powder
¼ teaspoon salt
1 teaspoon vanilla essence
A pinch of ground star anise
A pinch of freshly grated nutmeg
Cooking spray

1. Spray a baking pan with cooking spray.
2. With an electric mixer or hand mixer, beat the butter and Swerve until creamy. One at a time, mix in the eggs and whisk until fluffy. Add the remaining ingredients and stir to combine.
3. Transfer the batter to the prepared baking pan.
4. Select Bake, Super Convection, set temperature to 320ºF (160ºC), and set time to 30 minutes. Select Start/Stop to begin preheating.
5. Once the oven has preheated, place the pan on the bake position. Rotate the pan halfway through the cooking time.
6. When cooking is complete, the center of the cake should be springy.
7. Allow the cake to cool in the pan for 10 minutes before removing and serving.

Ultimate Chocolate Cheesecake

Prep time: 10 minutes | Cook time: 18 minutes | Serves 6

Crust:
½ cup butter, melted
½ cup coconut flour
2 tablespoons stevia
Cooking spray

Topping:
4 ounces (113 g) unsweetened baker's chocolate
1 cup mascarpone cheese, at room temperature
1 teaspoon vanilla extract
2 drops peppermint extract

1. Lightly coat a baking pan with cooking spray.
2. In a mixing bowl, whisk together the butter, flour, and stevia until well combined. Transfer the mixture to the prepared baking pan.
3. Select Bake, Super Convection, set temperature to 350ºF (180ºC), and set time to 18 minutes. Select Start/Stop to begin preheating.
4. Once the oven has preheated, place the pan on the bake position.
5. When done, a toothpick inserted in the center should come out clean.
6. Remove the crust from the oven to a wire rack to cool.
7. Once cooled completely, place it in the freezer for 20 minutes.
8. When ready, combine all the ingredients for the topping in a small bowl and stir to incorporate.
9. Spread this topping over the crust and let it sit for another 15 minutes in the freezer.
10. Serve chilled.

Pumpkin Pudding with Vanilla Wafers Topping

Prep time: 10 minutes | Cook time: 15 minutes | Serves 4

1 cup canned no-salt-added pumpkin purée (not pumpkin pie filling)
¼ cup packed brown sugar
3 tablespoons all-purpose flour
1 egg, whisked
2 tablespoons milk
1 tablespoon unsalted butter, melted
1 teaspoon pure vanilla extract
4 low-fat vanilla wafers, crumbled
Cooking spray

1. Coat a baking pan with cooking spray. Set aside.
2. Mix the pumpkin purée, brown sugar, flour, whisked egg, milk, melted butter, and vanilla in a medium bowl and whisk to combine. Transfer the mixture to the baking pan.
3. Select Bake, Super Convection, set temperature to 350°F (180°C), and set time to 15 minutes. Select Start/Stop to begin preheating.
4. Once the oven has preheated, place the pan on the bake position.
5. When cooking is complete, the pudding should be set.
6. Remove the pudding from the oven to a wire rack to cool.
7. Divide the pudding into four bowls and serve with the vanilla wafers sprinkled on top.

Blackberry Goden Cobbler

Prep time: 10 minutes | Cook time: 20 to 25 minutes | Serves 6

3 cups fresh or frozen blackberries
1¾ cups sugar, divided
1 teaspoon vanilla extract
8 tablespoons (1 stick) butter, melted
1 cup self-rising flour
Cooking spray

1. Spritz a baking pan with cooking spray.
2. Mix the blackberries, 1 cup of sugar, and vanilla in a medium bowl and stir to combine.
3. Stir together the melted butter, remaining sugar, and flour in a separate medium bowl.
4. Spread the blackberry mixture evenly in the prepared pan and top with the butter mixture.
5. Select Bake, Super Convection, set temperature to 350°F (180°C), and set time to 25 minutes. Select Start/Stop to begin preheating.
6. Once the oven has preheated, place the pan on the bake position.
7. After about 20 minutes, check if the cobbler has a golden crust and you can't see any batter bubbling while it cooks. If needed, bake for another 5 minutes.
8. Remove from the oven and place on a wire rack to cool to room temperature. Serve immediately.

Black and White Chocolate Cake

Prep time: 10 minutes | Cook time: 20 minutes | Makes 1 dozen brownies

1 egg
¼ cup brown sugar
2 tablespoons white sugar
2 tablespoons safflower oil
1 teaspoon vanilla
$1/3$ cup all-purpose flour
¼ cup cocoa powder
¼ cup white chocolate chips
Nonstick cooking spray

1. Spritz a baking pan with nonstick cooking spray.
2. Whisk together the egg, brown sugar, and white sugar in a medium bowl. Mix in the safflower oil and vanilla and stir to combine.
3. Add the flour and cocoa powder and stir just until incorporated. Fold in the white chocolate chips.
4. Scrape the batter into the prepared baking pan.
5. Select Bake, Super Convection, set temperature to 340°F (171°C), and set time to 20 minutes. Select Start/Stop to begin preheating.
6. Once the oven has preheated, place the pan on the bake position.
7. When done, the brownie should spring back when touched lightly with your fingers.
8. Transfer to a wire rack and let cool for 30 minutes before slicing to serve.

Caramelized Peach with Blueberry Yogurt

Prep time: 10 minutes | Cook time: 10 minutes | Serves 6

3 peaches, peeled, halved, and pitted
2 tablespoons packed brown sugar
1 cup plain Greek yogurt
¼ teaspoon ground cinnamon
1 teaspoon pure vanilla extract
1 cup fresh blueberries

1. Arrange the peaches in the air fry basket, cut-side up. Top with a generous sprinkle of brown sugar.
2. Select Bake, Super Convection, set temperature to 380ºF (193ºC), and set time to 10 minutes. Select Start/Stop to begin preheating.
3. Once the oven has preheated, place the basket on the bake position.
4. Meanwhile, whisk together the yogurt, cinnamon, and vanilla in a small bowl until smooth.
5. When cooking is complete, the peaches should be lightly browned and caramelized.
6. Remove the peaches from the oven to a plate. Serve topped with the yogurt mixture and fresh blueberries.

Maple Blackberry and Peach Cobbler

Prep time: 15 minutes | Cook time: 20 minutes | Serves 4

Filling:
1 (6-ounce / 170-g) package blackberries
1½ cups chopped peaches, cut into ½-inch thick slices
2 teaspoons arrowroot or cornstarch
2 tablespoons coconut sugar
1 teaspoon lemon juice

Topping:
2 tablespoons sunflower oil
1 tablespoon maple syrup
1 teaspoon vanilla
3 tablespoons coconut sugar
½ cup rolled oats
⅓ cup whole-wheat pastry flour
1 teaspoon cinnamon
¼ teaspoon nutmeg
⅛ teaspoon sea salt

Make the Filling:
1. Combine the blackberries, peaches, arrowroot, coconut sugar, and lemon juice in a baking pan.
2. Using a rubber spatula, stir until well incorporated. Set aside.

Make the Topping:
1. Combine the oil, maple syrup, and vanilla in a mixing bowl and stir well. Whisk in the remaining ingredients. Spread this mixture evenly over the filling.
2. Select Bake, Super Convection, set temperature to 320ºF (160ºC), and set time to 20 minutes. Select Start/Stop to begin preheating.
3. Once the oven has preheated, place the pan on the bake position.
4. When cooked, the topping should be crispy and golden brown. Serve warm

Triple Berry Crisp

Prep time: 10 minutes | Cook time: 12 minutes | Serves 4

½ cup fresh blueberries
½ cup chopped fresh strawberries
⅓ cup frozen raspberries, thawed
1 tablespoon honey
1 tablespoon freshly squeezed lemon juice
⅔ cup whole-wheat pastry flour
3 tablespoons packed brown sugar
2 tablespoons unsalted butter, melted

1. Place the blueberries, strawberries, and raspberries in a baking pan and drizzle the honey and lemon juice over the top.
2. Combine the pastry flour and brown sugar in a small mixing bowl.
3. Add the butter and whisk until the mixture is crumbly. Scatter the flour mixture on top of the fruit.
4. Select Bake, Super Convection, set temperature to 380ºF (193ºC), and set time to 12 minutes. Select Start/Stop to begin preheating.
5. Once the oven has preheated, place the pan on the bake position.
6. When cooking is complete, the fruit should be bubbly and the topping should be golden brown.
7. Remove from the oven and serve on a plate.

Fudgy Brownies

Prep time: 10 minutes | Cook time: 21 minutes | Serves 8

1 stick butter, melted
1 cup Swerve
2 eggs
1 cup coconut flour
½ cup unsweetened cocoa powder
2 tablespoons flaxseed meal
1 teaspoon baking powder
1 teaspoon vanilla essence
A pinch of salt
A pinch of ground cardamom
Cooking spray

1. Spray a baking pan with cooking spray.
2. Beat together the melted butter and Swerve in a large mixing dish until fluffy. Whisk in the eggs.
3. Add the coconut flour, cocoa powder, flaxseed meal, baking powder, vanilla essence, salt, and cardamom and stir with a spatula until well incorporated. Spread the mixture evenly into the prepared baking pan.
4. Select Bake, Super Convection, set temperature to 350°F (180°C), and set time to 21 minutes. Select Start/Stop to begin preheating.
5. Once the oven has preheated, place the pan on the bake position.
6. When cooking is complete, a toothpick inserted in the center should come out clean.
7. Remove from the oven and place on a wire rack to cool completely. Cut into squares and serve immediately.

Fried Banana with Chocolate Sauce

Prep time: 10 minutes | Cook time: 7 minutes | Serves 6

¼ cup cornstarch
¼ cup plain bread crumbs
1 large egg, beaten
3 bananas, halved crosswise
Cooking spray
Chocolate sauce, for serving

1. Place the cornstarch, bread crumbs, and egg in three separate bowls.
2. Roll the bananas in the cornstarch, then in the beaten egg, and finally in the bread crumbs to coat well.
3. Spritz the air fry basket with cooking spray.
4. Arrange the banana halves in the air fry basket and mist them with cooking spray.
5. Select Air Fry, Super Convection, set temperature to 350°F (180°C), and set time to 7 minutes. Select Start/Stop to begin preheating.
6. Once the oven has preheated, place the basket on the air fry position.
7. After about 5 minutes, flip the bananas and continue to air fry for another 2 minutes.
8. When cooking is complete, remove the bananas from the oven to a serving plate. Serve with the chocolate sauce drizzled over the top.

Blackberry Almond Muffins

Prep time: 10 minutes | Cook time: 12 minutes | Serves 8

½ cup fresh blackberries
Dry Ingredients:
1½ cups almond flour
1 teaspoon baking powder
½ teaspoon baking soda
½ cup Swerve
¼ teaspoon kosher salt

Wet Ingredients:
2 eggs
¼ cup coconut oil, melted
½ cup milk
½ teaspoon vanilla paste

1. Line an 8-cup muffin tin with paper liners.
2. Thoroughly combine the almond flour, baking powder, baking soda, Swerve, and salt in a mixing bowl.
3. Whisk together the eggs, coconut oil, milk, and vanilla in a separate mixing bowl until smooth.
4. Add the wet mixture to the dry and fold in the blackberries. Stir with a spatula just until well incorporated.
5. Spoon the batter into the prepared muffin cups, filling each about three-quarters full.
6. Select Bake, Super Convection, set temperature to 350°F (180°C), and set time to 12 minutes. Select Start/Stop to begin preheating.
7. Once the oven has preheated, place the muffin tin on the bake position.
8. When done, the tops should be golden and a toothpick inserted in the middle should come out clean.
9. Allow the muffins to cool in the muffin tin for 10 minutes before removing and serving

Southern Fudge Pie

Prep time: 10 minutes | Cook time: 26 minutes | Serves 8

1½ cups sugar
½ cup self-rising flour
⅓ cup unsweetened cocoa powder
3 large eggs, beaten
12 tablespoons (1½ sticks) butter, melted
1½ teaspoons vanilla extract
1 (9-inch) unbaked pie crust
¼ cup confectioners' sugar (optional)

1. Thoroughly combine the sugar, flour, and cocoa powder in a medium bowl. Add the beaten eggs and butter and whisk to combine. Stir in the vanilla.
2. Pour the prepared filling into the pie crust and transfer to the air fry basket.
3. Select Bake, Super Convection, set temperature to 350ºF (180ºC), and set time to 26 minutes. Select Start/Stop to begin preheating.
4. Once the oven has preheated, place the basket on the bake position.
5. When cooking is complete, the pie should be set.
6. Allow the pie to cool for 5 minutes. Sprinkle with the confectioners' sugar, if desired. Serve warm.

Blackberry Brownie

Prep time: 10 minutes | Cook time: 22 minutes | Serves 8

½ cup butter, at room temperature
2 ounces (57 g) Swerve
4 eggs
1 cup almond flour
1 teaspoon baking soda
⅓ teaspoon baking powder
½ cup cocoa powder
1 teaspoon orange zest
⅓ cup fresh blackberries

1. With an electric mixer or hand mixer, beat the butter and Swerve until creamy.
2. One at a time, mix in the eggs and beat again until fluffy.
3. Add the almond flour, baking soda, baking powder, cocoa powder, orange zest and mix well. Add the butter mixture to the almond flour mixture and stir until well blended. Fold in the blackberries.
4. Scrape the batter into a baking pan.
5. Select Bake, Super Convection, set temperature to 335ºF (168ºC), and set time to 22 minutes. Select Start/Stop to begin preheating.
6. Once the oven has preheated, place the pan on the bake position.
7. When cooking is complete, a toothpick inserted into the center of the cake should come out clean.
8. Allow the cake cool on a wire rack to room temperature. Serve immediately.

Blueberry Chocolate Cupcakes

Prep time: 15 minutes | Cook time: 15 minutes | Serves 6

¾ cup granulated erythritol
1¼ cups almond flour
1 teaspoon unsweetened baking powder
3 teaspoons cocoa powder
½ teaspoon baking soda
½ teaspoon ground cinnamon
¼ teaspoon grated nutmeg
⅛ teaspoon salt
½ cup milk
1 stick butter, at room temperature
3 eggs, whisked
1 teaspoon pure rum extract
½ cup blueberries
Cooking spray

1. Spray a 6-cup muffin tin with cooking spray.
2. In a mixing bowl, combine the erythritol, almond flour, baking powder, cocoa powder, baking soda, cinnamon, nutmeg, and salt and stir until well blended.
3. In another mixing bowl, mix together the milk, butter, egg, and rum extract until thoroughly combined. Slowly and carefully pour this mixture into the bowl of dry mixture. Stir in the blueberries.
4. Spoon the batter into the greased muffin cups, filling each about three-quarters full.
5. Select Bake, Super Convection, set temperature to 345ºF (174ºC), and set time to 15 minutes. Select Start/Stop to begin preheating.
6. Once the oven has preheated, place the muffin tin on the bake position.
7. When done, the center should be springy and a toothpick inserted in the middle should come out clean.
8. Remove from the oven and place on a wire rack to cool. Serve immediately.

Pear Tart with Caramel Sauce

Prep time: 10 minutes | Cook time: 25 minutes | Serves 8

Juice of 1 lemon
4 cups water
3 medium or 2 large ripe or almost ripe pears (preferably Bosc or Anjou), peeled, stemmed, and halved lengthwise
1 sheet (½ package) frozen puff pastry, thawed
All-purpose flour, for dusting
4 tablespoons caramel sauce such as Smucker's Salted Caramel, divided

1. Combine the lemon juice and water in a large bowl.
2. Remove the seeds from the pears with a melon baller and cut out the blossom end. Remove any tough fibers between the stem end and the center. As you work, place the pear halves in the acidulated water.
3. On a lightly floured cutting board, unwrap and unfold the puff pastry, roll it very lightly with a rolling pin so as to press the folds together. Place it on the sheet pan.
4. Roll about ½ inch of the pastry edges up to form a ridge around the perimeter. Crimp the corners together so as to create a solid rim around the pastry to hold in the liquid as the tart cooks.
5. Brush 2 tablespoons of caramel sauce over the bottom of the pastry.
6. Remove the pear halves from the water and blot off any remaining water with paper towels.
7. Place one of the halves on the board cut-side down and cut ¼-inch-thick slices radially. Repeat with the remaining halves. Arrange the pear slices over the pastry. Drizzle the remaining 2 tablespoons of caramel sauce over the top.
8. Select Bake, Super Convection, set temperature to 350ºF (180ºC), and set time to 25 minutes. Select Start/Stop to begin preheating.
9. Once the unit has preheated, place the basket on the bake position.
10. After 15 minutes, check the tart, rotating the pan if the crust is not browning evenly. Continue cooking for another 10 minutes, or until the pastry is golden brown, the pears are soft, and the caramel is bubbling.
11. When done, remove the pan from the oven and allow to cool for about 10 minutes.
12. Served warm.

Chocolate Chip and Oat Cookies

Prep time: 10 minutes | Cook time: 20 minutes | Makes 4 dozen (1-by-1½-inch) bars

1 cup unsalted butter, at room temperature
1 cup dark brown sugar
½ cup granulated sugar
2 large eggs
1 tablespoon vanilla extract
Pinch salt
2 cups old-fashioned rolled oats
1½ cups all-purpose flour
1 teaspoon baking powder
1 teaspoon baking soda
2 cups chocolate chips

1. Stir together the butter, brown sugar, and granulated sugar in a large mixing bowl until smooth and light in color.
2. Crack the eggs into the bowl, one at a time, mixing after each addition. Stir in the vanilla and salt.
3. Mix together the oats, flour, baking powder, and baking soda in a separate bowl. Add the mixture to the butter mixture and stir until mixed. Stir in the chocolate chips.
4. Spread the dough onto the sheet pan in an even layer.
5. Select Bake, Super Convection, set temperature to 350ºF (180ºC), and set time to 20 minutes. Select Start/Stop to begin preheating.
6. Once the unit has preheated, place the basket on the bake position.
7. After 15 minutes, check the cookie, rotating the pan if the crust is not browning evenly. Continue cooking for a total of 18 to 20 minutes or until golden brown.
8. When cooking is complete, remove the pan from the oven and allow to cool completely before slicing and serving.

Sweet Chocolate Cookies

Prep time: 10 minutes | Cook time: 22 minutes | Makes 30 cookies

⅓ cup (80g) organic brown sugar
⅓ cup (80g) organic cane sugar
4 ounces (112g) cashew-based vegan butter
½ cup coconut cream
1 teaspoon vanilla extract
2 tablespoons ground flaxseed
1 teaspoon baking powder
1 teaspoon baking soda
Pinch of salt
2¼ cups (220g) almond flour
½ cup (90g) dairy-free dark chocolate chips

1. Line a baking sheet with parchment paper.
2. Mix together the brown sugar, cane sugar, and butter in a medium bowl or the bowl of a stand mixer. Cream together with a mixer.
3. Fold in the coconut cream, vanilla, flaxseed, baking powder, baking soda, and salt. Stir well.
4. Add the almond flour, a little at a time, mixing after each addition until fully incorporated. Stir in the chocolate chips with a spatula.
5. Scoop the dough onto the prepared baking sheet.
6. Select Bake, Super Convection, set temperature to 325°F (160°C), and set the time to 22 minutes. Select Start/Stop to begin preheating.
7. Once the unit has preheated, place the baking sheet on the bake position.
8. Bake, Super Convection until the cookies are golden brown.
9. When cooking is complete, transfer the baking sheet onto a wire rack to cool completely before serving.

Monk Fruit and Hazelnut Cake

Prep time: 10 minutes | Cook time: 20 minutes | Serves 6

1 stick butter, at room temperature
5 tablespoons liquid monk fruit
2 eggs plus 1 egg yolk, beaten
⅓ cup hazelnuts, roughly chopped
3 tablespoons sugar-free orange marmalade
6 ounces (170 g) unbleached almond flour
1 teaspoon baking soda
½ teaspoon baking powder
½ teaspoon ground cinnamon
½ teaspoon ground allspice
½ ground anise seed
Cooking spray

1. Lightly spritz a baking pan with cooking spray.
2. In a mixing bowl, whisk the butter and liquid monk fruit until the mixture is pale and smooth. Mix in the beaten eggs, hazelnuts, and marmalade and whisk again until well incorporated.
3. Add the almond flour, baking soda, baking powder, cinnamon, allspice, anise seed and stir to mix well.
4. Scrape the batter into the prepared baking pan.
5. Select Bake, Super Convection, set temperature to 310ºF (154ºC), and set time to 20 minutes. Select Start/Stop to begin preheating.
6. Once the oven has preheated, place the pan on the bake position.
7. When cooking is complete, the top of the cake should spring back when gently pressed with your fingers.
8. Transfer to a wire rack and let the cake cool to room temperature. Serve immediately.

Blueberry and Peach Tart

Prep time: 10 minutes | Cook time: 30 minutes | Serves 6 to 8

4 peaches, pitted and sliced
1 cup fresh blueberries
2 tablespoons cornstarch
3 tablespoons sugar
1 tablespoon freshly squeezed lemon juice
Cooking spray
1 sheet frozen puff pastry, thawed
1 tablespoon nonfat or low-fat milk
Confectioners' sugar, for dusting

1. Add the peaches, blueberries, cornstarch, sugar, and lemon juice to a large bowl and toss to coat.
2. Spritz a round baking pan with cooking spray.
3. Unfold the pastry and put on the prepared baking pan.
4. Lay the peach slices on the pan, slightly overlapping them. Scatter the blueberries over the peach.
5. Drape the pastry over the outside of the fruit and press pleats firmly together. Brush the milk over the pastry.
6. Select Bake, Super Convection, set temperature to 400ºF (205ºC), and set time to 30 minutes. Select Start/Stop to begin preheating.
7. Once the unit has preheated, place the pan on the bake position.
8. Bake, Super Convection until the crust is golden brown and the fruit is bubbling.
9. When cooking is complete, remove the pan from the oven and allow to cool for 10 minutes.
10. Serve the tart with the confectioners' sugar sprinkled on top.

Chocolate-Coconut Cake

Prep time: 5 minutes | Cook time: 15 minutes | Serves 10

1¼ cups unsweetened bakers' chocolate
1 stick butter
1 teaspoon liquid stevia
1/3 cup shredded coconut
2 tablespoons coconut milk
2 eggs, beaten
Cooking spray

1. Lightly spritz a baking pan with cooking spray.
2. Place the chocolate, butter, and stevia in a microwave-safe bowl. Microwave for about 30 seconds until melted. Let the chocolate mixture cool to room temperature.
3. Add the remaining ingredients to the chocolate mixture and stir until well incorporated. Pour the batter into the prepared baking pan.
4. Select Bake, Super Convection, set temperature to 330ºF (166ºC), and set time to 15 minutes. Select Start/Stop to begin preheating.
5. Once the oven has preheated, place the pan on the bake position.
6. When cooking is complete, a toothpick inserted in the center should come out clean.
7. Remove from the oven and allow to cool for about 10 minutes before serving.

Chapter 9 Wraps and Sandwiches

Avocado and Cabbage Slaw Taco

Prep time: 15 minutes | Cook time: 6 minutes | Serves 4

¼ cup all-purpose flour
¼ teaspoon salt, plus more as needed
¼ teaspoon ground black pepper
2 large egg whites
1¼ cups panko bread crumbs
2 tablespoons olive oil
2 avocados, peeled and halved, cut into ½-inch-thick slices
½ small red cabbage, thinly sliced
1 deseeded jalapeño, thinly sliced
2 green onions, thinly sliced
½ cup cilantro leaves
¼ cup mayonnaise
Juice and zest of 1 lime
4 corn tortillas, warmed
½ cup sour cream
Cooking spray

1. Spritz the air fry basket with cooking spray.
2. Pour the flour in a large bowl and sprinkle with salt and black pepper, then stir to mix well.
3. Whisk the egg whites in a separate bowl. Combine the panko with olive oil on a shallow dish.
4. Dredge the avocado slices in the bowl of flour, then into the egg to coat. Shake the excess off, then roll the slices over the panko.
5. Arrange the avocado slices in a single layer in the basket and spritz the cooking spray.
6. Select Air Fry, Super Convection, set temperature to 400ºF (205ºC) and set time to 6 minutes. Select Start/Stop to begin preheating.
7. Once preheated, place the basket on the air fry position. Flip the slices halfway through with tongs.
8. When cooking is complete, the avocado slices should be tender and lightly browned.
9. Combine the cabbage, jalapeño, onions, cilantro leaves, mayo, lime juice and zest, and a touch of salt in a separate large bowl. Toss to mix well.
10. Unfold the tortillas on a clean work surface, then spread with cabbage slaw and air fried avocados. Top with sour cream and serve.

Tilapia Fillet Tacos

Prep time: 10 minutes | Cook time: 5 minutes | Serves 4

2 tablespoons milk
⅓ cup mayonnaise
¼ teaspoon garlic powder
1 teaspoon chili powder
1½ cups panko bread crumbs
½ teaspoon salt
4 teaspoons canola oil
1 pound (454 g) skinless tilapia fillets, cut into 3-inch-long and 1-inch-wide strips
4 small flour tortillas
Lemon wedges, for topping
Cooking spray

1. Spritz the air fry basket with cooking spray.
2. Combine the milk, mayo, garlic powder, and chili powder in a bowl. Stir to mix well. Combine the panko with salt and canola oil in a separate bowl. Stir to mix well.
3. Dredge the tilapia strips in the milk mixture first, then dunk the strips in the panko mixture to coat well. Shake the excess off.
4. Arrange the tilapia strips in the basket.
5. Select Air Fry, Super Convection, set temperature to 400ºF (205ºC) and set time to 5 minutes. Select Start/Stop to begin preheating.
6. Once the oven has preheated, place the basket on the air fry position. Flip the strips halfway through the cooking time.
7. When cooking is complete, the strips will be opaque on all sides and the panko will be golden brown.
8. Unfold the tortillas on a large plate, then divide the tilapia strips over the tortillas. Squeeze the lemon wedges on top before serving.

Mushroom, Veggies and Noodle Spring Rolls

Prep time: 15 minutes | Cook time: 14 minutes | Makes 14 spring rolls

2 tablespoons vegetable oil
4 cups sliced Napa cabbage
5 ounces (142 g) shiitake mushrooms, diced
3 carrots, cut into thin matchsticks
1 tablespoon minced fresh ginger
1 tablespoon minced garlic
1 bunch scallions, white and light green parts only, sliced
2 tablespoons soy sauce
1 (4-ounce / 113-g) package cellophane noodles
¼ teaspoon cornstarch
1 (12-ounce / 340-g) package frozen spring roll wrappers, thawed
Cooking spray

1. Heat the olive oil in a nonstick skillet over medium-high heat until shimmering.
2. Add the cabbage, mushrooms, and carrots and sauté for 3 minutes or until tender.
3. Add the ginger, garlic, and scallions and sauté for 1 minutes or until fragrant.
4. Mix in the soy sauce and turn off the heat. Discard any liquid remains in the skillet and allow to cool for a few minutes.
5. Bring a pot of water to a boil, then turn off the heat and pour in the noodles. Let sit for 10 minutes or until the noodles are al dente. Transfer 1 cup of the noodles in the skillet and toss with the cooked vegetables. Reserve the remaining noodles for other use.
6. Dissolve the cornstarch in a small dish of water, then place the wrappers on a clean work surface. Dab the edges of the wrappers with cornstarch.
7. Scoop up 3 tablespoons of filling in the center of each wrapper, then fold the corner in front of you over the filling. Tuck the wrapper under the filling, then fold the corners on both sides into the center. Keep rolling to seal the wrapper. Repeat with remaining wrappers.
8. Spritz the air fry basket with cooking spray. Arrange the wrappers in the basket and spritz with cooking spray.
9. Select Air Fry, Super Convection, set temperature to 400ºF (205ºC) and set time to 10 minutes. Select Start/Stop to begin preheating.
10. Once preheated, place the basket on the air fry position. Flip the wrappers halfway through the cooking time.
11. When cooking is complete, the wrappers will be golden brown.
12. Serve immediately.

Beef and Red Onion Taco

Prep time: 15 minutes | Cook time: 12 minutes | Serves 6

2 tablespoons gochujang
1 tablespoon soy sauce
2 tablespoons sesame seeds
2 teaspoons minced fresh ginger
2 cloves garlic, minced
2 tablespoons toasted sesame oil
2 teaspoons sugar
½ teaspoon kosher salt
1½ pounds (680 g) thinly sliced beef chuck
1 medium red onion, sliced
6 corn tortillas, warmed
¼ cup chopped fresh cilantro
½ cup kimchi
½ cup chopped green onions

1. Combine the gochujang, soy sauce, sesame seeds, ginger, garlic, sesame oil, sugar, and salt in a large bowl. Stir to mix well.
2. Dunk the beef chunk in the large bowl. Press to submerge, then wrap the bowl in plastic and refrigerate to marinate for at least 1 hour.
3. Remove the beef chunk from the marinade and transfer to the air fry basket. Add the onion to the basket.
4. Select Air Fry, Super Convection, set temperature to 400ºF (205ºC) and set time to 12 minutes. Select Start/Stop to begin preheating.
5. Once preheated, place the basket on the air fry position. Stir the mixture halfway through the cooking time.
6. When cooked, the beef will be well browned.
7. Unfold the tortillas on a clean work surface, then divide the fried beef and onion on the tortillas. Spread the cilantro, kimchi, and green onions on top.
8. Serve immediately.

Salsa Bacon and Egg Cheese Wraps

Prep time: 10 minutes | Cook time: 10 minutes | Serves 3

3 corn tortillas
3 slices bacon, cut into strips
2 scrambled eggs
3 tablespoons salsa
1 cup grated Pepper Jack cheese
3 tablespoons cream cheese, divided
Cooking spray

1. Spritz the air fry basket with cooking spray.
2. Unfold the tortillas on a clean work surface, divide the bacon and eggs in the middle of the tortillas, then spread with salsa and scatter with cheeses. Fold the tortillas over.
3. Arrange the tortillas in the basket.
4. Select Air Fry, Super Convection, set temperature to 390ºF (199ºC) and set time to 10 minutes. Select Start/Stop to begin preheating.
5. Once the oven has preheated, place the basket on the air fry position. Flip the tortillas halfway through the cooking time.
6. When cooking is complete, the cheeses will be melted and the tortillas will be lightly browned.
7. Serve immediately.

Cod Fillet Taco with Salsa

Prep time: 15 minutes | Cook time: 15 minutes | Serves 4

2 eggs
1¼ cups Mexican beer
1½ cups coconut flour
1½ cups almond flour
½ tablespoon chili powder
1 tablespoon cumin
Salt, to taste
1 pound (454 g) cod fillet, slice into large pieces
4 toasted corn tortillas
4 large lettuce leaves, chopped
¼ cup salsa
Cooking spray

1. Spritz the air fry basket with cooking spray.
2. Break the eggs in a bowl, then pour in the beer. Whisk to combine well.
3. Combine the coconut flour, almond flour, chili powder, cumin, and salt in a separate bowl. Stir to mix well.
4. Dunk the cod pieces in the egg mixture, then shake the excess off and dredge into the flour mixture to coat well. Arrange the cod in the basket.
5. Select Air Fry, Super Convection, set temperature to 375ºF (190ºC) and set time to 15 minutes. Select Start/Stop to begin preheating.
6. Once the oven has preheated, place the basket on the air fry position. Flip the cod halfway through the cooking time.
7. When cooking is complete, the cod should be golden brown.
8. Unwrap the toasted tortillas on a large plate, then divide the cod and lettuce leaves on top. Baste with salsa and wrap to serve.

Avocado and Tomato Egg Rolls Wrappers

Prep time: 10 minutes | Cook time: 5 minutes | Serves 5

10 egg roll wrappers
3 avocados, peeled and pitted
1 tomato, diced
Salt and ground black pepper, to taste
Cooking spray

1. Spritz the air fry basket with cooking spray.
2. Put the tomato and avocados in a food processor. Sprinkle with salt and ground black pepper. Pulse to mix and coarsely mash until smooth.
3. Unfold the wrappers on a clean work surface, then divide the mixture in the center of each wrapper. Roll the wrapper up and press to seal.
4. Transfer the rolls to the basket and spritz with cooking spray.
5. Select Air Fry, Super Convection, set temperature to 350ºF (180ºC) and set time to 5 minutes. Select Start/Stop to begin preheating.
6. Once the oven has preheated, place the basket on the air fry position. Flip the rolls halfway through the cooking time.
7. When cooked, the rolls should be golden brown.
8. Serve immediately.

Beef and Bell Pepper Cheese Fajitas

Prep time: 15 minutes | Cook time: 10 minutes | Serves 4

1 pound (454 g) beef sirloin steak, cut into strips
2 shallots, sliced
1 orange bell pepper, sliced
1 red bell pepper, sliced
2 garlic cloves, minced
2 tablespoons Cajun seasoning
1 tablespoon paprika
Salt and ground black pepper, to taste
4 corn tortillas
½ cup shredded Cheddar cheese
Cooking spray

1. Spritz the air fry basket with cooking spray.
2. Combine all the ingredients, except for the tortillas and cheese, in a large bowl. Toss to coat well.
3. Pour the beef and vegetables in the basket and spritz with cooking spray.
4. Select Air Fry, Super Convection, set temperature to 360°F (182°C) and set time to 10 minutes. Select Start/Stop to begin preheating.
5. Once preheated, place the basket on the air fry position. Stir the beef and vegetables halfway through the cooking time.
6. When cooking is complete, the meat will be browned and the vegetables will be soft and lightly wilted.
7. Unfold the tortillas on a clean work surface and spread the cooked beef and vegetables on top. Scatter with cheese and fold to serve.

Mexican Cheese Potato Taquitos

Prep time: 5 minutes | Cook time: 6 minutes | Makes 12 taquitos

2 cups mashed potatoes
½ cup shredded Mexican cheese
12 corn tortillas
Cooking spray

1. Line a baking pan with parchment paper.
2. In a bowl, combine the potatoes and cheese until well mixed. Microwave the tortillas on high heat for 30 seconds, or until softened. Add some water to another bowl and set alongside.
3. On a clean work surface, lay the tortillas. Scoop 3 tablespoons of the potato mixture in the center of each tortilla. Roll up tightly and secure with toothpicks if necessary.
4. Arrange the filled tortillas, seam side down, in the prepared baking pan. Spritz the tortillas with cooking spray.
5. Select Air Fry, Super Convection, set temperature to 400°F (205°C) and set time to 6 minutes. Select Start/Stop to begin preheating.
6. Once preheated, place the pan into the oven. Flip the tortillas halfway through the cooking time.
7. When cooked, the tortillas should be crispy and golden brown.
8. Serve hot.

Eggplant Parmesan Hoagies

Prep time: 15 minutes | Cook time: 12 minutes | Makes 3 hoagies

6 peeled eggplant slices (about ½ inch thick and 3 inches in diameter)
¼ cup jarred pizza sauce
6 tablespoons grated Parmesan cheese
3 Italian sub rolls, split open lengthwise, warmed
Cooking spray

1. Spritz the air fry basket with cooking spray.
2. Arrange the eggplant slices in the basket and spritz with cooking spray.
3. Select Air Fry, Super Convection, set temperature to 350°F (180°C) and set time to 10 minutes. Select Start/Stop to begin preheating.
4. Once the oven has preheated, place the basket on the air fry position. Flip the slices halfway through the cooking time.
5. When cooked, the eggplant slices should be lightly wilted and tender.
6. Divide and spread the pizza sauce and cheese on top of the eggplant slice
7. Select Air Fry, Super Convection, set temperature to 375°F (190°C) and set time to 2 minutes. Place the basket on the air fry position. When cooked, the cheese will be melted.
8. Assemble each sub roll with two slices of eggplant and serve immediately.

Mozzarella Chicken and Yogurt Taquitos

Prep time: 10 minutes | Cook time: 12 minutes | Serves 4

1 cup cooked chicken, shredded	Mozzarella cheese
¼ cup Greek yogurt	Salt and ground black pepper, to taste
¼ cup salsa	4 flour tortillas
1 cup shredded	Cooking spray

1. Spritz the air fry basket with cooking spray.
2. Combine all the ingredients, except for the tortillas, in a large bowl. Stir to mix well.
3. Make the taquitos: Unfold the tortillas on a clean work surface, then scoop up 2 tablespoons of the chicken mixture in the middle of each tortilla. Roll the tortillas up to wrap the filling.
4. Arrange the taquitos in the basket and spritz with cooking spray.
5. Select Air Fry, Super Convection, set temperature to 380°F (193°C) and set time to 12 minutes. Select Start/Stop to begin preheating.
6. Once preheated, place the basket on the air fry position. Flip the taquitos halfway through the cooking time.
7. When cooked, the taquitos should be golden brown and the cheese should be melted.
8. Serve immediately.

Thai Curried Pork Burgers

Prep time: 10 minutes | Cook time: 14 minutes | Makes 6 sliders

1 pound (454 g) ground pork	peeled fresh ginger
1 tablespoon Thai curry paste	1 tablespoon light brown sugar
1½ tablespoons fish sauce	1 teaspoon ground black pepper
¼ cup thinly sliced scallions, white and green parts	6 slider buns, split open lengthwise, warmed
2 tablespoons minced	Cooking spray

1. Spritz the air fry basket with cooking spray.
2. Combine all the ingredients, except for the buns in a large bowl. Stir to mix well.
3. Divide and shape the mixture into six balls, then bash the balls into six 3-inch-diameter patties.
4. Arrange the patties in the basket and spritz with cooking spray.
5. Select Air Fry, Super Convection, set temperature to 375°F (190°C) and set time to 14 minutes. Select Start/Stop to begin preheating.
6. Once the oven has preheated, place the basket on the air fry position. Flip the patties halfway through the cooking time.
7. When cooked, the patties should be well browned.
8. Assemble the buns with patties to make the sliders and serve immediately.

Pork and Carrot Momos

Prep time: 10 minutes | Cook time: 20 minutes | Serves 4

2 tablespoons olive oil	1 teaspoon soy sauce
1 pound (454 g) ground pork	16 wonton wrappers
1 shredded carrot	Salt and ground black pepper, to taste
1 onion, chopped	Cooking spray

1. Heat the olive oil in a nonstick skillet over medium heat until shimmering.
2. Add the ground pork, carrot, onion, soy sauce, salt, and ground black pepper and sauté for 10 minutes or until the pork is well browned and carrots are tender.
3. Unfold the wrappers on a clean work surface, then divide the cooked pork and vegetables on the wrappers. Fold the edges around the filling to form momos. Nip the top to seal the momos.
4. Arrange the momos in the air fry basket and spritz with cooking spray.
5. Select Air Fry, Super Convection, set temperature to 320°F (160°C) and set time to 10 minutes. Select Start/Stop to begin preheating.
6. Once the oven has preheated, place the basket on the air fry position.
7. When cooking is complete, the wrappers will be lightly browned.
8. Serve immediately.

Turkey and Leek Hamburger

Prep time: 10 minutes | Cook time: 20 minutes | Serves 4

1 cup leftover turkey, cut into bite-sized chunks
1 leek, sliced
1 Serrano pepper, deveined and chopped
2 bell peppers, deveined and chopped
2 tablespoons Tabasco sauce
½ cup sour cream
1 heaping tablespoon fresh cilantro, chopped
1 teaspoon hot paprika
¾ teaspoon kosher salt
½ teaspoon ground black pepper
4 hamburger buns
Cooking spray

1. Spritz a baking pan with cooking spray.
2. Mix all the ingredients, except for the buns, in a large bowl. Toss to combine well.
3. Pour the mixture in the baking pan.
4. Select Bake, Super Convection, set temperature to 385ºF (196ºC) and set time to 20 minutes. Select Start/Stop to begin preheating.
5. Once preheated, place the pan on the bake position.
6. When done, the turkey will be well browned and the leek will be tender.
7. Assemble the hamburger buns with the turkey mixture and serve immediately.

Greek Lamb and Feta Hamburgers

Prep time: 15 minutes | Cook time: 16 minutes | Makes 4 burgers

1½ pounds (680 g) ground lamb
¼ cup crumbled Feta
1½ teaspoons tomato paste
1½ teaspoons minced garlic
1 teaspoon ground dried ginger
1 teaspoon ground coriander
¼ teaspoon salt
¼ teaspoon cayenne pepper
4 kaiser rolls or hamburger buns, split open lengthwise, warmed
Cooking spray

1. Spritz the air fry basket with cooking spray.
2. Combine all the ingredients, except for the buns, in a large bowl. Coarsely stir to mix well.
3. Shape the mixture into four balls, then pound the balls into four 5-inch diameter patties.
4. Arrange the patties in the basket and spritz with cooking spray.
5. Select Air Fry, Super Convection, set temperature to 375ºF (190ºC) and set time to 16 minutes. Select Start/Stop to begin preheating.
6. Once preheated, place the basket on the air fry position. Flip the patties halfway through the cooking time.
7. When cooking is complete, the patties should be well browned.
8. Assemble the buns with patties to make the burgers and serve immediately.

Curried Shrimp and Zucchini Potstickers

Prep time: 10 minutes | Cook time: 5 minutes | Serves 10

½ pound (227 g) peeled and deveined shrimp, finely chopped
1 medium zucchini, coarsely grated
1 tablespoon fish sauce
1 tablespoon green curry paste
2 scallions, thinly sliced
¼ cup basil, chopped
30 round dumpling wrappers
Cooking spray

1. Combine the chopped shrimp, zucchini, fish sauce, curry paste, scallions, and basil in a large bowl. Stir to mix well.
2. Unfold the dumpling wrappers on a clean work surface, dab a little water around the edges of each wrapper, then scoop up 1 teaspoon of filling in the middle of each wrapper.
3. Make the potstickers: Fold the wrappers in half and press the edges to seal.
4. Spritz the air fry basket with cooking spray.
5. Transfer the potstickers to the basket and spritz with cooking spray.
6. Select Air Fry, Super Convection, set temperature to 350ºF (180ºC) and set time to 5 minutes. Select Start/Stop to begin preheating.
7. Once preheated, place the basket on the air fry position. Flip the potstickers halfway through the cooking time.
8. When cooking is complete, the potstickers should be crunchy and lightly browned.
9. Serve immediately.

English Pea and Potato Samosas

Prep time: 25 minutes | Cook time: 22 minutes | Makes 16 samosas

Dough:
- 4 cups all-purpose flour, plus more for flouring the work surface
- ¼ cup plain yogurt
- ½ cup cold unsalted butter, cut into cubes
- 2 teaspoons kosher salt
- 1 cup ice water

Filling:
- 2 tablespoons vegetable oil
- 1 onion, diced
- 1½ teaspoons coriander
- 1½ teaspoons cumin
- 1 clove garlic, minced
- 1 teaspoon turmeric
- 1 teaspoon kosher salt
- ½ cup peas, thawed if frozen
- 2 cups mashed potatoes
- 2 tablespoons yogurt
- Cooking spray

Chutney:
- 1 cup mint leaves, lightly packed
- 2 cups cilantro leaves, lightly packed
- 1 green chile pepper, deseeded and minced
- ½ cup minced onion
- Juice of 1 lime
- 1 teaspoon granulated sugar
- 1 teaspoon kosher salt
- 2 tablespoons vegetable oil

1. Put the flour, yogurt, butter, and salt in a food processor. Pulse to combine until grainy. Pour in the water and pulse until a smooth and firm dough forms.
2. Transfer the dough on a clean and lightly floured working surface. Knead the dough and shape it into a ball. Cut in half and flatten the halves into 2 discs. Wrap them in plastic and let sit in refrigerator until ready to use.
3. Meanwhile, make the filling: Heat the vegetable oil in a saucepan over medium heat.
4. Add the onion and sauté for 5 minutes or until lightly browned.
5. Add the coriander, cumin, garlic, turmeric, and salt and sauté for 2 minutes or until fragrant.
6. Add the peas, potatoes, and yogurt and stir to combine well. Turn off the heat and allow to cool.
7. Meanwhile, combine the ingredients for the chutney in a food processor. Pulse to mix well until glossy. Pour the chutney in a bowl and refrigerate until ready to use.
8. Make the samosas: Remove the dough discs from the refrigerator and cut each disc into 8 parts. Shape each part into a ball, then roll the ball into a 6-inch circle. Cut the circle in half and roll each half into a cone.
9. Scoop up 2 tablespoons of the filling into the cone, press the edges of the cone to seal and form into a triangle. Repeat with remaining dough and filling.
10. Spritz the air fry basket with cooking spray. Arrange the samosas in the basket and spritz with cooking spray.
11. Select Air Fry, Super Convection, set temperature to 360°F (182°C) and set time to 15 minutes. Select Start/Stop to begin preheating.
12. Once the oven has preheated, place the basket on the air fry position. Flip the samosas halfway through the cooking time.
13. When cooked, the samosas will be golden brown and crispy.
14. Serve the samosas with the chutney.

Cream Cheese Wontons

Prep time: 5 minutes | Cook time: 6 minutes | Serves 4

- 2 ounces (57 g) cream cheese, softened
- 1 tablespoon sugar
- 16 square wonton wrappers
- Cooking spray

1. Spritz the air fry basket with cooking spray.
2. In a mixing bowl, stir together the cream cheese and sugar until well mixed. Prepare a small bowl of water alongside.
3. On a clean work surface, lay the wonton wrappers. Scoop ¼ teaspoon of cream cheese in the center of each wonton wrapper. Dab the water over the wrapper edges. Fold each wonton wrapper diagonally in half over the filling to form a triangle.
4. Arrange the wontons in the basket. Spritz the wontons with cooking spray.
5. Select Air Fry, Super Convection, set temperature to 350°F (180°C) and set time to 6 minutes. Select Start/Stop to begin preheating.
6. Once preheated, place the basket on the air fry position. Flip the wontons halfway through the cooking time.
7. When cooking is complete, the wontons will be golden brown and crispy.
8. Divide the wontons among four plates. Let rest for 5 minutes before serving.

Potato, Spinach and Black Bean Burritos

Prep time: 15 minutes | Cook time: 30 minutes | Makes 6 burritos

2 sweet potatoes, peeled and cut into a small dice
1 tablespoon vegetable oil
Kosher salt and ground black pepper, to taste
6 large flour tortillas
1 (16-ounce / 454-g) can refried black beans, divided
1½ cups baby spinach, divided
6 eggs, scrambled
¾ cup grated Cheddar cheese, divided
¼ cup salsa
¼ cup sour cream
Cooking spray

1. Put the sweet potatoes in a large bowl, then drizzle with vegetable oil and sprinkle with salt and black pepper. Toss to coat well.
2. Place the potatoes in the air fry basket.
3. Select Air Fry, Super Convection, set temperature to 400°F (205°C) and set time to 10 minutes. Select Start/Stop to begin preheating.
4. Once preheated, place the basket on the air fry position. Flip the potatoes halfway through the cooking time.
5. When done, the potatoes should be lightly browned. Remove the potatoes from the oven.
6. Unfold the tortillas on a clean work surface. Divide the black beans, spinach, air fried sweet potatoes, scrambled eggs, and cheese on top of the tortillas.
7. Fold the long side of the tortillas over the filling, then fold in the shorter side to wrap the filling to make the burritos.
8. Wrap the burritos in the aluminum foil and put in the basket.
9. Select Air Fry, Super Convection, set temperature to 350°F (180°C) and set time to 20 minutes. Place the basket on the air fry position. Flip the burritos halfway through the cooking time.
10. Remove the burritos from the oven and spread with sour cream and salsa. Serve immediately.

Prawn and Cabbage Egg Wrappers

Prep time: 15 minutes | Cook time: 18 minutes | Serves 4

2 tablespoons olive oil
1 carrot, cut into strips
1-inch piece fresh ginger, grated
1 tablespoon minced garlic
2 tablespoons soy sauce
¼ cup chicken broth
1 tablespoon sugar
1 cup shredded Napa cabbage
1 tablespoon sesame oil
8 cooked prawns, minced
8 egg roll wrappers
1 egg, beaten
Cooking spray

1. Spritz the air fry basket with cooking spray. Set aside.
2. Heat the olive oil in a nonstick skillet over medium heat until shimmering.
3. Add the carrot, ginger, and garlic and sauté for 2 minutes or until fragrant.
4. Pour in the soy sauce, broth, and sugar. Bring to a boil. Keep stirring.
5. Add the cabbage and simmer for 4 minutes or until the cabbage is tender.
6. Turn off the heat and mix in the sesame oil. Let sit for 15 minutes.
7. Use a strainer to remove the vegetables from the liquid, then combine with the minced prawns.
8. Unfold the egg roll wrappers on a clean work surface, then divide the prawn mixture in the center of wrappers.
9. Dab the edges of a wrapper with the beaten egg, then fold a corner over the filling and tuck the corner under the filling. Fold the left and right corner into the center. Roll the wrapper up and press to seal. Repeat with remaining wrappers.
10. Arrange the wrappers in the basket and spritz with cooking spray.
11. Select Air Fry, Super Convection, set temperature to 370°F (188°C) and set time to 12 minutes. Select Start/Stop to begin preheating.
12. Once the oven has preheated, place the basket on the air fry position. Flip the wrappers halfway through the cooking time.
13. When cooking is complete, the wrappers should be golden.
14. Serve immediately.

Spinach and Tomato Pockets

Prep time: 10 minutes | Cook time: 10 minutes | Makes 8 pockets

2 large eggs, divided
1 tablespoon water
1 cup baby spinach, roughly chopped
¼ cup sun-dried tomatoes, finely chopped
1 cup ricotta cheese
1 cup basil, chopped
¼ teaspoon red pepper flakes
¼ teaspoon kosher salt
2 refrigerated rolled pie crusts
2 tablespoons sesame seeds

1. Spritz the air fry basket with cooking spray.
2. Whisk an egg with water in a small bowl.
3. Combine the spinach, tomatoes, the other egg, ricotta cheese, basil, red pepper flakes, and salt in a large bowl. Whisk to mix well.
4. Unfold the pie crusts on a clean work surface and slice each crust into 4 wedges. Scoop up 3 tablespoons of the spinach mixture on each crust and leave ½ inch space from edges.
5. Fold the crust wedges in half to wrap the filling and press the edges with a fork to seal.
6. Arrange the wraps in the basket and spritz with cooking spray. Sprinkle with sesame seeds.
7. Select Air Fry, Super Convection, set temperature to 380°F (193°C) and set time to 10 minutes. Select Start/Stop to begin preheating.
8. Once the oven has preheated, place the basket on the air fry position. Flip the wraps halfway through the cooking time.
9. When cooked, the wraps will be crispy and golden.
10. Serve immediately.

Vegetable Spring Rolls

Prep time: 10 minutes | Cook time: 18 minutes | Serves 4

4 spring roll wrappers
½ cup cooked vermicelli noodles
1 teaspoon sesame oil
1 tablespoon freshly minced ginger
1 tablespoon soy sauce
1 clove garlic, minced
½ red bell pepper, deseeded and chopped
½ cup chopped carrot
½ cup chopped mushrooms
¼ cup chopped scallions
Cooking spray

1. Spritz the air fry basket with cooking spray and set aside.
2. Heat the sesame oil in a saucepan on medium heat. Sauté the ginger and garlic in the sesame oil for 1 minute, or until fragrant. Add soy sauce, red bell pepper, carrot, mushrooms and scallions. Sauté for 5 minutes or until the vegetables become tender. Mix in vermicelli noodles. Turn off the heat and remove them from the saucepan. Allow to cool for 10 minutes.
3. Lay out one spring roll wrapper with a corner pointed toward you. Scoop the noodle mixture on spring roll wrapper and fold corner up over the mixture. Fold left and right corners toward the center and continue to roll to make firmly sealed rolls.
4. Arrange the spring rolls in the basket and spritz with cooking spray.
5. Select Air Fry, Super Convection, set temperature to 340°F (171°C) and set time to 12 minutes. Select Start/Stop to begin preheating.
6. Once the oven has preheated, place the basket on the air fry position. Flip the spring rolls halfway through the cooking time.
7. When done, the spring rolls will be golden brown and crispy.
8. Serve warm.

Chicken and Cabbage Egg Rolls

Prep time: 10 minutes | Cook time: 23 to 24 minutes | Serves 4

1 pound (454 g) ground chicken	2 cups white cabbage, shredded
2 teaspoons olive oil	1 onion, chopped
2 garlic cloves, minced	¼ cup soy sauce
1 teaspoon grated fresh ginger	8 egg roll wrappers
	1 egg, beaten
	Cooking spray

1. Spritz the air fry basket with cooking spray.
2. Heat olive oil in a saucepan over medium heat. Sauté the garlic and ginger in the olive oil for 1 minute, or until fragrant. Add the ground chicken to the saucepan. Sauté for 5 minutes, or until the chicken is cooked through. Add the cabbage, onion and soy sauce and sauté for 5 to 6 minutes, or until the vegetables become soft. Remove the saucepan from the heat.
3. Unfold the egg roll wrappers on a clean work surface. Divide the chicken mixture among the wrappers and brush the edges of the wrappers with the beaten egg. Tightly roll up the egg rolls, enclosing the filling. Arrange the rolls in the basket.
4. Select Air Fry, Super Convection, set temperature to 370ºF (188ºC) and set time to 12 minutes. Select Start/Stop to begin preheating.
5. Once the oven has preheated, place the basket on the air fry position. Flip the rolls halfway through the cooking time.
6. When cooked, the rolls will be crispy and golden brown.
7. Transfer to a platter and let cool for 5 minutes before serving.

Chicken and Spring Onion Wraps

Prep time: 10 minutes | Cook time: 5 minutes | Serves 12

2 large-sized chicken breasts, cooked and shredded	molasses
2 spring onions, chopped	1 teaspoon grated fresh ginger
10 ounces (284 g) Ricotta cheese	¼ cup soy sauce
1 tablespoon rice vinegar	$^1/_3$ teaspoon sea salt
1 tablespoon	¼ teaspoon ground black pepper, or more to taste
	48 wonton wrappers
	Cooking spray

1. Spritz the air fry basket with cooking spray.
2. Combine all the ingredients, except for the wrappers in a large bowl. Toss to mix well.
3. Unfold the wrappers on a clean work surface, then divide and spoon the mixture in the middle of the wrappers.
4. Dab a little water on the edges of the wrappers, then fold the edge close to you over the filling. Tuck the edge under the filling and roll up to seal.
5. Arrange the wraps in the basket.
6. Select Air Fry, Super Convection, set temperature to 375ºF (190ºC) and set time to 5 minutes. Select Start/Stop to begin preheating.
7. Once preheated, place the basket on the air fry position. Flip the wraps halfway through the cooking time.
8. When cooking is complete, the wraps should be lightly browned.
9. Serve immediately.

Beer-Battered Cod Tacos

Prep time: 20 minutes | Cook time: 17 minutes | Makes 6 tacos

1 egg
5 ounces (142 g) Mexican beer
¾ cup all-purpose flour
¾ cup cornstarch
¼ teaspoon chili powder
½ teaspoon ground cumin
½ pound (227 g) cod, cut into large pieces
6 corn tortillas
Cooking spray

Salsa:
1 mango, peeled and diced
¼ red bell pepper, diced
½ small jalapeño, diced
¼ red onion, minced
Juice of half a lime
Pinch chopped fresh cilantro
¼ teaspoon salt
¼ teaspoon ground black pepper

1. Spritz the air fry basket with cooking spray.
2. Whisk the egg with beer in a bowl. Combine the flour, cornstarch, chili powder, and cumin in a separate bowl.
3. Dredge the cod in the egg mixture first, then in the flour mixture to coat well. Shake the excess off.
4. Arrange the cod in the air fry basket and spritz with cooking spray.
5. Select Air Fry, Super Convection, set temperature to 380ºF (193ºC) and set time to 17 minutes. Select Start/Stop to begin preheating.
6. Once preheated, place the basket on the air fry position. Flip the cod halfway through the cooking time.
7. When cooked, the cod should be golden brown and crunchy.
8. Meanwhile, combine the ingredients for the salsa in a small bowl. Stir to mix well.
9. Unfold the tortillas on a clean work surface, then divide the fish on the tortillas and spread the salsa on top. Fold to serve.

Philly Cheese Steaks

Prep time: 15 minutes | Cook time: 20 minutes | Serves 2

12 ounces (340 g) boneless rib-eye steak, sliced thinly
½ teaspoon Worcestershire sauce
½ teaspoon soy sauce
Kosher salt and ground black pepper, to taste
½ green bell pepper, stemmed, deseeded, and thinly sliced
½ small onion, halved and thinly sliced
1 tablespoon vegetable oil
2 soft hoagie rolls, split three-fourths of the way through
1 tablespoon butter, softened
2 slices provolone cheese, halved

1. Combine the steak, Worcestershire sauce, soy sauce, salt, and ground black pepper in a large bowl. Toss to coat well. Set aside.
2. Combine the bell pepper, onion, salt, ground black pepper, and vegetable oil in a separate bowl. Toss to coat the vegetables well.
3. Pour the steak and vegetables in the air fry basket.
4. Select Air Fry, Super Convection, set temperature to 400ºF (205ºC) and set time to 15 minutes. Select Start/Stop to begin preheating.
5. Once preheated, place the basket on the air fry position.
6. When cooked, the steak will be browned and vegetables will be tender. Transfer them on a plate. Set aside.
7. Brush the hoagie rolls with butter and place in the basket.
8. Select Toast, Super Convection and set time to 3 minutes. Place the basket on the toast position. When done, the rolls should be lightly browned.
9. Transfer the rolls to a clean work surface and divide the steak and vegetable mix in between the rolls. Spread with cheese. Place the stuffed rolls back in the basket.
10. Select Air Fry, Super Convection and set time to 2 minutes. Place the basket on the air fry position. When done, the cheese should be melted.
11. Serve immediately.

Crab Meat and Cream Cheese Wontons

Prep time: 10 minutes | Cook time: 10 minutes | Serves 6 to 8

24 wonton wrappers, thawed if frozen
Filling:
5 ounces (142 g) lump crabmeat, drained and patted dry
4 ounces (113 g) cream cheese, at room temperature
2 scallions, sliced
Cooking spray
1½ teaspoons toasted sesame oil
1 teaspoon Worcestershire sauce
Kosher salt and ground black pepper, to taste

1. Spritz the air fry basket with cooking spray.
2. In a medium-size bowl, place all the ingredients for the filling and stir until well mixed. Prepare a small bowl of water alongside.
3. On a clean work surface, lay the wonton wrappers. Scoop 1 teaspoon of the filling in the center of each wrapper. Wet the edges with a touch of water. Fold each wonton wrapper diagonally in half over the filling to form a triangle.
4. Arrange the wontons in the basket. Spritz the wontons with cooking spray.
5. Select Air Fry, Super Convection, set temperature to 350°F (180°C) and set time to 10 minutes. Select Start/Stop to begin preheating.
6. Once preheated, place the basket on the air fry position. Flip the wontons halfway through the cooking time.
7. When cooking is complete, the wontons will be crispy and golden brown.
8. Serve immediately.

Japanese Pork and Cabbage Gyoza

Prep time: 10 minutes | Cook time: 10 minutes | Makes 48 gyozas

1 pound (454 g) ground pork
1 head Napa cabbage (about 1 pound / 454 g), sliced thinly and minced
½ cup minced scallions
1 teaspoon minced fresh chives
1 teaspoon soy sauce
1 teaspoon minced fresh ginger
1 tablespoon minced garlic
1 teaspoon granulated sugar
2 teaspoons kosher salt
48 to 50 wonton or dumpling wrappers
Cooking spray

1. Spritz the air fry basket with cooking spray. Set aside.
2. Make the filling: Combine all the ingredients, except for the wrappers in a large bowl. Stir to mix well.
3. Unfold a wrapper on a clean work surface, then dab the edges with a little water. Scoop up 2 teaspoons of the filling mixture in the center.
4. Make the gyoza: Fold the wrapper over to filling and press the edges to seal. Pleat the edges if desired. Repeat with remaining wrappers and fillings.
5. Arrange the gyozas in the basket and spritz with cooking spray.
6. Select Air Fry, Super Convection, set temperature to 360°F (182°C) and set time to 10 minutes. Select Start/Stop to begin preheating.
7. Once preheated, place the basket on the air fry position. Flip the gyozas halfway through the cooking time.
8. When cooked, the gyozas will be golden brown.
9. Serve immediately.

Turkey Sliders with Chive Mayonnaise

Prep time: 15 minutes | Cook time: 15 minutes | Serves 6

12 burger buns	Cooking spray
Turkey Sliders:	
¾ pound (340 g) turkey, minced	chopped scallions
1 tablespoon oyster sauce	1 tablespoon chopped fresh cilantro
¼ cup pickled jalapeno, chopped	1 to 2 cloves garlic, minced
2 tablespoons	Sea salt and ground black pepper, to taste
Chive Mayo:	
1 tablespoon chives	Zest of 1 lime
1 cup mayonnaise	1 teaspoon salt

1. Spritz the air fry basket with cooking spray.
2. Combine the ingredients for the turkey sliders in a large bowl. Stir to mix well. Shape the mixture into 6 balls, then bash the balls into patties.
3. Arrange the patties in the basket and spritz with cooking spray.
4. Select Air Fry, Super Convection, set temperature to 365ºF (185ºC) and set time to 15 minutes. Select Start/Stop to begin preheating.
5. Once preheated, place the basket on the air fry position. Flip the patties halfway through the cooking time.
6. Meanwhile, combine the ingredients for the chive mayo in a small bowl. Stir to mix well.
7. When cooked, the patties will be well browned.
8. Smear the patties with chive mayo, then assemble the patties between two buns to make the sliders. Serve immediately.

Cheesy Vegetable Wraps

Prep time: 15 minutes | Cook time: 9 minutes | Serves 4

8 ounces (227 g) green beans	3 tablespoons lemon juice
2 portobello mushroom caps, sliced	¼ teaspoon ground black pepper
1 large red pepper, sliced	4 (6-inch) whole-grain wraps
2 tablespoons olive oil, divided	4 ounces (113 g) fresh herb or garlic goat cheese, crumbled
¼ teaspoon salt	
1 (15-ounce / 425-g) can chickpeas, drained	1 lemon, cut into wedges

1. Add the green beans, mushrooms, red pepper to a large bowl. Drizzle with 1 tablespoon olive oil and season with salt. Toss until well coated.
2. Transfer the vegetable mixture to a baking pan.
3. Select Air Fry, Super Convection, set temperature to 400ºF (205ºC) and set time to 9 minutes. Select Start/Stop to begin preheating.
4. Once preheated, slide the pan into the oven. Stir the vegetable mixture three times during cooking.
5. When cooked, the vegetables should be tender.
6. Meanwhile, mash the chickpeas with lemon juice, pepper and the remaining 1 tablespoon oil until well blended
7. Unfold the wraps on a clean work surface. Spoon the chickpea mash on the wraps and spread all over.
8. Divide the cooked veggies among wraps. Sprinkle 1 ounce crumbled goat cheese on top of each wrap. Fold to wrap. Squeeze the lemon wedges on top and serve.

Montreal Steak Hamburgers

Prep time: 15 minutes | Cook time: 10 minutes | Serves 4

1 teaspoon cumin seeds	salt
1 teaspoon mustard seeds	2 teaspoons ground black pepper
1 teaspoon coriander seeds	1 pound (454 g) 85% lean ground beef
1 teaspoon dried minced garlic	2 tablespoons Worcestershire sauce
1 teaspoon dried red pepper flakes	4 hamburger buns
1 teaspoon kosher	Mayonnaise, for serving
	Cooking spray

1. Spritz the air fry basket with cooking spray.
2. Put the seeds, garlic, red pepper flakes, salt, and ground black pepper in a food processor. Pulse to coarsely ground the mixture.
3. Put the ground beef in a large bowl. Pour in the seed mixture and drizzle with Worcestershire sauce. Stir to mix well.
4. Divide the mixture into four parts and shape each part into a ball, then bash each ball into a patty. Arrange the patties in the basket.
5. Select Air Fry, Super Convection, set temperature to 350ºF (180ºC) and set time to 10 minutes. Select Start/Stop to begin preheating.
6. Once the oven has preheated, place the basket on the air fry position. Flip the patties with tongs halfway through the cooking time.
7. When cooked, the patties will be well browned.
8. Assemble the buns with the patties, then drizzle the mayo over the patties to make the burgers. Serve immediately.

Korean Bulgogi Burgers

Prep time: 15 minutes | Cook time: 10 minutes | Serves 4

Burgers:

1 pound (454 g) 85% lean ground beef	1 tablespoon soy sauce
2 tablespoons gochujang	1 tablespoon toasted sesame oil
¼ cup chopped scallions	2 teaspoons sugar
2 teaspoons minced garlic	½ teaspoon kosher salt
2 teaspoons minced fresh ginger	4 hamburger buns
	Cooking spray

Korean Mayo:

1 tablespoon gochujang	¼ cup chopped scallions
¼ cup mayonnaise	1 tablespoon toasted sesame oil
2 teaspoons sesame seeds	

1. Combine the ingredients for the burgers, except for the buns, in a large bowl. Stir to mix well, then wrap the bowl in plastic and refrigerate to marinate for at least an hour.
2. Spritz the air fry basket with cooking spray.
3. Divide the meat mixture into four portions and form into four balls. Bash the balls into patties.
4. Arrange the patties in the basket and spritz with cooking spray.
5. Select Air Fry, Super Convection, set temperature to 350ºF (180ºC) and set time to 10 minutes. Select Start/Stop to begin preheating.
6. Once the oven has preheated, place the basket on the air fry position. Flip the patties halfway through the cooking time.
7. Meanwhile, combine the ingredients for the Korean mayo in a small bowl. Stir to mix well.
8. When cooking is complete, the patties should be golden brown.
9. Remove the patties from the oven and assemble with the buns, then spread the Korean mayo over the patties to make the burgers. Serve immediately.

Mexican Spiced Chicken Burgers

Prep time: 15 minutes | Cook time: 20 minutes | Serves 6 to 8

4 skinless and boneless chicken breasts
1 small head of cauliflower, sliced into florets
1 jalapeño pepper
3 tablespoons smoked paprika
1 tablespoon thyme
1 tablespoon oregano
1 tablespoon mustard powder
1 teaspoon cayenne pepper
1 egg
Salt and ground black pepper, to taste
2 tomatoes, sliced
2 lettuce leaves, chopped
6 to 8 brioche buns, sliced lengthwise
¾ cup taco sauce
Cooking spray

1. Spritz the air fry basket with cooking spray. Set aside.
2. In a blender, add the cauliflower florets, jalapeño pepper, paprika, thyme, oregano, mustard powder and cayenne pepper and blend until the mixture has a texture similar to bread crumbs.
3. Transfer ¾ of the cauliflower mixture to a medium bowl and set aside. Beat the egg in a different bowl and set aside.
4. Add the chicken breasts to the blender with remaining cauliflower mixture. Sprinkle with salt and pepper. Blend until finely chopped and well mixed.
5. Remove the mixture from the blender and form into 6 to 8 patties. One by one, dredge each patty in the reserved cauliflower mixture, then into the egg. Dip them in the cauliflower mixture again for additional coating.
6. Place the coated patties into the basket and spritz with cooking spray.
7. Select Air Fry, Super Convection, set temperature to 350ºF (180ºC) and set time to 20 minutes. Select Start/Stop to begin preheating.
8. Once preheated, place the basket on the air fry position. Flip the patties halfway through the cooking time.
9. When cooking is complete, the patties should be golden and crispy.
10. Transfer the patties to a clean work surface and assemble with the buns, tomato slices, chopped lettuce leaves and taco sauce to make burgers. Serve and enjoy.

Empanadas de Pollo Verde

Prep time: 10 minutes | Cook time: 12 minutes | Makes 12 empanadas

1 cup boneless, skinless rotisserie chicken breast meat, chopped finely
¼ cup salsa verde
⅔ cup shredded Cheddar cheese
1 teaspoon ground cumin
1 teaspoon ground black pepper
2 purchased refrigerated pie crusts, from a minimum 14.1-ounce (400 g) box
1 large egg
2 tablespoons water
Cooking spray

1. Spritz the air fry basket with cooking spray. Set aside.
2. Combine the chicken meat, salsa verde, Cheddar, cumin, and black pepper in a large bowl. Stir to mix well. Set aside.
3. Unfold the pie crusts on a clean work surface, then use a large cookie cutter to cut out 3½-inch circles as much as possible.
4. Roll the remaining crusts to a ball and flatten into a circle which has the same thickness of the original crust. Cut out more 3½-inch circles until you have 12 circles in total.
5. Make the empanadas: Divide the chicken mixture in the middle of each circle, about 1½ tablespoons each. Dab the edges of the circle with water. Fold the circle in half over the filling to shape like a half-moon and press to seal, or you can press with a fork.
6. Whisk the egg with water in a small bowl.
7. Arrange the empanadas in the basket and spritz with cooking spray. Brush with whisked egg.
8. Select Air Fry, Super Convection, set temperature to 350ºF (180ºC) and set time to 12 minutes. Select Start/Stop to begin preheating.
9. Once preheated, place the basket on the air fry position. Flip the empanadas halfway through the cooking time.
10. When cooking is complete, the empanadas will be golden and crispy.
11. Serve immediately.

Chapter 3 Vegan and Vegetarian

Chapter 10 Casseroles, Frittata, and Quiche

Pimento and Turkey Casserole

Prep time: 10 minutes | Cook time: 32 minutes | Serves 4

1 pound (454 g) turkey breasts
1 tablespoon olive oil
2 boiled eggs, chopped
2 tablespoons chopped pimentos
¼ cup slivered almonds, chopped
¼ cup mayonnaise
½ cup diced celery
2 tablespoons chopped green onion
¼ cup cream of chicken soup
¼ cup bread crumbs
Salt and ground black pepper, to taste

1. Put the turkey breasts in a large bowl. Sprinkle with salt and ground black pepper and drizzle with olive oil. Toss to coat well.
2. Transfer the turkey in the air fry basket.
3. Select Air Fry, Super Convection. Set temperature to 390°F (199°C) and set time to 12 minutes. Press Start/Stop to begin preheating.
4. Once preheated, place the basket on the air fry position. Flip the turkey halfway through.
5. When cooking is complete, the turkey should be well browned.
6. Remove the turkey breasts from the oven and cut into cubes, then combine the chicken cubes with eggs, pimentos, almonds, mayo, celery, green onions, and chicken soup in a large bowl. Stir to mix.
7. Pour the mixture into a baking pan, then spread with bread crumbs.
8. Select Bake, Super Convection. Set time to 20 minutes. Place the pan on the bake position.
9. When cooking is complete, the eggs should be set.
10. Remove the baking pan from the oven and serve immediately.

Creamy Cauliflower and Pumpkin Casserole

Prep time: 15 minutes | Cook time: 50 minutes | Serves 6

1 cup chicken broth
2 cups cauliflower florets
1 cup canned pumpkin purée
¼ cup heavy cream
1 teaspoon vanilla extract
2 large eggs, beaten
$1/3$ cup unsalted butter, melted, plus more for greasing the pan
¼ cup sugar
1 teaspoon fine sea salt
Chopped fresh parsley leaves, for garnish

TOPPING:
½ cup blanched almond flour
1 cup chopped pecans
$1/3$ cup unsalted butter, melted
½ cup sugar

1. Pour the chicken broth in a baking pan, then add the cauliflower.
2. Select Bake, Super Convection, set temperature to 350°F (180°C) and set time to 20 minutes. Press Start/Stop to begin preheating.
3. Once preheated, place the pan on the bake position.
4. When cooking is complete, the cauliflower should be soft.
5. Meanwhile, combine the ingredients for the topping in a large bowl. Stir to mix well.
6. Pat the cauliflower dry with paper towels, then place in a food processor and pulse with pumpkin purée, heavy cream, vanilla extract, eggs, butter, sugar, and salt until smooth.
7. Clean the baking pan and grease with more butter, then pour the purée mixture in the pan. Spread the topping over the mixture.
8. Place the baking pan back to the oven. Select Bake, Super Convection and set time to 30 minutes.
9. When baking is complete, the topping of the casserole should be lightly browned.
10. Remove the casserole from the oven and serve with fresh parsley on top.

Pastrami and Bell Pepper Casserole

Prep time: 10 minutes | Cook time: 8 minutes | Serves 2

1 cup pastrami, sliced
1 bell pepper, chopped
¼ cup Greek yogurt
2 spring onions, chopped
½ cup Cheddar cheese, grated
4 eggs
¼ teaspoon ground black pepper
Sea salt, to taste
Cooking spray

1. Spritz a baking pan with cooking spray.
2. Whisk together all the ingredients in a large bowl. Stir to mix well. Pour the mixture into the baking pan.
3. Select Bake, Super Convection, set temperature to 330ºF (166ºC) and set time to 8 minutes. Press Start/Stop to begin preheating.
4. Once preheated, place the pan on the bake position.
5. When cooking is complete, the eggs should be set and the casserole edges should be lightly browned.
6. Remove the baking pan from the oven and allow to cool for 10 minutes before serving.

Ranch Cheddar Broccoli Casserole

Prep time: 5 minutes | Cook time: 30 minutes | Serves 6

4 cups broccoli florets
¼ cup heavy whipping cream
½ cup sharp Cheddar cheese, shredded
¼ cup ranch dressing
Kosher salt and ground black pepper, to taste

1. Combine all the ingredients in a large bowl. Toss to coat well broccoli well.
2. Pour the mixture into a baking pan.
3. Select Bake, Super Convection, set temperature to 375ºF (190ºC) and set time to 30 minutes. Press Start/Stop to begin preheating.
4. Once preheated, place the pan on the bake position.
5. When cooking is complete, the broccoli should be tender.
6. Remove the baking pan from the oven and serve immediately.

Mushroom and Spinach Frittata

Prep time: 10 minutes | Cook time: 8 minutes | Serves 2

1 cup chopped mushrooms
2 cups spinach, chopped
4 eggs, lightly beaten
3 ounces (85 g) Feta cheese, crumbled
2 tablespoons heavy cream
A handful of fresh parsley, chopped
Salt and ground black pepper, to taste
Cooking spray

1. Spritz a baking pan with cooking spray.
2. Whisk together all the ingredients in a large bowl. Stir to mix well.
3. Pour the mixture in the prepared baking pan.
4. Select Bake, Super Convection, set temperature to 350ºF (180ºC) and set time to 8 minutes. Press Start/Stop to begin preheating.
5. Once preheated, place the pan on the bake position. Stir the mixture halfway through.
6. When cooking is complete, the eggs should be set.
7. Serve immediately.

Half-and-Half Frittata

Prep time: 10 minutes | Cook time: 20 minutes | Serves 4

½ cup shredded Cheddar cheese
½ cup half-and-half
4 large eggs
2 tablespoons chopped scallion greens
2 tablespoons chopped fresh parsley
½ teaspoon kosher salt
½ teaspoon ground black pepper
Cooking spray

1. Spritz a baking pan with cooking spray.
2. Whisk together all the ingredients in a large bowl, then pour the mixture into the prepared baking pan.
3. Select Bake, Super Convection, set temperature to 300ºF (150ºC) and set time to 20 minutes. Press Start/Stop to begin preheating.
4. Once preheated, place the pan on the bake position. Stir the mixture halfway through.
5. When cooking is complete, the eggs should be set.
6. Serve immediately.

Sausage and Broccoli Egg Casserole

Prep time: 10 minutes | Cook time: 20 minutes | Serves 8

10 eggs
1 cup Cheddar cheese, shredded and divided
¾ cup heavy whipping cream
1 (12-ounce / 340-g) package cooked chicken sausage
1 cup broccoli, chopped
2 cloves garlic, minced
½ tablespoon salt
¼ tablespoon ground black pepper
Cooking spray

1. Spritz a baking pan with cooking spray.
2. Whisk the eggs with Cheddar and cream in a large bowl to mix well.
3. Combine the cooked sausage, broccoli, garlic, salt, and ground black pepper in a separate bowl. Stir to mix well.
4. Pour the sausage mixture into the baking pan, then spread the egg mixture over to cover.
5. Select Bake, Super Convection, set temperature to 400ºF (205ºC) and set time to 20 minutes. Press Start/Stop to begin preheating.
6. Once preheated, place the pan on the bake position.
7. When cooking is complete, the egg should be set and a toothpick inserted in the center should come out clean.
8. Serve immediately.

Ritzy Seafood Casserole

Prep time: 10 minutes | Cook time: 22 minutes | Serves 2

1 tablespoon olive oil
1 small yellow onion, chopped
2 garlic cloves, minced
4 ounces (113 g) tilapia pieces
4 ounces (113 g) rockfish pieces
½ teaspoon dried basil
Salt and ground white pepper, to taste
4 eggs, lightly beaten
1 tablespoon dry sherry
4 tablespoons cheese, shredded

1. Heat the olive oil in a nonstick skillet over medium-high heat until shimmering.
2. Add the onion and garlic and sauté for 2 minutes or until fragrant.
3. Add the tilapia, rockfish, basil, salt, and white pepper to the skillet. Sauté to combine well and transfer them on a baking pan.
4. Combine the eggs, sherry and cheese in a large bowl. Stir to mix well. Pour the mixture in the baking pan over the fish mixture.
5. Select Bake, Super Convection, set temperature to 360ºF (182ºC) and set time to 20 minutes. Press Start/Stop to begin preheating.
6. Once preheated, place the pan on the bake position.
7. When cooking is complete, the eggs should be set and the casserole edges should be lightly browned.
8. Serve immediately.

Beef and Mushroom Casserole

Prep time: 10 minutes | Cook time: 25 minutes | Serves 4

1½ pounds (680 g) beef steak
1 ounce (28 g) dry onion soup mix
2 cups sliced mushrooms
1 (14.5-ounce / 411-g) can cream of mushroom soup
½ cup beef broth
¼ cup red wine
3 garlic cloves, minced
1 whole onion, chopped

1. Put the beef steak in a large bowl, then sprinkle with dry onion soup mix. Toss to coat well.
2. Combine the mushrooms with mushroom soup, beef broth, red wine, garlic, and onion in a large bowl. Stir to mix well.
3. Transfer the beef steak in a baking pan, then pour in the mushroom mixture.
4. Select Bake, Super Convection, set temperature to 360ºF (182ºC) and set time to 25 minutes. Press Start/Stop to begin preheating.
5. Once preheated, place the pan on the bake position.
6. When cooking is complete, the mushrooms should be soft and the beef should be well browned.
7. Remove the baking pan from the oven and serve immediately.

Corn Kernels and Bell Pepper Casserole

Prep time: 10 minutes | Cook time: 20 minutes | Serves 4

1 cup corn kernels
¼ cup bell pepper, finely chopped
½ cup low-fat milk
1 large egg, beaten
½ cup yellow cornmeal
½ cup all-purpose flour
½ teaspoon baking powder
2 tablespoons melted unsalted butter
1 tablespoon granulated sugar
Pinch of cayenne pepper
¼ teaspoon kosher salt
Cooking spray

1. Spritz a baking pan with cooking spray.
2. Combine all the ingredients in a large bowl. Stir to mix well. Pour the mixture into the baking pan.
3. Select Bake, Super Convection, set temperature to 330ºF (166ºC) and set time to 20 minutes. Press Start/Stop to begin preheating.
4. Once preheated, place the pan on the bake position.
5. When cooking is complete, the casserole should be lightly browned and set.
6. Remove the baking pan from the oven and serve immediately.

Asparagus and Grits Casserole

Prep time: 5 minutes | Cook time: 30 minutes | Serves 4

10 fresh asparagus spears, cut into 1-inch pieces
2 cups cooked grits, cooled to room temperature
2 teaspoons Worcestershire sauce
1 egg, beaten
½ teaspoon garlic powder
¼ teaspoon salt
2 slices provolone cheese, crushed
Cooking spray

1. Spritz a baking pan with cooking spray.
2. Set the asparagus in the air fry basket. Spritz the asparagus with cooking spray.
3. Select Air Fry, Super Convection. Set temperature to 390ºF (199ºC) and set time to 5 minutes. Press Start/Stop to begin preheating.
4. Once preheated, place the basket on the air fry position. Flip the asparagus halfway through.
5. When cooking is complete, the asparagus should be lightly browned and crispy.
6. Meanwhile, combine the grits, Worcestershire sauce, egg, garlic powder, and salt in a bowl. Stir to mix well.
7. Pour half of the grits mixture in the prepared baking pan, then spread with fried asparagus.
8. Spread the cheese over the asparagus and pour the remaining grits over.
9. Select Bake, Super Convection. Set time to 25 minutes. Place the pan on the bake position.
10. When cooking is complete, the egg should be set.
11. Serve immediately.

Breakfast Sausage and Colorful Peppers Casserole

Prep time: 10 minutes | Cook time: 25 minutes | Serves 6

1 pound (454 g) minced breakfast sausage
1 yellow pepper, diced
1 red pepper, diced
1 green pepper, diced
1 sweet onion, diced
2 cups Cheddar cheese, shredded
6 eggs
Salt and freshly ground black pepper, to taste
Fresh parsley, for garnish

1. Cook the sausage in a nonstick skillet over medium heat for 10 minutes or until well browned. Stir constantly.
2. When the cooking is finished, transfer the cooked sausage to a baking pan and add the peppers and onion. Scatter with Cheddar cheese.
3. Whisk the eggs with salt and ground black pepper in a large bowl, then pour the mixture into the baking pan.
4. Select Bake, Super Convection, set temperature to 360ºF (182ºC) and set time to 15 minutes. Press Start/Stop to begin preheating.
5. Once preheated, place the pan on the bake position.
6. When cooking is complete, the egg should be set and the edges of the casserole should be lightly browned.
7. Remove the baking pan from the oven and top with fresh parsley before serving.

Double Cheese Green Bean Casserole

Prep time: 5 minutes | Cook time: 6 minutes | Serves 4

1 tablespoon melted butter
1 cup green beans
6 ounces (170 g) Cheddar cheese, shredded
7 ounces (198 g) Parmesan cheese, shredded
¼ cup heavy cream
Sea salt, to taste

1. Grease a baking pan with the melted butter.
2. Add the green beans, Cheddar, salt, and black pepper to the prepared baking pan. Stir to mix well, then spread the Parmesan and cream on top.
3. Select Bake, Super Convection, set temperature to 400ºF (205ºC) and set time to 6 minutes. Press Start/Stop to begin preheating.
4. Once preheated, place the pan on the bake position.
5. When cooking is complete, the beans should be tender and the cheese should be melted.
6. Serve immediately.

Smoky Trout and Crème Fraiche Frittata

Prep time: 10 minutes | Cook time: 17 minutes | Serves 4

2 tablespoons olive oil
1 onion, sliced
1 egg, beaten
½ tablespoon horseradish sauce
6 tablespoons crème fraiche
1 cup diced smoked trout
2 tablespoons chopped fresh dill
Cooking spray

1. Spritz a baking pan with cooking spray.
2. Heat the olive oil in a nonstick skillet over medium heat until shimmering.
3. Add the onion and sauté for 3 minutes or until translucent.
4. Combine the egg, horseradish sauce, and crème fraiche in a large bowl. Stir to mix well, then mix in the sautéed onion, smoked trout, and dill.
5. Pour the mixture in the prepared baking pan.
6. Select Bake, Super Convection, set temperature to 350ºF (180ºC) and set time to 14 minutes. Press Start/Stop to begin preheating.
7. Once preheated, place the pan on the bake position. Stir the mixture halfway through.
8. When cooking is complete, the egg should be set and the edges should be lightly browned.
9. Serve immediately.

Asparagus and Goat Cheese Frittata

Prep time: 10 minutes | Cook time: 25 minutes | Serves 2 to 4

1 cup asparagus spears, cut into 1-inch pieces
1 teaspoon vegetable oil
1 tablespoon milk
6 eggs, beaten
2 ounces (57 g) goat cheese, crumbled
1 tablespoon minced chives, optional
Kosher salt and pepper, to taste

1. Add the asparagus spears to a small bowl and drizzle with the vegetable oil. Toss until well coated and transfer to the air fry basket.
2. Select Air Fry, Super Convection. Set temperature to 400ºF (205ºC) and set time to 5 minutes. Press Start/Stop to begin preheating.
3. Once preheated, place the basket on the air fry position. Flip the asparagus halfway through.
4. When cooking is complete, the asparagus should be tender and slightly wilted.
5. Remove the asparagus from the oven to a baking pan.
6. Stir together the milk and eggs in a medium bowl. Pour the mixture over the asparagus in the pan. Sprinkle with the goat cheese and the chives (if using) over the eggs. Season with salt and pepper.
7. Select Bake, Super Convection, set temperature to 320ºF (160ºC) and set time to 20 minutes. Press Start/Stop. Place the pan on the bake position.
8. When cooking is complete, the top should be golden and the eggs should be set.
9. Transfer to a serving dish. Slice and serve.

Okra and Cauliflower Casserole

Prep time: 8 minutes | Cook time: 12 minutes | Serves 4

1 head cauliflower, cut into florets
1 cup okra, chopped
1 yellow bell pepper, chopped
2 eggs, beaten
½ cup chopped onion
1 tablespoon soy sauce
2 tablespoons olive oil
Salt and ground black pepper, to taste

1. Spritz a baking pan with cooking spray.
2. Put the cauliflower in a food processor and pulse to rice the cauliflower.
3. Pour the cauliflower rice in the baking pan and add the remaining ingredients. Stir to mix well.
4. Select Bake, Super Convection, set temperature to 380ºF (193ºC) and set time to 12 minutes. Press Start/Stop to begin preheating.
5. Once preheated, place the pan on the bake position.
6. When cooking is complete, the eggs should be set.
7. Remove the baking pan from the oven and serve immediately.

Chicken Broccoli Divan

Prep time: 5 minutes | Cook time: 24 minutes | Serves 4

4 chicken breasts
Salt and ground black pepper, to taste
1 head broccoli, cut into florets
½ cup cream of mushroom soup
1 cup shredded Cheddar cheese
½ cup croutons
Cooking spray

1. Spritz the air fry basket with cooking spray.
2. Put the chicken breasts in the air fry basket and sprinkle with salt and ground black pepper.
3. Select Air Fry, Super Convection. Set temperature to 390ºF (199ºC) and set time to 14 minutes. Press Start/Stop to begin preheating.
4. Once preheated, place the basket on the air fry position. Flip the breasts halfway through the cooking time.
5. When cooking is complete, the breasts should be well browned and tender.
6. Remove the breasts from the oven and allow to cool for a few minutes on a plate, then cut the breasts into bite-size pieces.
7. Combine the chicken, broccoli, mushroom soup, and Cheddar cheese in a large bowl. Stir to mix well.
8. Spritz a baking pan with cooking spray. Pour the chicken mixture into the pan. Spread the croutons over the mixture.
9. Select Bake, Super Convection. Set time to 10 minutes. Place the pan on the bake position.
10. When cooking is complete, the croutons should be lightly browned and the mixture should be set.
11. Remove the baking pan from the oven and serve immediately.

Beef and Green Chile Casserole

Prep time: 10 minutes | Cook time: 15 minutes | Serves 4

1 pound (454 g) 85% lean ground beef
1 tablespoon taco seasoning
1 (7-ounce / 198-g) can diced mild green chiles
½ cup milk
2 large eggs
1 cup shredded Mexican cheese blend
2 tablespoons all-purpose flour
½ teaspoon kosher salt
Cooking spray

1. Spritz a baking pan with cooking spray.
2. Toss the ground beef with taco seasoning in a large bowl to mix well. Pour the seasoned ground beef in the prepared baking pan.
3. Combing the remaining ingredients in a medium bowl. Whisk to mix well, then pour the mixture over the ground beef.
4. Select Bake, Super Convection, set temperature to 350ºF (180ºC) and set time to 15 minutes. Press Start/Stop to begin preheating.
5. Once preheated, place the pan on the bake position.
6. When cooking is complete, a toothpick inserted in the center should come out clean.
7. Remove the casserole from the oven and allow to cool for 5 minutes, then slice to serve.

Swiss Chicken and Ham Casserole

Prep time: 10 minutes | Cook time: 15 minutes | Serves 4 to 6

2 cups diced cooked chicken
1 cup diced ham
¼ teaspoon ground nutmeg
½ cup half-and-half
½ teaspoon ground black pepper
6 slices Swiss cheese
Cooking spray

1. Spritz a baking pan with cooking spray.
2. Combine the chicken, ham, nutmeg, half-and-half, and ground black pepper in a large bowl. Stir to mix well.
3. Pour half of the mixture into the baking pan, then top the mixture with 3 slices of Swiss cheese, then pour in the remaining mixture and top with remaining cheese slices.
4. Select Bake, Super Convection, set temperature to 350ºF (180ºC) and set time to 15 minutes. Press Start/Stop to begin preheating.
5. Once preheated, place the pan on the bake position.
6. When cooking is complete, the egg should be set and the cheese should be melted.
7. Serve immediately.

Classic Mediterranean Quiche

Prep time: 10 minutes | Cook time: 30 minutes | Serves 4

4 eggs
¼ cup chopped Kalamata olives
½ cup chopped tomatoes
¼ cup chopped onion
½ cup milk
1 cup crumbled feta cheese
½ tablespoon chopped oregano
½ tablespoon chopped basil
Salt and ground black pepper, to taste
Cooking spray

1. Spritz a baking pan with cooking spray.
2. Whisk the eggs with remaining ingredients in a large bowl. Stir to mix well.
3. Pour the mixture into the prepared baking pan.
4. Select Bake, Super Convection, set temperature to 340ºF (171ºC) and set time to 30 minutes. Press Start/Stop to begin preheating.
5. Once preheated, place the pan on the bake position.
6. When cooking is complete, the eggs should be set and a toothpick inserted in the center should come out clean.
7. Serve immediately.

Beef and Cannellini Casserole

Prep time: 15 minutes | Cook time: 31 minutes | Serves 4

1 tablespoon olive oil
½ cup finely chopped bell pepper
½ cup chopped celery
1 onion, chopped
2 garlic cloves, minced
1 pound (454 g) ground beef
1 can diced tomatoes
½ teaspoon parsley
½ tablespoon chili powder
1 teaspoon chopped cilantro
1½ cups vegetable broth
1 (8-ounce / 227-g) can cannellini beans
Salt and ground black pepper, to taste

1. Heat the olive oil in a nonstick skillet over medium heat until shimmering.
2. Add the bell pepper, celery, onion, and garlic to the skillet and sauté for 5 minutes or until the onion is translucent.
3. Add the ground beef and sauté for an additional 6 minutes or until lightly browned.
4. Mix in the tomatoes, parsley, chili powder, cilantro and vegetable broth, then cook for 10 more minutes. Stir constantly.
5. Pour them in a baking pan, then mix in the beans and sprinkle with salt and ground black pepper.
6. Select Bake, Super Convection, set temperature to 350ºF (180ºC) and set time to 10 minutes. Press Start/Stop to begin preheating.
7. Once preheated, place the pan on the bake position.
8. When cooking is complete, the vegetables should be tender and the beef should be well browned.
9. Remove the baking pan from the oven and serve immediately.

Chicken and Veggies Casserole

Prep time: 15 minutes | Cook time: 15 minutes | Serves 4

4 boneless and skinless chicken breasts, cut into cubes
2 carrots, sliced
1 yellow bell pepper, cut into strips
1 red bell pepper, cut into strips
15 ounces (425 g) broccoli florets
1 cup snow peas
1 scallion, sliced
Cooking spray

Sauce:
1 teaspoon Sriracha
3 tablespoons soy sauce
2 tablespoons oyster sauce
1 tablespoon rice wine vinegar
1 teaspoon cornstarch
1 tablespoon grated ginger
2 garlic cloves, minced
1 teaspoon sesame oil
1 tablespoon brown sugar

1. Spritz a baking pan with cooking spray.
2. Combine the chicken, carrot, and bell peppers in a large bowl. Stir to mix well.
3. Combine the ingredients for the sauce in a separate bowl. Stir to mix well.
4. Pour the chicken mixture into the baking pan, then pour the sauce over. Stir to coat well.
5. Select Bake, Super Convection, set temperature to 370ºF (188ºC) and set time to 13 minutes. Press Start/Stop to begin preheating.
6. Once preheated, place the pan on the bake position. Add the broccoli and snow peas to the pan halfway through.
7. When cooking is complete, the vegetables should be tender.
8. Remove the pan from the oven and sprinkle with sliced scallion before serving.

Shrimp and Baby Spinach Frittata

Prep time: 6 minutes | Cook time: 14 minutes | Serves 4

4 whole eggs
1 teaspoon dried basil
½ cup shrimp, cooked and chopped
½ cup baby spinach
½ cup rice, cooked
½ cup Monterey Jack cheese, grated
Salt, to taste
Cooking spray

1. Spritz a baking pan with cooking spray.
2. Whisk the eggs with basil and salt in a large bowl until bubbly, then mix in the shrimp, spinach, rice, and cheese.
3. Pour the mixture into the baking pan.
4. Select Bake, Super Convection, set temperature to 360ºF (182ºC) and set time to 14 minutes. Press Start/Stop to begin preheating.
5. Once preheated, place the pan on the bake position. Stir the mixture halfway through.
6. When cooking is complete, the eggs should be set and the frittata should be golden brown.
7. Slice to serve.

Spinach, Chickpea and Tomato Casserole

Prep time: 10 minutes | Cook time: 21 to 22 minutes | Serves 4

2 tablespoons olive oil
2 garlic cloves, minced
1 tablespoon ginger, minced
1 onion, chopped
1 chili pepper, minced
Salt and ground black pepper, to taste
1 pound (454 g) spinach
1 can coconut milk
½ cup dried tomatoes, chopped
1 (14-ounce / 397-g) can chickpeas, drained

1. Heat the olive oil in a saucepan over medium heat. Sauté the garlic and ginger in the olive oil for 1 minute, or until fragrant.
2. Add the onion, chili pepper, salt and pepper to the saucepan. Sauté for 3 minutes.
3. Mix in the spinach and sauté for 3 to 4 minutes or until the vegetables become soft. Remove from heat.
4. Pour the vegetable mixture into a baking pan. Stir in coconut milk, dried tomatoes and chickpeas until well blended.
5. Select Bake, Super Convection, set temperature to 370ºF (188ºC) and set time to 15 minutes. Press Start/Stop to begin preheating.
6. Once preheated, place the pan on the bake position.
7. When cooking is complete, transfer the casserole to a serving dish. Let cool for 5 minutes before serving.

Broccoli, Tomato, and Carrot Quiche

Prep time: 10 minutes | Cook time: 14 minutes | Serves 4

4 eggs
1 teaspoon dried thyme
1 cup whole milk
1 steamed carrots, diced
2 cups steamed broccoli florets
2 medium tomatoes, diced
¼ cup crumbled feta cheese
1 cup grated Cheddar cheese
1 teaspoon chopped parsley
Salt and ground black pepper, to taste
Cooking spray

1. Spritz a baking pan with cooking spray.
2. Whisk together the eggs, thyme, salt, and ground black pepper in a bowl and fold in the milk while mixing.
3. Put the carrots, broccoli, and tomatoes in the prepared baking pan, then spread with feta cheese and ½ cup Cheddar cheese. Pour the egg mixture over, then scatter with remaining Cheddar on top.
4. Select Bake, Super Convection, set temperature to 350ºF (180ºC) and set time to 14 minutes. Press Start/Stop to begin preheating.
5. Once preheated, place the pan on the bake position.
6. When cooking is complete, the egg should be set and the quiche should be puffed.
7. Remove the quiche from the oven and top with chopped parsley, then slice to serve.

Pork Gratin

Prep time: 10 minutes | Cook time: 21 minutes | Serves 4

2 tablespoons olive oil
2 pounds (907 g) pork tenderloin, cut into serving-size pieces
1 teaspoon dried marjoram
¼ teaspoon chili powder
1 teaspoon coarse sea salt
½ teaspoon freshly ground black pepper
1 cup Ricotta cheese
1½ cups chicken broth
1 tablespoon mustard
Cooking spray

1. Spritz a baking pan with cooking spray.
2. Heat the olive oil in a nonstick skillet over medium-high heat until shimmering.
3. Add the pork and sauté for 6 minutes or until lightly browned.
4. Transfer the pork to the prepared baking pan and sprinkle with marjoram, chili powder, salt, and ground black pepper.
5. Combine the remaining ingredients in a large bowl. Stir to mix well. Pour the mixture over the pork in the pan.
6. Select Bake, Super Convection, set temperature to 350ºF (180ºC) and set time to 15 minutes. Press Start/Stop to begin preheating.
7. Once preheated, place the pan on the bake position. Stir the mixture halfway through.
8. When cooking is complete, the mixture should be frothy and the cheese should be melted.
9. Serve immediately.

Chorizo, Potato, and Corn Frittata

Prep time: 10 minutes | Cook time: 12 minutes | Serves 4

2 tablespoons olive oil
1 chorizo, sliced
4 eggs
½ cup corn
1 large potato, boiled and cubed
1 tablespoon chopped parsley
½ cup Feta cheese, crumbled
Salt and ground black pepper, to taste

1. Heat the olive oil in a nonstick skillet over medium heat until shimmering.
2. Add the chorizo and cook for 4 minutes or until golden brown.
3. Whisk the eggs in a bowl, then sprinkle with salt and ground black pepper.
4. Mix the remaining ingredients in the egg mixture, then pour the chorizo and its fat into a baking pan. Pour in the egg mixture.
5. Select Bake, Super Convection, set temperature to 330ºF (166ºC) and set time to 8 minutes. Press Start/Stop to begin preheating.
6. Once preheated, place the pan on the bake position. Stir the mixture halfway through.
7. When cooking is complete, the eggs should be set.
8. Serve immediately.

Lush Veggies Frittata

Prep time: 15 minutes | Cook time: 20 minutes | Serves 2

4 eggs
1/3 cup milk
2 teaspoons olive oil
1 large zucchini, sliced
2 asparagus, sliced thinly
1/3 cup sliced mushrooms
1 cup baby spinach
1 small red onion, sliced
1/3 cup crumbled Feta cheese
1/3 cup grated Cheddar cheese
¼ cup chopped chives
Salt and ground black pepper, to taste

1. Line a baking pan with parchment paper.
2. Whisk together the eggs, milk, salt, and ground black pepper in a large bowl. Set aside.
3. Heat the olive oil in a nonstick skillet over medium heat until shimmering.
4. Add the zucchini, asparagus, mushrooms, spinach, and onion to the skillet and sauté for 5 minutes or until tender.
5. Pour the sautéed vegetables into the prepared baking pan, then spread the egg mixture over and scatter with cheeses.
6. Select Bake, Super Convection, set temperature to 380ºF (193ºC) and set time to 15 minutes. Press Start/Stop to begin preheating.
7. Once preheated, place the pan on the bake position. Stir the mixture halfway through.
8. When cooking is complete, the egg should be set and the edges should be lightly browned.
9. Remove the frittata from the oven and sprinkle with chives before serving.

Keto Cheesy Quiche

Prep time: 20 minutes | Cook time: 1 hour | Serves 8

Crust:
1¼ cups blanched almond flour
1 large egg, beaten
1¼ cups grated Parmesan cheese
¼ teaspoon fine sea salt

Filling:
4 ounces (113 g) cream cheese
1 cup shredded Swiss cheese
1/3 cup minced leeks
4 large eggs, beaten
½ cup chicken broth
1/8 teaspoon cayenne pepper
¾ teaspoon fine sea salt
1 tablespoon unsalted butter, melted
Chopped green onions, for garnish
Cooking spray

1. Spritz a pie pan with cooking spray.
2. Combine the flour, egg, Parmesan, and salt in a large bowl. Stir to mix until a satiny and firm dough forms.
3. Arrange the dough between two grease parchment papers, then roll the dough into a 1/16-inch thick circle.
4. Make the crust: Transfer the dough into the prepared pie pan and press to coat the bottom.
5. Select Bake, Super Convection, set temperature to 325ºF (163ºC) and set time to 12 minutes. Press Start/Stop to begin preheating.
6. Once preheated, place the pan on the bake position.
7. When cooking is complete, the edges of the crust should be lightly browned.
8. Meanwhile, combine the ingredient for the filling, except for the green onions in a large bowl.
9. Pour the filling over the cooked crust and cover the edges of the crust with aluminum foil.
10. Select Bake, Super Convection. Set time to 15 minutes. Press Start/Stop. Place the pan on the bake position.
11. When cooking is complete, reduce the heat to 300ºF (150ºC) and set time to 30 minutes.
12. When cooking is complete, a toothpick inserted in the center should come out clean.
13. Remove the pie pan from the oven and allow to cool for 10 minutes before serving.

Chapter 11 Holiday Specials

Mexican Churros

Prep time: 10 minutes | Cook time: 10 minutes | Makes 12 churros

- 4 tablespoons butter
- ¼ teaspoon salt
- ½ cup water
- ½ cup all-purpose flour
- 2 large eggs
- 2 teaspoons ground cinnamon
- ¼ cup granulated white sugar
- Cooking spray

1. Put the butter, salt, and water in a saucepan. Bring to a boil until the butter is melted on high heat. Keep stirring.
2. Reduce the heat to medium and fold in the flour to form a dough. Keep cooking and stirring until the dough is dried out and coat the pan with a crust.
3. Turn off the heat and scrape the dough in a large bowl. Allow to cool for 15 minutes.
4. Break and whisk the eggs into the dough with a hand mixer until the dough is sanity and firm enough to shape.
5. Scoop up 1 tablespoon of the dough and roll it into a ½-inch-diameter and 2-inch-long cylinder. Repeat with remaining dough to make 12 cylinders in total.
6. Combine the cinnamon and sugar in a large bowl and dunk the cylinders into the cinnamon mix to coat.
7. Arrange the cylinders on a plate and refrigerate for 20 minutes.
8. Spritz the air fry basket with cooking spray. Place the cylinders in the air fry basket and spritz with cooking spray.
9. Select Air Fry, Super Convection, set temperature to 375ºF (190ºC) and set time to 10 minutes. Select Start/Stop to begin preheating.
10. Once preheated, place the basket on the air fry position. Flip the cylinders halfway through the cooking time.
11. When cooked, the cylinders should be golden brown and fluffy.
12. Serve immediately.

Buttermilk Banana Cake

Prep time: 15 minutes | Cook time: 20 minutes | Serves 8

- 1 cup plus 1 tablespoon all-purpose flour
- ¼ teaspoon baking soda
- ¾ teaspoon baking powder
- ¼ teaspoon salt
- 9½ tablespoons granulated white sugar
- 5 tablespoons butter, at room temperature
- 2½ small ripe bananas, peeled
- 2 large eggs
- 5 tablespoons buttermilk
- 1 teaspoon vanilla extract
- Cooking spray

1. Spritz a baking pan with cooking spray.
2. Combine the flour, baking soda, baking powder, and salt in a large bowl. Stir to mix well.
3. Beat the sugar and butter in a separate bowl with a hand mixer on medium speed for 3 minutes.
4. Beat in the bananas, eggs, buttermilk, and vanilla extract into the sugar and butter mix with a hand mixer.
5. Pour in the flour mixture and whip with hand mixer until sanity and smooth.
6. Scrape the batter into the pan and level the batter with a spatula.
7. Select Bake, Super Convection, set temperature to 325ºF (163ºC) and set time to 20 minutes. Select Start/Stop to begin preheating.
8. Once the oven has preheated, place the pan on the bake position.
9. After 15 minutes, remove the pan from the oven. Check the doneness. Return the pan to the oven and continue cooking.
10. When done, a toothpick inserted in the center should come out clean.
11. Invert the cake on a cooling rack and allow to cool for 15 minutes before slicing to serve.

Pork, Cabbage and Mushroom Egg Rolls

Prep time: 20 minutes | Cook time: 33 minutes | Makes 25 egg rolls

Egg Rolls:
1 tablespoon mirin
3 tablespoons soy sauce, divided
1 pound (454 g) ground pork
3 tablespoons vegetable oil, plus more for brushing
5 ounces (142 g) shiitake mushrooms, minced
4 cups shredded Napa cabbage
¼ cup sliced scallions
1 teaspoon grated fresh ginger
1 clove garlic, minced
¼ teaspoon cornstarch
1 (1-pound / 454-g) package frozen egg roll wrappers, thawed

Dipping Sauce:
1 scallion, white and light green parts only, sliced
¼ cup rice vinegar
¼ cup soy sauce
Pinch sesame seeds
Pinch red pepper flakes
1 teaspoon granulated sugar

1. Line the air fry basket with parchment paper. Set aside.
2. Combine the mirin and 1 tablespoon of soy sauce in a large bowl. Stir to mix well.
3. Dunk the ground pork in the mixture and stir to mix well. Wrap the bowl in plastic and marinate in the refrigerator for at least 10 minutes.
4. Heat the vegetable oil in a nonstick skillet over medium-high heat until shimmering. Add the mushrooms, cabbage, and scallions and sauté for 5 minutes or until tender.
5. Add the marinated meat, ginger, garlic, and remaining 2 tablespoons of soy sauce. Sauté for 3 minutes or until the pork is lightly browned. Turn off the heat and allow to cool until ready to use.
6. Put the cornstarch in a small bowl and pour in enough water to dissolve the cornstarch. Put the bowl alongside a clean work surface.
7. Put the egg roll wrappers in the air fry basket.
8. Select Air Fry, Super Convection, set temperature to 400ºF (205ºC) and set time to 15 minutes. Select Start/Stop to begin preheating.
9. Once preheated, place the basket on the air fry position. Flip the wrappers halfway through the cooking time.
10. When cooked, the wrappers will be golden brown. Remove the egg roll wrappers from the oven and allow to cool for 10 minutes or until you can handle them with your hands.
11. Lay out one egg roll wrapper on the work surface with a corner pointed toward you. Place 2 tablespoons of the pork mixture on the egg roll wrapper and fold corner up over the mixture. Fold left and right corners toward the center and continue to roll. Brush a bit of the dissolved cornstarch on the last corner to help seal the egg wrapper. Repeat with remaining wrappers to make 25 egg rolls in total.
12. Arrange the rolls in the basket and brush the rolls with more vegetable oil.
13. Select Air Fry and set time to 10 minutes. Place the basket on the air fry position When done, the rolls should be well browned and crispy.
14. Meanwhile, combine the ingredients for the dipping sauce in a small bowl. Stir to mix well.
15. Serve the rolls with the dipping sauce immediately.

Blistered Cherry Tomatoes

Prep time: 5 minutes | Cook time: 10 minutes | Serves 4 to 6

2 pounds (907 g) cherry tomatoes
2 tablespoons olive oil
2 teaspoons balsamic vinegar
½ teaspoon salt
½ teaspoon ground black pepper

1. Toss the cherry tomatoes with olive oil in a large bowl to coat well. Pour the tomatoes in a baking pan.
2. Select Air Fry, Super Convection, set temperature to 400ºF (205ºC) and set time to 10 minutes. Select Start/Stop to begin preheating.
3. Once preheated, slide the pan into the oven. Stir the tomatoes halfway through the cooking time.
4. When cooking is complete, the tomatoes will be blistered and lightly wilted.
5. Transfer the blistered tomatoes to a large bowl and toss with balsamic vinegar, salt, and black pepper before serving.

Baked Butter Cake

Prep time: 10 minutes | Cook time: 20 minutes | Serves 8

1 cup all-purpose flour	9½ tablespoons butter, at room temperature
1¼ teaspoons baking powder	2 large eggs
¼ teaspoon salt	1 large egg yolk
½ cup plus 1½ tablespoons granulated white sugar	2½ tablespoons milk
	1 teaspoon vanilla extract
	Cooking spray

1. Spritz a baking pan with cooking spray.
2. Combine the flour, baking powder, and salt in a large bowl. Stir to mix well.
3. Whip the sugar and butter in a separate bowl with a hand mixer on medium speed for 3 minutes.
4. Whip the eggs, egg yolk, milk, and vanilla extract into the sugar and butter mix with a hand mixer.
5. Pour in the flour mixture and whip with hand mixer until sanity and smooth.
6. Scrape the batter into the baking pan and level the batter with a spatula.
7. Select Bake, Super Convection, set temperature to 325ºF (163ºC) and set time to 20 minutes. Select Start/Stop to begin preheating.
8. Once the oven has preheated, place the pan on the bake position.
9. After 15 minutes, remove the pan from the oven. Check the doneness. Return the pan to the oven and continue cooking.
10. When done, a toothpick inserted in the center should come out clean.
11. Invert the cake on a cooling rack and allow to cool for 15 minutes before slicing to serve.

Chocolate Glazed Custard Donut Holes

Prep time: 20 minutes | Cook time: 4 minutes | Makes 24 donut holes

Dough:

1½ cups bread flour	vanilla extract
2 egg yolks	2 tablespoons butter, melted
1 teaspoon active dry yeast	1 tablespoon sugar
½ cup warm milk	¼ teaspoon salt
½ teaspoon pure	Cooking spray

Custard Filling:

1 (3.4-ounce / 96-g) box French vanilla instant pudding mix	¾ cup whole milk
¼ cup heavy cream	**Chocolate Glaze:**
	⅓ cup heavy cream
	1 cup chocolate chips

Special Equipment:
A pastry bag with a long tip

1. Combine the ingredients for the dough in a food processor, then pulse until a satiny dough ball forms.
2. Transfer the dough on a lightly floured work surface, then knead for 2 minutes by hand and shape the dough back to a ball.
3. Spritz a large bowl with cooking spray, then transfer the dough ball into the bowl. Wrap the bowl in plastic and let it rise for 1½ hours or until it doubled in size.
4. Transfer the risen dough on a floured work surface, then shape it into a 24-inch long log. Cut the log into 24 parts and shape each part into a ball.
5. Transfer the balls on two baking sheets and let sit to rise for 30 more minutes.
6. Spritz the balls with cooking spray.
7. Select Bake, Super Convection, set temperature to 400ºF (205ºC) and set time to 4 minutes. Select Start/Stop to begin preheating.
8. Once preheated, place the baking sheets on the bake position. Flip the balls halfway through the cooking time.
9. When cooked, the balls should be golden brown.
10. Meanwhile, combine the ingredients for the filling in a large bowl and whisk for 2 minutes with a hand mixer until well combined.
11. Pour the heavy cream in a saucepan, then bring to a boil. Put the chocolate chips in a small bowl and pour in the boiled heavy cream immediately. Mix until the chocolate chips are melted and the mixture is smooth.
12. Transfer the baked donut holes to a large plate, then pierce a hole into each donut hole and lightly hollow them.
13. Pour the filling in a pastry bag with a long tip and gently squeeze the filling into the donut holes. Then top the donut holes with chocolate glaze.
14. Allow to sit for 10 minutes, then serve.

Pickle Spears with Buttermilk Dressing

Prep time: 25 minutes | Cook time: 8 minutes | Serves 6 to 8

Buttermilk Dressing:
- ¼ cup buttermilk
- ¼ cup chopped scallions
- ¾ cup mayonnaise
- ½ cup sour cream
- ½ teaspoon cayenne pepper
- ½ teaspoon onion powder
- ½ teaspoon garlic powder
- 1 tablespoon chopped chives
- 2 tablespoons chopped fresh dill
- Kosher salt and ground black pepper, to taste

Fried Dill Pickles:
- ¾ cup all-purpose flour
- 1 (2-pound / 907-g) jar kosher dill pickles, cut into 4 spears, drained
- 2½ cups panko bread crumbs
- 2 eggs, beaten with 2 tablespoons water
- Kosher salt and ground black pepper, to taste
- Cooking spray

1. Combine the ingredients for the dressing in a bowl. Stir to mix well.
2. Wrap the bowl in plastic and refrigerate for 30 minutes or until ready to serve.
3. Pour the flour in a bowl and sprinkle with salt and ground black pepper. Stir to mix well. Put the bread crumbs in a separate bowl. Pour the beaten eggs in a third bowl.
4. Dredge the pickle spears in the flour, then into the eggs, and then into the panko to coat well. Shake the excess off.
5. Arrange the pickle spears in a single layer in the air fry basket and spritz with cooking spray.
6. Select Air Fry, Super Convection, set temperature to 400ºF (205ºC) and set time to 8 minutes. Select Start/Stop to begin preheating.
7. Once the oven has preheated, place the basket on the air fry position. Flip the pickle spears halfway through the cooking time.
8. When cooking is complete, remove the pan from the oven.
9. Serve the pickle spears with buttermilk dressing.

Marinated Olive Stromboli

Prep time: 10 minutes | Cook time: 25 minutes | Serves 8

- 4 large cloves garlic, unpeeled
- 3 tablespoons grated Parmesan cheese
- ½ cup packed fresh basil leaves
- ½ cup marinated, pitted green and black olives
- ¼ teaspoon crushed red pepper
- ½ pound (227 g) pizza dough, at room temperature
- 4 ounces (113 g) sliced provolone cheese (about 8 slices)
- Cooking spray

1. Spritz the air fry basket with cooking spray. Put the unpeeled garlic in the air fry basket.
2. Select Air Fry, Super Convection, set temperature to 370ºF (188ºC) and set time to 10 minutes. Select Start/Stop to begin preheating.
3. Once preheated, place the basket on the air fry position.
4. When cooked, the garlic will be softened completely. Remove from the oven and allow to cool until you can handle.
5. Peel the garlic and place into a food processor with 2 tablespoons of Parmesan, basil, olives, and crushed red pepper. Pulse to mix well. Set aside.
6. Arrange the pizza dough on a clean work surface, then roll it out with a rolling pin into a rectangle. Cut the rectangle in half.
7. Sprinkle half of the garlic mixture over each rectangle half, and leave ½-inch edges uncover. Top them with the provolone cheese.
8. Brush one long side of each rectangle half with water, then roll them up. Spritz the air fry basket with cooking spray. Transfer the rolls to the air fry basket. Spritz with cooking spray and scatter with remaining Parmesan.
9. Select Air Fry and set time to 15 minutes. Place the basket on the air fry position. Flip the rolls halfway through the cooking time. When done, the rolls should be golden brown.
10. Remove the rolls from the oven and allow to cool for a few minutes before serving.

Mini Crescent Dogs

Prep time: 10 minutes | Cook time: 8 minutes | Makes 16 rolls

1 can refrigerated crescent roll dough
1 small package mini smoked sausages, patted dry
2 tablespoons melted butter
2 teaspoons sesame seeds
1 teaspoon onion powder

1. Place the crescent roll dough on a clean work surface and separate into 8 pieces. Cut each piece in half and you will have 16 triangles.
2. Make the pigs in the blanket: Arrange each sausage on each dough triangle, then roll the sausages up.
3. Brush the pigs with melted butter and place of the pigs in the blanket in the air fry basket. Sprinkle with sesame seeds and onion powder.
4. Select Bake, Super Convection, set temperature to 330ºF (166ºC) and set time to 8 minutes. Select Start/Stop to begin preheating.
5. Once the oven has preheated, place the basket on the bake position. Flip the pigs halfway through the cooking time.
6. When cooking is complete, the pigs should be fluffy and golden brown.
7. Serve immediately.

Coconut Chocolate Macaroons

Prep time: 10 minutes | Cook time: 8 minutes | Makes 24 macaroons

3 large egg whites, at room temperature
¼ teaspoon salt
¾ cup granulated white sugar
4½ tablespoons unsweetened cocoa powder
2¼ cups unsweetened shredded coconut

1. Line the air fry basket with parchment paper.
2. Whisk the egg whites with salt in a large bowl with a hand mixer on high speed until stiff peaks form.
3. Whisk in the sugar with the hand mixer on high speed until the mixture is thick. Mix in the cocoa powder and coconut.
4. Scoop 2 tablespoons of the mixture and shape the mixture in a ball. Repeat with remaining mixture to make 24 balls in total.
5. Arrange the balls in a single layer in the air fry basket and leave a little space between each two balls.
6. Select Air Fry, Super Convection, set temperature to 375ºF (190ºC) and set time to 8 minutes. Select Start/Stop to begin preheating.
7. Once the oven has preheated, place the basket on the air fry position.
8. When cooking is complete, the balls should be golden brown.
9. Serve immediately.

Blintzes

Prep time: 5 minutes | Cook time: 10 minutes | Makes 8 blintzes

2 (7½-ounce / 213-g) packages farmer cheese, mashed
¼ cup cream cheese
¼ teaspoon vanilla extract
¼ cup granulated white sugar
8 egg roll wrappers
4 tablespoons butter, melted

1. Combine the farmer cheese, cream cheese, vanilla extract, and sugar in a bowl. Stir to mix well.
2. Unfold the egg roll wrappers on a clean work surface, spread ¼ cup of the filling at the edge of each wrapper and leave a ½-inch edge uncovering.
3. Wet the edges of the wrappers with water and fold the uncovered edge over the filling. Fold the left and right sides in the center, then tuck the edge under the filling and fold to wrap the filling.
4. Brush the wrappers with melted butter, then arrange the wrappers in a single layer in the air fry basket, seam side down. Leave a little space between each two wrappers.
5. Select Air Fry, Super Convection, set temperature to 375ºF (190ºC) and set time to 10 minutes. Select Start/Stop to begin preheating.
6. Once preheated, place the basket on the air fry position.
7. When cooking is complete, the wrappers will be golden brown.
8. Serve immediately.

Arancini Balls

Prep time: 5 minutes | Cook time: 30 minutes | Makes 10 balls

2/3 cup raw white Arborio rice
2 teaspoons butter
½ teaspoon salt
1 1/3 cups water
2 large eggs, well beaten
1¼ cups seasoned Italian-style dried bread crumbs
10 ¾-inch semi-firm Mozzarella cubes
Cooking spray

1. Pour the rice, butter, salt, and water in a pot. Stir to mix well and bring a boil over medium-high heat. Keep stirring.
2. Reduce the heat to low and cover the pot. Simmer for 20 minutes or until the rice is tender.
3. Turn off the heat and let sit, covered, for 10 minutes, then open the lid and fluffy the rice with a fork. Allow to cool for 10 more minutes.
4. Pour the beaten eggs in a bowl, then pour the bread crumbs in a separate bowl.
5. Scoop 2 tablespoons of the cooked rice up and form it into a ball, then press the Mozzarella into the ball and wrap.
6. Dredge the ball in the eggs first, then shake the excess off the dunk the ball in the bread crumbs. Roll to coat evenly. Repeat to make 10 balls in total with remaining rice.
7. Transfer the balls in the air fry basket and spritz with cooking spray.
8. Select Air Fry, Super Convection, set temperature to 375ºF (190ºC) and set time to 10 minutes. Select Start/Stop to begin preheating.
9. Once preheated, place the basket on the air fry position.
10. When cooking is complete, the balls should be lightly browned and crispy.
11. Remove the balls from the oven and allow to cool before serving.

Nuggets

Prep time: 10 minutes | Cook time: 4 minutes | Makes 20 nuggets

1 cup all-purpose flour, plus more for dusting
1 teaspoon baking powder
½ teaspoon butter, at room temperature, plus more for brushing
¼ teaspoon salt
¼ cup water
1/8 teaspoon onion powder
¼ teaspoon garlic powder
1/8 teaspoon seasoning salt
Cooking spray

1. Line the air fry basket with parchment paper.
2. Mix the flour, baking powder, butter, and salt in a large bowl. Stir to mix well. Gradually whisk in the water until a sanity dough forms.
3. Put the dough on a lightly floured work surface, then roll it out into a ½-inch thick rectangle with a rolling pin.
4. Cut the dough into about twenty 1- or 2-inch squares, then arrange the squares in a single layer in the air fry basket. Spritz with cooking spray.
5. Combine onion powder, garlic powder, and seasoning salt in a small bowl. Stir to mix well, then sprinkle the squares with the powder mixture.
6. Select Air Fry, Super Convection, set temperature to 370ºF (188ºC) and set time to 4 minutes. Select Start/Stop to begin preheating.
7. Once the oven has preheated, place the basket on the air fry position. Flip the squares halfway through the cooking time.
8. When cooked, the dough squares should be golden brown.
9. Remove the golden nuggets from the oven and brush with more butter immediately. Serve warm.

Cream Glazed Cinnamon Rolls

Prep time: 10 minutes | Cook time: 5 minutes | Serves 8

1 pound (454 g) frozen bread dough, thawed
2 tablespoons melted butter
Cream Glaze:
4 ounces (113 g) softened cream cheese
½ teaspoon vanilla extract
1½ tablespoons cinnamon
¾ cup brown sugar
Cooking spray
2 tablespoons melted butter
1¼ cups powdered erythritol

1. Place the bread dough on a clean work surface, then roll the dough out into a rectangle with a rolling pin.
2. Brush the top of the dough with melted butter and leave 1-inch edges uncovered.
3. Combine the cinnamon and sugar in a small bowl, then sprinkle the dough with the cinnamon mixture.
4. Roll the dough over tightly, then cut the dough log into 8 portions. Wrap the portions in plastic, better separately, and let sit to rise for 1 or 2 hours.
5. Meanwhile, combine the ingredients for the glaze in a separate small bowl. Stir to mix well.
6. Spritz the air fry basket with cooking spray. Transfer the risen rolls to the air fry basket.
7. Select Air Fry, Super Convection, set temperature to 350ºF (180ºC) and set time to 5 minutes. Select Start/Stop to begin preheating.
8. Once the oven has preheated, place the basket on the air fry position. Flip the rolls halfway through the cooking time.
9. When cooking is complete, the rolls will be golden brown.
10. Serve the rolls with the glaze.

Brazilian Cheese Bread

Prep time: 10 minutes | Cook time: 12 minutes | Makes 12 balls

2 tablespoons butter, plus more for greasing
½ cup milk
1½ cups tapioca flour
½ teaspoon salt
1 large egg
⅔ cup finely grated aged Asiago cheese

1. Put the butter in a saucepan and pour in the milk, heat over medium heat until the liquid boils. Keep stirring.
2. Turn off the heat and mix in the tapioca flour and salt to form a soft dough. Transfer the dough in a large bowl, then wrap the bowl in plastic and let sit for 15 minutes.
3. Break the egg in the bowl of dough and whisk with a hand mixer for 2 minutes or until a sanity dough forms. Fold the cheese in the dough. Cover the bowl in plastic again and let sit for 10 more minutes.
4. Grease a baking pan with butter.
5. Scoop 2 tablespoons of the dough into the baking pan. Repeat with the remaining dough to make dough 12 balls. Keep a little distance between each two balls.
6. Select Bake, Super Convection, set temperature to 375ºF (190ºC) and set time to 12 minutes. Select Start/Stop to begin preheating.
7. Once preheated, place the pan on the bake position. Flip the balls halfway through the cooking time.
8. When cooking is complete, the balls should be golden brown and fluffy.
9. Remove the balls from the oven and allow to cool for 5 minutes before serving.

Panko-Kale Salad Sushi Rolls

Prep time: 15 minutes | Cook time: 10 minutes | Serves 12

Kale Salad:
1½ cups chopped kale
1 tablespoon sesame seeds
¾ teaspoon soy sauce
¾ teaspoon toasted sesame oil
½ teaspoon rice vinegar
¼ teaspoon ginger
⅛ teaspoon garlic powder

Sushi Rolls:
3 sheets sushi nori
1 batch cauliflower rice
½ avocado, sliced

Sriracha Mayonnaise:
¼ cup Sriracha sauce
¼ cup vegan mayonnaise

Coating:
½ cup panko bread crumbs

1. In a medium bowl, toss all the ingredients for the salad together until well coated and set aside.
2. Place a sheet of nori on a clean work surface and spread the cauliflower rice in an even layer on the nori. Scoop 2 to 3 tablespoon of kale salad on the rice and spread over. Place 1 or 2 avocado slices on top. Roll up the sushi, pressing gently to get a nice, tight roll. Repeat to make the remaining 2 rolls.
3. In a bowl, stir together the Sriracha sauce and mayonnaise until smooth. Add bread crumbs to a separate bowl.
4. Dredge the sushi rolls in Sriracha Mayonnaise, then roll in bread crumbs till well coated.
5. Place the coated sushi rolls in the air fry basket.
6. Select Air Fry, Super Convection, set temperature to 390°F (199°C) and set time to 10 minutes. Select Start/Stop to begin preheating.
7. Once the oven has preheated, place the basket on the air fry position. Flip the sushi rolls halfway through the cooking time.
8. When cooking is complete, the sushi rolls will be golden brown and crispy. .
9. Transfer to a platter and rest for 5 minutes before slicing each roll into 8 pieces. Serve warm.

Sweet Pecan Tart

Prep time: 15 minutes | Cook time: 26 minutes | Serves 8

Tart Crust:
¼ cup firmly packed brown sugar
⅓ cup butter, softened
1 cup all-purpose flour
¼ teaspoon kosher salt

Filling:
¼ cup whole milk
4 tablespoons butter, diced
½ cup packed brown sugar
¼ cup pure maple syrup
1½ cups finely chopped pecans
¼ teaspoon pure vanilla extract
¼ teaspoon sea salt

1. Line a baking pan with aluminum foil, then spritz the pan with cooking spray.
2. Stir the brown sugar and butter in a bowl with a hand mixer until puffed, then add the flour and salt and stir until crumbled.
3. Pour the mixture in the prepared baking pan and tilt the pan to coat the bottom evenly.
4. Select Bake, Super Convection, set temperature to 350°F (180°C) and set time to 13 minutes. Select Start/Stop to begin preheating.
5. Once the oven has preheated, place the pan on the bake position.
6. When done, the crust will be golden brown.
7. Meanwhile, pour the milk, butter, sugar, and maple syrup in a saucepan. Stir to mix well. Bring to a simmer, then cook for 1 more minute. Stir constantly.
8. Turn off the heat and mix the pecans and vanilla into the filling mixture.
9. Pour the filling mixture over the golden crust and spread with a spatula to coat the crust evenly.
10. Select Bake, Super Convection and set time to 12 minutes. Place the pan on the bake position. When cooked, the filling mixture should be set and frothy.
11. Remove the baking pan from the oven and sprinkle with salt. Allow to sit for 10 minutes or until cooled.
12. Transfer the pan to the refrigerator to chill for at least 2 hours, then remove the aluminum foil and slice to serve.

Sriracha Panko-Crusted Shrimp

Prep time: 15 minutes | Cook time: 10 minutes | Serves 4

1 tablespoon Sriracha sauce
1 teaspoon Worcestershire sauce
2 tablespoons sweet chili sauce
¾ cup mayonnaise
1 egg, beaten
1 cup panko bread crumbs
1 pound (454 g) raw shrimp, shelled and deveined, rinsed and drained
Lime wedges, for serving
Cooking spray

1. Spritz the air fry basket with cooking spray.
2. Combine the Sriracha sauce, Worcestershire sauce, chili sauce, and mayo in a bowl. Stir to mix well. Reserve ⅓ cup of the mixture as the dipping sauce.
3. Combine the remaining sauce mixture with the beaten egg. Stir to mix well. Put the panko in a separate bowl.
4. Dredge the shrimp in the sauce mixture first, then into the panko. Roll the shrimp to coat well. Shake the excess off.
5. Place the shrimp in the air fry basket, then spritz with cooking spray.
6. Select Air Fry, Super Convection, set temperature to 360°F (182°C) and set time to 10 minutes. Select Start/Stop to begin preheating.
7. Once preheated, place the basket on the air fry position. Flip the shrimp halfway through the cooking time.
8. When cooking is complete, the shrimp should be opaque.
9. Remove the shrimp from the oven and serve with reserve sauce mixture and squeeze the lime wedges over.

Teriyaki Panko-Shrimp Skewers

Prep time: 10 minutes | Cook time: 6 minutes | Makes 12 skewered shrimp

1½ tablespoons mirin
1½ teaspoons ginger juice
1½ tablespoons soy sauce
12 large shrimp (about 20 shrimps per pound), peeled and deveined
1 large egg
¾ cup panko bread crumbs
Cooking spray

1. Combine the mirin, ginger juice, and soy sauce in a large bowl. Stir to mix well.
2. Dunk the shrimp in the bowl of mirin mixture, then wrap the bowl in plastic and refrigerate for 1 hour to marinate.
3. Spritz the air fry basket with cooking spray.
4. Run twelve 4-inch skewers through each shrimp.
5. Whisk the egg in the bowl of marinade to combine well. Pour the bread crumbs on a plate.
6. Dredge the shrimp skewers in the egg mixture, then shake the excess off and roll over the bread crumbs to coat well.
7. Arrange the shrimp skewers in the air fry basket and spritz with cooking spray.
8. Select Air Fry, Super Convection, set temperature to 400°F (205°C) and set time to 6 minutes. Select Start/Stop to begin preheating.
9. Once preheated, place the basket on the air fry position. Flip the shrimp skewers halfway through the cooking time.
10. When done, the shrimp will be opaque and firm.
11. Serve immediately.

Risotto Croquettes

Prep time: 25 minutes | Cook time: 54 minutes | Serves 6

Risotto Croquettes:
- 4 tablespoons unsalted butter
- 1 small yellow onion, minced
- 1 cup Arborio rice
- 3½ cups chicken stock
- ½ cup dry white wine
- 3 eggs
- Zest of 1 lemon
- ½ cup grated Parmesan cheese
- 2 ounces (57 g) fresh Mozzarella cheese
- ¼ cup peas
- 2 tablespoons water
- ½ cup all-purpose flour
- 1½ cups panko bread crumbs
- Kosher salt and ground black pepper, to taste
- Cooking spray

Tomato Sauce:
- 2 tablespoons extra-virgin olive oil
- 4 cloves garlic, minced
- ¼ teaspoon red pepper flakes
- 1 (28-ounce / 794-g) can crushed tomatoes
- 2 teaspoons granulated sugar
- Kosher salt and ground black pepper, to taste

1. Melt the butter in a pot over medium heat, then add the onion and salt to taste. Sauté for 5 minutes or until the onion in translucent.
2. Add the rice and stir to coat well. Cook for 3 minutes or until the rice is lightly browned. Pour in the chicken stock and wine.
3. Bring to a boil. Then cook for 20 minutes or until the rice is tender and liquid is almost absorbed.
4. Make the risotto: When the rice is cooked, break the egg into the pot. Add the lemon zest and Parmesan cheese. Sprinkle with salt and ground black pepper. Stir to mix well.
5. Pour the risotto in a baking sheet, then level with a spatula to spread the risotto evenly. Wrap the baking sheet in plastic and refrigerate for 1 hour.
6. Meanwhile, heat the olive oil in a saucepan over medium heat until shimmering.
7. Add the garlic and sprinkle with red pepper flakes. Sauté for a minute or until fragrant.
8. Add the crushed tomatoes and sprinkle with sugar. Stir to mix well. Bring to a boil. Reduce the heat to low and simmer for 15 minutes or until lightly thickened. Sprinkle with salt and pepper to taste. Set aside until ready to serve.
9. Remove the risotto from the refrigerator. Scoop the risotto into twelve 2-inch balls, then flatten the balls with your hands.
10. Arrange a about ½-inch piece of Mozzarella and 5 peas in the center of each flattened ball, then wrap them back into balls.
11. Transfer the balls to a baking sheet lined with parchment paper, then refrigerate for 15 minutes or until firm.
12. Whisk the remaining 2 eggs with 2 tablespoons of water in a bowl. Pour the flour in a second bowl and pour the panko in a third bowl.
13. Dredge the risotto balls in the bowl of flour first, then into the eggs, and then into the panko. Shake the excess off.
14. Transfer the balls to the air fry basket and spritz with cooking spray.
15. Select Bake, Super Convection, set temperature to 400ºF (205ºC) and set time to 10 minutes. Select Start/Stop to begin preheating.
16. Once the oven has preheated, place the basket on the bake position. Flip the balls halfway through the cooking time.
17. When cooking is complete, the balls should be until golden brown.
18. Serve the risotto balls with the tomato sauce.

Chapter 12 Fast and Easy Everyday Favorites

Quick Edamame

Prep time: 5 minutes | Cook time: 7 minutes | Serves 6

1½ pounds (680 g) unshelled edamame
2 tablespoons olive oil
1 teaspoon sea salt

1. Place the edamame in a large bowl, then drizzle with olive oil. Toss to coat well. Transfer the edamame to the air fry basket.
2. Select Air Fry, Super Convection, set temperature to 400ºF (205ºC) and set time to 7 minutes. Select Start/Stop to begin preheating.
3. Once preheated, place the basket on the air fry position. Stir the edamame at least three times during cooking.
4. When done, the edamame will be tender and warmed through.
5. Transfer the cooked edamame onto a plate and sprinkle with salt. Toss to combine well and set aside for 3 minutes to infuse before serving.

Okra Chips

Prep time: 5 minutes | Cook time: 16 minutes | Serves 6

2 pounds (907 g) fresh okra pods, cut into 1-inch pieces
2 tablespoons canola oil
1 teaspoon coarse sea salt

1. Stir the oil and salt in a bowl to mix well. Add the okra and toss to coat well. Place the okra in the air fry basket.
2. Select Air Fry, Super Convection, set temperature to 400ºF (205ºC) and set time to 16 minutes. Select Start/Stop to begin preheating.
3. Once the oven has preheated, place the basket on the air fry position. Flip the okra at least three times during cooking.
4. When cooked, the okra should be lightly browned. Remove from the oven.
5. Serve immediately.

Cinnamon-Sugar Chickpeas

Prep time: 5 minutes | Cook time: 10 minutes | Serves 2

1 tablespoon cinnamon
1 tablespoon sugar
1 cup chickpeas, soaked in water overnight, rinsed and drained

1. Combine the cinnamon and sugar in a bowl. Stir to mix well.
2. Add the chickpeas to the bowl, then toss to coat well.
3. Pour the chickpeas in the air fry basket.
4. Select Air Fry, Super Convection, set temperature to 390ºF (199ºC) and set time to 10 minutes. Select Start/Stop to begin preheating.
5. Once the oven has preheated, place the basket on the air fry position. Stir the chickpeas three times during cooking.
6. When cooked, the chickpeas should be golden brown and crispy. Remove the basket from the oven.
7. Serve immediately.

Hot Chicken Wings

Prep time: 5 minutes | Cook time: 15 minutes | Makes 16 wings

16 chicken wings
3 tablespoons hot sauce
Cooking spray

1. Spritz the air fry basket with cooking spray.
2. Arrange the chicken wings in the air fry basket.
3. Select Air Fry, Super Convection, set temperature to 360ºF (182ºC) and set time to 15 minutes. Select Start/Stop to begin preheating.
4. Once preheated, place the basket on the air fry position. Flip the wings at lease three times during cooking.
5. When cooking is complete, the chicken wings will be well browned. Remove the pan from the oven.
6. Transfer the air fried wings to a plate and serve with hot sauce.

Crunchy Tortilla Chips

Prep time: 5 minutes | Cook time: 10 minutes | Serves 4

4 six-inch corn tortillas, cut in half and slice into thirds
1 tablespoon canola oil
¼ teaspoon kosher salt
Cooking spray

1. Spritz the air fry basket with cooking spray.
2. On a clean work surface, brush the tortilla chips with canola oil, then transfer the chips to the air fry basket.
3. Select Air Fry, Super Convection, set temperature to 360°F (182°C) and set time to 10 minutes. Select Start/Stop to begin preheating.
4. Once preheated, place the basket on the air fry position. Flip the chips and sprinkle with salt halfway through the cooking time.
5. When cooked, the chips will be crunchy and lightly browned. Transfer the chips to a plate lined with paper towels. Serve immediately.

Blistered Shishito Peppers

Prep time: 5 minutes | Cook time: 5 minutes | Serves 4

½ pound (227 g) shishito peppers (about 24)
1 tablespoon olive oil
Coarse sea salt, to taste
Lemon wedges, for serving
Cooking spray

1. Spritz the air fry basket with cooking spray.
2. Toss the peppers with olive oil in a large bowl to coat well.
3. Arrange the peppers in the air fry basket.
4. Select Air Fry, Super Convection, set temperature to 400°F (205°C) and set time to 5 minutes. Select Start/Stop to begin preheating.
5. Once preheated, place the basket on the air fry position. Flip the peppers and sprinkle the peppers with salt halfway through the cooking time.
6. When cooked, the peppers should be blistered and lightly charred. Transfer the peppers onto a plate and squeeze the lemon wedges on top before serving.

Canadian Poutine

Prep time: 15 minutes | Cook time: 33 minutes | Serves 2

2 russet potatoes, scrubbed and cut into ½-inch sticks
2 teaspoons vegetable oil
2 tablespoons butter
¼ onion, minced
¼ teaspoon dried thyme
1 clove garlic, smashed
3 tablespoons all-purpose flour
1 teaspoon tomato paste
1½ cups beef stock
2 teaspoons Worcestershire sauce
Salt and freshly ground black pepper, to taste
⅔ cup chopped string cheese

1. Bring a pot of water to a boil, then put in the potato sticks and blanch for 4 minutes.
2. Drain the potato sticks and rinse under running cold water, then pat dry with paper towels.
3. Transfer the sticks in a large bowl and drizzle with vegetable oil. Toss to coat well. Place the potato sticks in the air fry basket.
4. Select Air Fry, Super Convection, set temperature to 400°F (205°C) and set time to 25 minutes. Select Start/Stop to begin preheating.
5. Once preheated, place the basket on the air fry position. Stir the potato sticks at least three times during cooking.
6. Meanwhile, make the gravy: Heat the butter in a saucepan over medium heat until melted.
7. Add the onion, thyme, and garlic and sauté for 5 minutes or until the onion is translucent.
8. Add the flour and sauté for an additional 2 minutes. Pour in the tomato paste and beef stock and cook for 1 more minute or until lightly thickened.
9. Drizzle the gravy with Worcestershire sauce and sprinkle with salt and ground black pepper. Reduce the heat to low to keep the gravy warm until ready to serve.
10. When done, the sticks should be golden brown. Remove the basket from the oven. Transfer the fried potato sticks onto a plate, then sprinkle with salt and ground black pepper. Scatter with string cheese and pour the gravy over. Serve warm.

Crispy Zucchini

Prep time: 5 minutes | Cook time: 10 minutes | Serves 4

1 medium zucchini, cut into 48 sticks
¼ cup seasoned bread crumbs
1 tablespoon melted buttery spread
Cooking spray

1. Spritz the air fry basket with cooking spray and set aside.
2. In 2 different shallow bowls, add the seasoned bread crumbs and the buttery spread.
3. One by one, dredge the zucchini sticks into the buttery spread, then roll in the bread crumbs to coat evenly. Arrange the crusted sticks in the air fry basket.
4. Select Air Fry, Super Convection, set temperature to 360°F (182°C) and set time to 10 minutes. Select Start/Stop to begin preheating.
5. When preheated, place the basket on the air fry position. Stir the sticks halfway through the cooking time.
6. When done, the sticks should be golden brown and crispy. Transfer the fries to a plate. Rest for 5 minutes and serve warm.

Beer Battered Onion Rings

Prep time: 10 minutes | Cook time: 16 minutes | Serves 2 to 4

⅔ cup all-purpose flour
1 teaspoon paprika
½ teaspoon baking soda
1 teaspoon salt
½ teaspoon freshly ground black pepper
1 egg, beaten
¾ cup beer
1½ cups bread crumbs
1 tablespoons olive oil
1 large Vidalia onion, peeled and sliced into ½-inch rings
Cooking spray

1. Spritz the air fry basket with cooking spray.
2. Combine the flour, paprika, baking soda, salt, and ground black pepper in a bowl. Stir to mix well.
3. Combine the egg and beer in a separate bowl. Stir to mix well.
4. Make a well in the center of the flour mixture, then pour the egg mixture in the well. Stir to mix everything well.
5. Pour the bread crumbs and olive oil in a shallow plate. Stir to mix well.
6. Dredge the onion rings gently into the flour and egg mixture, then shake the excess off and put into the plate of bread crumbs. Flip to coat the both sides well. Arrange the onion rings in the air fry basket.
7. Select Air Fry, Super Convection, set temperature to 360°F (182°C) and set time to 16 minutes. Select Start/Stop to begin preheating.
8. Once preheated, place the basket on the air fry position. Flip the rings and put the bottom rings to the top halfway through.
9. When cooked, the rings will be golden brown and crunchy. Remove the pan from the oven.
10. Serve immediately.

Fast Corn on the Cob

Prep time: 10 minutes | Cook time: 10 minutes | Serves 4

2 tablespoons mayonnaise
2 teaspoons minced garlic
½ teaspoon sea salt
1 cup panko bread crumbs
4 (4-inch length) ears corn on the cob, husk and silk removed
Cooking spray

1. Spritz the air fry basket with cooking spray.
2. Combine the mayonnaise, garlic, and salt in a bowl. Stir to mix well. Pour the panko on a plate.
3. Brush the corn on the cob with mayonnaise mixture, then roll the cob in the bread crumbs and press to coat well.
4. Transfer the corn on the cob in the air fry basket and spritz with cooking spray.
5. Select Air Fry, Super Convection, set temperature to 400°F (205°C) and set time to 10 minutes. Select Start/Stop to begin preheating.
6. Once the oven has preheated, place the basket on the air fry position. Flip the corn on the cob at least three times during the cooking.
7. When cooked, the corn kernels on the cob should be almost browned. Remove the basket from the oven.
8. Serve immediately.

Butternut Squash with Fried-Hazelnuts

Prep time: 10 minutes | Cook time: 23 minutes | Makes 3 cups

2 tablespoons whole hazelnuts
3 cups butternut squash, peeled, deseeded and cubed
¼ teaspoon kosher salt
¼ teaspoon freshly ground black pepper
2 teaspoons olive oil
Cooking spray

1. Spritz the air fry basket with cooking spray. Spread the hazelnuts in the basket.
2. Select Air Fry, Super Convection, set temperature to 300°F (150°C) and set time to 3 minutes. Select Start/Stop to begin preheating.
3. Once preheated, place the basket on the air fry position.
4. When done, the hazelnuts should be soft. Remove from the oven. Chopped the hazelnuts roughly and transfer to a small bowl. Set aside.
5. Put the butternut squash in a large bowl, then sprinkle with salt and pepper and drizzle with olive oil. Toss to coat well. Transfer the squash to the lightly greased basket.
6. Select Air Fry, Super Convection, set temperature to 360°F (182°C) and set time to 20 minutes.
7. Place the basket on the air fry position. Flip the squash halfway through the cooking time.
8. When cooking is complete, the squash will be soft. Transfer the squash to a plate and sprinkle with the chopped hazelnuts before serving.

Jalapeño Cheddar Cornbread

Prep time: 10 minutes | Cook time: 20 minutes | Serves 8

⅔ cup cornmeal
⅓ cup all-purpose flour
¾ teaspoon baking powder
2 tablespoons buttery spread, melted
½ teaspoon kosher salt
1 tablespoon granulated sugar
¾ cup whole milk
1 large egg, beaten
1 jalapeño pepper, thinly sliced
⅓ cup shredded sharp Cheddar cheese
Cooking spray

1. Spritz a baking pan with cooking spray.
2. Combine all the ingredients in a large bowl. Stir to mix well. Pour the mixture in the baking pan.
3. Select Bake, Super Convection, set temperature to 300°F (150°C) and set time to 20 minutes. Select Start/Stop to begin preheating.
4. Once preheated, place the pan on the bake position.
5. When the cooking is complete, a toothpick inserted in the center of the bread should come out clean.
6. Remove the baking pan from the oven and allow the bread to cool for 5 minutes before slicing to serve.

Maple Bacon Pinwheels

Prep time: 5 minutes | Cook time: 10 minutes | Makes 8 pinwheels

1 sheet puff pastry
2 tablespoons maple syrup
¼ cup brown sugar
8 slices bacon
Ground black pepper, to taste
Cooking spray

1. Spritz the air fry basket with cooking spray.
2. Roll the puff pastry into a 10-inch square with a rolling pin on a clean work surface, then cut the pastry into 8 strips.
3. Brush the strips with maple syrup and sprinkle with sugar, leaving a 1-inch far end uncovered.
4. Arrange each slice of bacon on each strip, leaving a ⅛-inch length of bacon hang over the end close to you. Sprinkle with black pepper.
5. From the end close to you, roll the strips into pinwheels, then dab the uncovered end with water and seal the rolls.
6. Arrange the pinwheels in the air fry basket and spritz with cooking spray.
7. Select Air Fry, Super Convection, set temperature to 360°F (182°C) and set time to 10 minutes. Select Start/Stop to begin preheating.
8. Once preheated, place the basket on the air fry position. Flip the pinwheels halfway through.
9. When cooking is complete, the pinwheels should be golden brown. Remove the pan from the oven.
10. Serve immediately.

French Fries with Ketchup

Prep time: 5 minutes | Cook time: 25 minutes | Serves 2

2 russet potatoes, peeled and cut into ½-inch sticks
2 teaspoons olive oil
Salt, to taste
¼ cup ketchup, for serving

1. Bring a pot of salted water to a boil. Put the potato sticks into the pot and blanch for 4 minutes.
2. Rinse the potatoes under running cold water and pat dry with paper towels.
3. Put the potato sticks in a large bowl and drizzle with olive oil. Toss to coat well.
4. Transfer the potato sticks to the air fry basket.
5. Select Air Fry, Super Convection, set temperature to 400°F (205°C) and set time to 25 minutes. Select Start/Stop to begin preheating.
6. Once the oven has preheated, place the basket on the air fry position. Stir the potato sticks and sprinkle with salt halfway through.
7. When cooked, the potato sticks will be crispy and golden brown. Remove the French fries from the oven and serve with ketchup.

Greek Spinach Pie with Feta

Prep time: 10 minutes | Cook time: 8 minutes | Serves 6

½ (10-ounce / 284-g) package frozen spinach, thawed and squeezed dry
1 egg, lightly beaten
¼ cup pine nuts, toasted
¼ cup grated Parmesan cheese
¾ cup crumbled feta cheese
⅛ teaspoon ground nutmeg
½ teaspoon salt
Freshly ground black pepper, to taste
6 sheets phyllo dough
½ cup butter, melted

1. Combine all the ingredients, except for the phyllo dough and butter, in a large bowl. Whisk to combine well. Set aside.
2. Place a sheet of phyllo dough on a clean work surface. Brush with butter then top with another layer sheet of phyllo. Brush with butter, then cut the layered sheets into six 3-inch-wide strips.
3. Top each strip with 1 tablespoon of the spinach mixture, then fold the bottom left corner over the mixture towards the right strip edge to make a triangle. Keep folding triangles until each strip is folded over.
4. Brush the triangles with butter and repeat with remaining strips and phyllo dough.
5. Place the triangles in the baking pan.
6. Select Air Fry, Super Convection, set temperature to 350°F (180°C) and set time to 8 minutes. Select Start/Stop to begin preheating.
7. Once the oven has preheated, place the pan into the oven. Flip the triangles halfway through the cooking time.
8. When cooking is complete, the triangles should be golden brown. Remove the pan from the oven.
9. Serve immediately.

Parmesan Cauliflower Patties

Prep time: 5 minutes | Cook time: 8 minutes | Serves 6

2 cups cooked cauliflower
1 cup panko bread crumbs
1 large egg, beaten
½ cup grated Parmesan cheese
1 tablespoon chopped fresh chives
Cooking spray

1. Spritz the air fry basket with cooking spray.
2. Put the cauliflower, panko bread crumbs, egg, Parmesan, and chives in a food processor, then pulse to lightly mash and combine the mixture until chunky and thick.
3. Shape the mixture into 6 flat patties, then arrange them in the air fry basket and spritz with cooking spray.
4. Select Air Fry, Super Convection, set temperature to 390°F (199°C) and set time to 8 minutes. Select Start/Stop to begin preheating.
5. Once preheated, place the basket on the air fry position. Flip the patties halfway through the cooking time.
6. When done, the patties should be crispy and golden brown. Remove the basket from the oven.
7. Serve immediately.

Candy Coated Pecans

Prep time: 5 minutes | Cook time: 10 minutes | Makes 4 cups

2 egg whites
1 tablespoon cumin
2 teaspoons smoked paprika
½ cup brown sugar
2 teaspoons kosher salt
1 pound (454 g) pecan halves
Cooking spray

1. Spritz the air fry basket with cooking spray.
2. Combine the egg whites, cumin, paprika, sugar, and salt in a large bowl. Stir to mix well. Add the pecans to the bowl and toss to coat well.
3. Transfer the pecans to the air fry basket.
4. Select Air Fry, Super Convection, set temperature to 300°F (150°C) and set time to 10 minutes. Select Start/Stop to begin preheating.
5. Once the oven has preheated, place the basket on the air fry position. Stir the pecans at least two times during the cooking.
6. When cooking is complete, the pecans should be lightly caramelized. Remove the basket from the oven.
7. Serve immediately.

Panko-Green Tomatoes Slices

Prep time: 10 minutes | Cook time: 8 minutes | Makes 12 slices

½ cup all-purpose flour
1 egg
½ cup buttermilk
1 cup cornmeal
1 cup panko
2 green tomatoes, cut into ¼-inch-thick slices, patted dry
½ teaspoon salt
½ teaspoon ground black pepper
Cooking spray

1. Spritz a baking sheet with cooking spray.
2. Pour the flour in a bowl. Whisk the egg and buttermilk in a second bowl. Combine the cornmeal and panko in a third bowl.
3. Dredge the tomato slices in the bowl of flour first, then into the egg mixture, and then dunk the slices into the cornmeal mixture. Shake the excess off.
4. Transfer the well-coated tomato slices in the baking sheet and sprinkle with salt and ground black pepper. Spritz the tomato slices with cooking spray.
5. Select Air Fry, Super Convection, set temperature to 400°F (205°C) and set time to 8 minutes. Select Start/Stop to begin preheating.
6. Once preheated, slide the baking sheet into the oven. Flip the slices halfway through the cooking time.
7. When cooking is complete, the tomato slices should be crispy and lightly browned. Remove the baking sheet from the oven.
8. Serve immediately.

Buttered Knots with Parsley

Prep time: 5 minutes | Cook time: 5 minutes | Makes 8 knots

1 teaspoon dried parsley
¼ cup melted butter
2 teaspoons garlic powder
1 (11-ounce / 312-g) tube refrigerated French bread dough, cut into 8 slices

1. Combine the parsley, butter, and garlic powder in a bowl. Stir to mix well.
2. Place the French bread dough slices on a clean work surface, then roll each slice into a 6-inch long rope. Tie the ropes into knots and arrange them on a plate.
3. Transfer the knots into a baking pan. Brush the knots with butter mixture.
4. Select Air Fry, Super Convection, set temperature to 350°F (180°C) and set time to 5 minutes. Select Start/Stop to begin preheating.
5. Once the oven has preheated, slide the pan into the oven. Flip the knots halfway through the cooking time.
6. When done, the knots should be golden brown. Remove the pan from the oven.
7. Serve immediately.

Parsnip Fries with Creamy Yogurt Dip

Prep time: 10 minutes | Cook time: 10 minutes | Serves 4

3 medium parsnips, peeled, cut into sticks
¼ teaspoon kosher salt
Dip:
¼ cup plain Greek yogurt
⅛ teaspoon garlic powder
1 tablespoon sour cream
¼ teaspoon kosher salt
Freshly ground black pepper, to taste
1 teaspoon olive oil
1 garlic clove, unpeeled
Cooking spray

1. Spritz the air fry basket with cooking spray.
2. Put the parsnip sticks in a large bowl, then sprinkle with salt and drizzle with olive oil.
3. Transfer the parsnip into the air fry basket and add the garlic.
4. Select Air Fry, Super Convection, set temperature to 360°F (182°C) and set time to 10 minutes. Select Start/Stop to begin preheating.
5. Once preheated, place the basket on the air fry position. Stir the parsnip halfway through the cooking time.
6. Meanwhile, peel the garlic and crush it. Combine the crushed garlic with the ingredients for the dip. Stir to mix well.
7. When cooked, the parsnip sticks should be crisp. Remove the parsnip fries from the oven and serve with the dipping sauce.

Potato Latkes

Prep time: 5 minutes | Cook time: 10 minutes | Makes 4 latkes

1 egg
2 tablespoons all-purpose flour
2 medium potatoes, peeled and shredded, rinsed and drained
¼ teaspoon granulated garlic
½ teaspoon salt
Cooking spray

1. Spritz the air fry basket with cooking spray.
2. Whisk together the egg, flour, potatoes, garlic, and salt in a large bowl. Stir to mix well.
3. Divide the mixture into four parts, then flatten them into four circles. Arrange the circles onto the air fry basket and spritz with cooking spray.
4. Select Air Fry, Super Convection, set temperature to 380°F (193°C) and set time to 10 minutes. Select Start/Stop to begin preheating.
5. Once the oven has preheated, place the basket on the air fry position. Flip the latkes halfway through.
6. When cooked, the latkes will be golden brown and crispy. Remove the basket from the oven.
7. Serve immediately.

Southwest Lemony Corn and Bell Pepper

Prep time: 10 minutes | Cook time: 10 minutes | Serves 4

Corn:
1½ cups thawed frozen corn kernels
1 cup mixed diced bell peppers
1 jalapeño, diced
1 cup diced yellow onion
½ teaspoon ancho chile powder
1 tablespoon fresh lemon juice
1 teaspoon ground cumin
½ teaspoon kosher salt
Cooking spray
For Serving:
¼ cup feta cheese
¼ cup chopped fresh cilantro
1 tablespoon fresh lemon juice

1. Spritz the air fry basket with cooking spray.
2. Combine the ingredients for the corn in a large bowl. Stir to mix well.
3. Pour the mixture into the air fry basket.
4. Select Air Fry, Super Convection, set temperature to 375°F (190°C) and set time to 10 minutes. Select Start/Stop to begin preheating.
5. Once the oven has preheated, place the basket on the air fry position. Stir the mixture halfway through the cooking time.
6. When done, the corn and bell peppers should be soft.
7. Transfer them onto a large plate, then spread with feta cheese and cilantro. Drizzle with lemon juice and serve.

Cherry Tomato with Basil

Prep time: 5 minutes | Cook time: 5 minutes | Serves 2

2 cups cherry tomatoes
1 clove garlic, thinly sliced
1 teaspoon olive oil
⅛ teaspoon kosher salt
1 tablespoon freshly chopped basil, for topping
Cooking spray

1. Spritz a baking pan with cooking spray and set aside.
2. In a large bowl, toss together the cherry tomatoes, sliced garlic, olive oil, and kosher salt. Spread the mixture in an even layer in the prepared pan.
3. Select Bake, Super Convection, set temperature to 360ºF (182ºC) and set time to 5 minutes. Select Start/Stop to begin preheating.
4. Once the oven has preheated, place the pan on the bake position.
5. When cooking is complete, the tomatoes should be the soft and wilted.
6. Transfer to a bowl and rest for 5 minutes. Top with the chopped basil and serve warm.

Air-Fried Brussels Sprouts

Prep time: 5 minutes | Cook time: 20 minutes | Serves 4

¼ teaspoon salt
⅛ teaspoon ground black pepper
1 tablespoon extra-virgin olive oil
1 pound (454 g) Brussels sprouts, trimmed and halved
Lemon wedges, for garnish

1. Combine the salt, black pepper, and olive oil in a large bowl. Stir to mix well.
2. Add the Brussels sprouts to the bowl of mixture and toss to coat well. Arrange the Brussels sprouts in the air fry basket.
3. Select Air Fry, Super Convection, set temperature to 350ºF (180ºC) and set time to 20 minutes. Select Start/Stop to begin preheating.
4. Once preheated, place the basket on the air fry position. Stir the Brussels sprouts two times during cooking.
5. When cooked, the Brussels sprouts will be lightly browned and wilted. Remove from the oven.
6. Transfer the cooked Brussels sprouts to a large plate and squeeze the lemon wedges on top to serve.

Vanilla Cinnamon Toast

Prep time: 5 minutes | Cook time: 5 minutes | Serves 6

1½ teaspoons cinnamon
1½ teaspoons vanilla extract
½ cup sugar
2 teaspoons ground black pepper
2 tablespoons melted coconut oil
12 slices whole wheat bread

1. Combine all the ingredients, except for the bread, in a large bowl. Stir to mix well.
2. Dunk the bread in the bowl of mixture gently to coat and infuse well. Shake the excess off. Arrange the bread slices in the air fry basket.
3. Select Air Fry, Super Convection, set temperature to 400ºF (205ºC) and set time to 5 minutes. Select Start/Stop to begin preheating.
4. Once the oven has preheated, place the basket on the air fry position. Flip the bread halfway through.
5. When cooking is complete, the bread should be golden brown.
6. Remove the bread slices from the oven and slice to serve.

Manchego Cheese Wafers

Prep time: 5 minutes | Cook time: 5 minutes | Serves 2

1 cup shredded aged Manchego cheese
1 teaspoon all-purpose flour
½ teaspoon cumin seeds
¼ teaspoon cracked black pepper

1. Line the air fry basket with parchment paper.
2. Combine the cheese and flour in a bowl. Stir to mix well. Spread the mixture in the basket into a 4-inch round.
3. Combine the cumin and black pepper in a small bowl. Stir to mix well. Sprinkle the cumin mixture over the cheese round.
4. Select Air Fry, Super Convection, set temperature to 375ºF (190ºC) and set time to 5 minutes. Select Start/Stop to begin preheating.
5. Once preheated, place the basket on the air fry position.
6. When cooked, the cheese will be lightly browned and frothy.
7. Use tongs to transfer the cheese wafer onto a plate and slice to serve.

Parmesan Shrimps

Prep time: 10 minutes | Cook time: 8 minutes | Serves 4 to 6

⅔ cup grated Parmesan cheese
4 minced garlic cloves
1 teaspoon onion powder
½ teaspoon oregano
1 teaspoon basil
1 teaspoon ground black pepper
2 tablespoons olive oil
2 pounds (907 g) cooked large shrimps, peeled and deveined
Lemon wedges, for topping
Cooking spray

1. Spritz the air fry basket with cooking spray.
2. Combine all the ingredients, except for the shrimps, in a large bowl. Stir to mix well.
3. Dunk the shrimps in the mixture and toss to coat well. Shake the excess off. Arrange the shrimps in the air fry basket.
4. Select Air Fry, Super Convection, set temperature to 350ºF (180ºC) and set time to 8 minutes. Select Start/Stop to begin preheating.
5. Once the oven has preheated, place the basket on the air fry position. Flip the shrimps halfway through the cooking time.
6. When cooking is complete, the shrimps should be opaque. Remove the pan from the oven.
7. Transfer the cooked shrimps on a large plate and squeeze the lemon wedges over before serving.

Chips with Lemony Cream Dip

Prep time: 10 minutes | Cook time: 15 minutes | Serves 2 to 4

2 large russet potatoes, sliced into ⅛-inch slices, rinsed
Sea salt and freshly ground black pepper, to taste
Cooking spray
Lemony Cream Dip:
½ cup sour cream
¼ teaspoon lemon juice
2 scallions, white part only, minced
1 tablespoon olive oil
¼ teaspoon salt
Freshly ground black pepper, to taste

1. Soak the potato slices in water for 10 minutes, then pat dry with paper towels.
2. Transfer the potato slices in the air fry basket. Spritz the slices with cooking spray.
3. Select Air Fry, Super Convection, set temperature to 300ºF (150ºC) and set time to 15 minutes. Select Start/Stop to begin preheating.
4. Once the oven has preheated, place the basket on the air fry position. Stir the potato slices three times during cooking. Sprinkle with salt and ground black pepper in the last minute.
5. Meanwhile, combine the ingredients for the dip in a small bowl. Stir to mix well.
6. When cooking is complete, the potato slices will be crispy and golden brown. Remove the basket from the oven.
7. Serve the potato chips immediately with the dip.

Shrimp, Sausage and Corn Bake

Prep time: 10 minutes | Cook time: 18 minutes | Serves 2

1 ear corn, husk and silk removed, cut into 2-inch rounds
8 ounces (227 g) red potatoes, unpeeled, cut into 1-inch pieces
2 teaspoons Old Bay Seasoning, divided
2 teaspoons vegetable oil, divided
¼ teaspoon ground black pepper
8 ounces (227 g) large shrimps (about 12 shrimps), deveined
6 ounces (170 g) andouille or chorizo sausage, cut into 1-inch pieces
2 garlic cloves, minced
1 tablespoon chopped fresh parsley

1. Put the corn rounds and potatoes in a large bowl. Sprinkle with 1 teaspoon of Old Bay seasoning and drizzle with vegetable oil. Toss to coat well.
2. Transfer the corn rounds and potatoes onto a baking pan.
3. Select Bake, Super Convection, set temperature to 400°F (205°C) and set time to 18 minutes. Select Start/Stop to begin preheating.
4. Once preheated, place the pan on the bake position.
5. After 6 minutes, remove the pan from the oven. Stir the corn rounds and potatoes. Return the pan to the oven and continue cooking.
6. Meanwhile, cut slits into the shrimps but be careful not to cut them through. Combine the shrimps, sausage, remaining Old Bay seasoning, and remaining vegetable oil in the large bowl. Toss to coat well.
7. After 6 minutes, remove the pan from the oven. Add the shrimps and sausage to the pan. Return the pan to the oven and continue cooking for 6 minutes. Stir the shrimp mixture halfway through the cooking time.
8. When done, the shrimps should be opaque. Remove the pan from the oven.
9. Transfer the dish to a plate and spread with parsley before serving.

Lime Avocado Wedge

Prep time: 10 minutes | Cook time: 8 minutes | Makes 12 fries

1 cup all-purpose flour
3 tablespoons lime juice
¾ cup orange juice
1¼ cups plain dried bread crumbs
1 cup yellow cornmeal
1½ tablespoons chile powder
2 large Hass avocados, peeled, pitted, and cut into wedges
Coarse sea salt, to taste
Cooking spray

1. Spritz the air fry basket with cooking spray.
2. Pour the flour in a bowl. Mix the lime juice with orange juice in a second bowl. Combine the bread crumbs, cornmeal, and chile powder in a third bowl.
3. Dip the avocado wedges in the bowl of flour to coat well, then dredge the wedges into the bowl of juice mixture, and then dunk the wedges in the bread crumbs mixture. Shake the excess off.
4. Arrange the coated avocado wedges in a single layer in the air fry basket. Spritz with cooking spray.
5. Select Air Fry, Super Convection, set temperature to 400°F (205°C) and set time to 8 minutes. Select Start/Stop to begin preheating.
6. Once preheated, place the basket on the air fry position. Stir the avocado wedges and sprinkle with salt halfway through the cooking time.
7. When cooking is complete, the avocado wedges should be tender and crispy.
8. Serve immediately.

Chapter 13 Basic Sauce and Dressing

Roast Mushrooms with Butter

Prep time: 8 minutes | Cook time: 30 minutes | Makes about 1½ cups

1 pound (454 g) button or cremini mushrooms, washed, stems trimmed, and cut into quarters or thick slices
¼ cup water
1 teaspoon kosher salt or ½ teaspoon fine salt
3 tablespoons unsalted butter, cut into pieces, or extra-virgin olive oil

1. Place a large piece of aluminum foil on the sheet pan. Place the mushroom pieces in the middle of the foil. Spread them out into an even layer. Pour the water over them, season with the salt, and add the butter. Wrap the mushrooms in the foil.
2. Select Roast, Super Convection, set the temperature to 325ºF (163ºC), and set the time for 15 minutes. Select Start/Stop to begin preheating.
3. Once the unit has preheated, place the pan on the roast position.
4. After 15 minutes, remove the pan from the oven. Transfer the foil packet to a cutting board and carefully unwrap it. Pour the mushrooms and cooking liquid from the foil onto the sheet pan.
5. Select Roast, Super Convection, set the temperature to 350ºF (180ºC), and set the time for 15 minutes. Place the basket on the roast position. Select Start/Stop to begin.
6. After about 10 minutes, remove the pan from the oven and stir the mushrooms. Return the pan to the oven and continue cooking for anywhere from 5 to 15 more minutes, or until the liquid is mostly gone and the mushrooms start to brown.
7. Serve immediately.

Teriyaki Sauce

Prep time: 5 minutes | Cook time: 0 minutes | Makes ¾ cup

½ cup soy sauce
3 tablespoons honey
1 tablespoon rice wine or dry sherry
1 tablespoon rice vinegar
2 teaspoons minced fresh ginger
2 garlic cloves, smashed

1. Beat together all the ingredients in a small bowl.
2. Use immediately.

Enchilada Sauce

Prep time: 15 minutes | Cook time: 0 minutes | Makes 2 cups

3 large ancho chiles, stems and seeds removed, torn into pieces
1½ cups very hot water
2 garlic cloves, peeled and lightly smashed
2 tablespoons wine vinegar
1½ teaspoons sugar
½ teaspoon dried oregano
½ teaspoon ground cumin
2 teaspoons kosher salt or 1 teaspoon fine salt

1. Mix together the chile pieces and hot water in a bowl and let stand for 10 to 15 minutes.
2. Pour the chiles and water into a blender jar. Fold in the garlic, vinegar, sugar, oregano, cumin, and salt and blend until smooth.
3. Use immediately.

Spice Mix with Cumin

Prep time: 5 minutes | Cook time: 0 minutes | Makes about 1 tablespoon

1 teaspoon smoked paprika
1 teaspoon cumin
¼ teaspoon turmeric
¼ teaspoon kosher salt or ⅛ teaspoon fine salt
¼ teaspoon cinnamon
¼ teaspoon allspice
¼ teaspoon red pepper flakes
¼ teaspoon freshly ground black pepper

1. Stir together all the ingredients in a small bowl.
2. Use immediately or place in an airtight container in the pantry.

Tomato Marinara Sauce

Prep time: 15 minutes | Cook time: 30 minutes | Makes about 3 cups

¼ cup extra-virgin olive oil
3 garlic cloves, minced
1 small onion, chopped (about ½ cup)
2 tablespoons minced or puréed sun-dried tomatoes (optional)
1 (28-ounce / 794-g) can crushed tomatoes
½ teaspoon dried basil
½ teaspoon dried oregano
¼ teaspoon red pepper flakes
1 teaspoon kosher salt or ½ teaspoon fine salt, plus more as needed

1. Heat the oil in a medium saucepan over medium heat.
2. Add the garlic and onion and sauté for 2 to 3 minutes, or until the onion is softened. Add the sun-dried tomatoes (if desired) and cook for 1 minute until fragrant. Stir in the crushed tomatoes, scraping any brown bits from the bottom of the pot. Fold in the basil, oregano, red pepper flakes, and salt. Stir well.
3. Bring to a simmer. Cook covered for about 30 minutes, stirring occasionally.
4. Turn off the heat and allow the sauce to cool for about 10 minutes.
5. Taste and adjust the seasoning, adding more salt if needed.
6. Use immediately.

Baked Rice

Prep time: 3 minutes | Cook time: 35 minutes | Makes about 4 cups

1 cup long-grain white rice, rinsed and drained
1 tablespoon unsalted butter, melted, or 1 tablespoon extra-virgin olive oil
2 cups water
1 teaspoon kosher salt or ½ teaspoon fine salt

1. Add the butter and rice to the baking pan and stir to coat. Pour in the water and sprinkle with the salt. Stir until the salt is dissolved.
2. Select Bake, Super Convection, set the temperature to 325°F (163°C), and set the time for 35 minutes. Select Start/Stop to begin preheating.
3. Once the unit has preheated, place the pan on the bake position.
4. After 20 minutes, remove the pan from the oven. Stir the rice. Transfer the pan back to the oven and continue cooking for 10 to 15 minutes, or until the rice is mostly cooked through and the water is absorbed.
5. When done, remove the pan from the oven and cover with aluminum foil. Let stand for 10 minutes. Using a fork, gently fluff the rice.
6. Serve immediately.

Chile Seasoning

Prep time: 5 minutes | Cook time: 0 minutes | Makes about ¾ cups

3 tablespoons ancho chile powder
3 tablespoons paprika
2 tablespoons dried oregano
2 tablespoons freshly ground black pepper
2 teaspoons cayenne
2 teaspoons cumin
1 tablespoon granulated onion
1 tablespoon granulated garlic

1. Stir together all the ingredients in a small bowl.
2. Use immediately or place in an airtight container in the pantry.

Chapter 3 Vegan and Vegetarian

Easy Dipping Sauce

Prep time: 15 minutes | Cook time: 0 minutes | Makes about 1 cup

¼ cup rice vinegar
¼ cup hoisin sauce
¼ cup low-sodium chicken or vegetable stock
3 tablespoons soy sauce
1 tablespoon minced or grated ginger
1 tablespoon minced or pressed garlic
1 teaspoon chili-garlic sauce or sriracha (or more to taste)

1. Stir together all the ingredients in a small bowl, or place in a jar with a tight-fitting lid and shake until well mixed.
2. Use immediately.

Salad Dressing

Prep time: 5 minutes | Cook time: 0 minutes | Makes about ⅔ cup

½ cup extra-virgin olive oil
2 tablespoons freshly squeezed lemon juice
1 teaspoon anchovy paste
¼ teaspoon kosher salt or ⅛ teaspoon fine salt
¼ teaspoon minced or pressed garlic
1 egg, beaten

1. Add all the ingredients to a tall, narrow container.
2. Purée the mixture with an immersion blender until smooth.
3. Use immediately.

Polenta with Butter

Prep time: 3 minutes | Cook time: 1 hour 5 minutes | Makes about 4 cups

1 cup grits or polenta (not instant or quick cook)
2 cups chicken or vegetable stock
2 cups milk
2 tablespoons unsalted butter, cut into 4 pieces
1 teaspoon kosher salt or ½ teaspoon fine salt

1. Add the grits to the baking pan. Stir in the stock, milk, butter, and salt.
2. Select Bake, Super Convection, set the temperature to 325°F (163°C), and set the time for 1 hour and 5 minutes. Select Start/Stop to begin preheating.
3. Once the unit has preheated, place the pan on the bake position.
4. After 15 minutes, remove the pan from the oven and stir the polenta. Return the pan to the oven and continue cooking.
5. After 30 minutes, remove the pan again and stir the polenta again. Return the pan to the oven and continue cooking for 15 to 20 minutes, or until the polenta is soft and creamy and the liquid is absorbed.
6. When done, remove the pan from the oven.
7. Serve immediately.

Appendix 1 Measurement Conversion Chart

VOLUME EQUIVALENTS(DRY)

US STANDARD	METRIC (APPROXIMATE)
1/8 teaspoon	0.5 mL
1/4 teaspoon	1 mL
1/2 teaspoon	2 mL
3/4 teaspoon	4 mL
1 teaspoon	5 mL
1 tablespoon	15 mL
1/4 cup	59 mL
1/2 cup	118 mL
3/4 cup	177 mL
1 cup	235 mL
2 cups	475 mL
3 cups	700 mL
4 cups	1 L

VOLUME EQUIVALENTS(LIQUID)

US STANDARD	US STANDARD (OUNCES)	METRIC (APPROXIMATE)
2 tablespoons	1 fl.oz.	30 mL
1/4 cup	2 fl.oz.	60 mL
1/2 cup	4 fl.oz.	120 mL
1 cup	8 fl.oz.	240 mL
1 1/2 cup	12 fl.oz.	355 mL
2 cups or 1 pint	16 fl.oz.	475 mL
4 cups or 1 quart	32 fl.oz.	1 L
1 gallon	128 fl.oz.	4 L

TEMPERATURES EQUIVALENTS

FAHRENHEIT(F)	CELSIUS(C) (APPROXIMATE)
225 °F	107 °C
250 °F	120 °C
275 °F	135 °C
300 °F	150 °C
325 °F	160 °C
350 °F	180 °C
375 °F	190 °C
400 °F	205 °C
425 °F	220 °C
450 °F	235 °C
475 °F	245 °C
500 °F	260 °C

WEIGHT EQUIVALENTS

US STANDARD	METRIC (APPROXIMATE)
1 ounce	28 g
2 ounces	57 g
5 ounces	142 g
10 ounces	284 g
15 ounces	425 g
16 ounces (1 pound)	455 g
1.5 pounds	680 g
2 pounds	907 g

Appendix 2: Air Fryer Cooking Timetable

Beef

Item	Temp (°F)	Time (mins)	Item	Temp (°F)	Time (mins)
Beef Eye Round Roast (4 lbs.)	400 °F	45 to 55	Meatballs (1-inch)	370 °F	7
Burger Patty (4 oz.)	370 °F	16 to 20	Meatballs (3-inch)	380 °F	10
Filet Mignon (8 oz.)	400 °F	18	Ribeye, bone-in (1-inch, 8 oz)	400 °F	10 to 15
Flank Steak (1.5 lbs.)	400 °F	12	Sirloin steaks (1-inch, 12 oz)	400 °F	9 to 14
Flank Steak (2 lbs.)	400 °F	20 to 28			

Chicken

Item	Temp (°F)	Time (mins)	Item	Temp (°F)	Time (mins)
Breasts, bone in (1 ¼ lb.)	370 °F	25	Legs, bone-in (1 ¾ lb.)	380 °F	30
Breasts, boneless (4 oz)	380 °F	12	Thighs, boneless (1 ½ lb.)	380 °F	18 to 20
Drumsticks (2 ½ lb.)	370 °F	20	Wings (2 lb.)	400 °F	12
Game Hen (halved 2 lb.)	390 °F	20	Whole Chicken	360 °F	75
Thighs, bone-in (2 lb.)	380 °F	22	Tenders	360 °F	8 to 10

Pork & Lamb

Item	Temp (°F)	Time (mins)	Item	Temp (°F)	Time (mins)
Bacon (regular)	400 °F	5 to 7	Pork Tenderloin	370 °F	15
Bacon (thick cut)	400 °F	6 to 10	Sausages	380 °F	15
Pork Loin (2 lb.)	360 °F	55	Lamb Loin Chops (1-inch thick)	400 °F	8 to 12
Pork Chops, bone in (1-inch, 6.5 oz)	400 °F	12	Rack of Lamb (1.5 – 2 lb.)	380 °F	22

Fish & Seafood

Item	Temp (°F)	Time (mins)	Item	Temp (°F)	Time (mins)
Calamari (8 oz)	400 °F	4	Tuna Steak	400 °F	7 to 10
Fish Fillet (1-inch, 8 oz)	400 °F	10	Scallops	400 °F	5 to 7
Salmon, fillet (6 oz)	380 °F	12	Shrimp	400 °F	5
Swordfish steak	400 °F	10			

Vegetables

INGREDIENT	AMOUNT	PREPARATION	OIL	TEMP	COOK TIME
Asparagus	2 bunches	Cut in half, trim stems	2 Tbsp	420°F	12-15 mins
Beets	1½ lbs	Peel, cut in ½-inch cubes	1 Tbsp	390°F	28-30 mins
Bell peppers (for roasting)	4 peppers	Cut in quarters, remove seeds	1 Tbsp	400°F	15-20 mins
Broccoli	1 large head	Cut in 1-2-inch florets	1 Tbsp	400°F	15-20 mins
Brussels sprouts	1 lb	Cut in half, remove stems	1 Tbsp	425°F	15-20 mins
Carrots	1 lb	Peel, cut in ¼-inch rounds	1 Tbsp	425°F	10-15 mins
Cauliflower	1 head	Cut in 1-2-inch florets	2 Tbsp	400°F	20-22 mins
Corn on the cob	7 ears	Whole ears, remove husks	1 Tbps	400°F	14-17 mins
Green beans	1 bag (12 oz)	Trim	1 Tbps	420°F	18-20 mins
Kale (for chips)	4 oz	Tear into pieces, remove stems	None	325°F	5-8 mins
Mushrooms	16 oz	Rinse, slice thinly	1 Tbps	390°F	25-30 mins
Potatoes, russet	1½ lbs	Cut in 1-inch wedges	1 Tbps	390°F	25-30 mins
Potatoes, russet	1 lb	Hand-cut fries, soak 30 mins in cold water, then pat dry	½ -3 Tbps	400°F	25-28 mins
Potatoes, sweet	1 lb	Hand-cut fries, soak 30 mins in cold water, then pat dry	1 Tbps	400°F	25-28 mins
Zucchini	1 lb	Cut in eighths lengthwise, then cut in half	1 Tbps	400°F	15-20 mins

Appendix 3: Recipe Index

A

Air Fried Zucchini Sticks 43
Air-Fried Apricot-Glazed Drumsticks 74
Air-Fried Brussels Sprouts 164
Air-Fried Chicken and Fingerling Potato 84
Air-Fried Chicken Wings 70
Air-Fried Duck Leg 69
Air-Fried Old Bay Chicken Wings 100
Apple Chips 93
Apple Wedges with Apricots and Cinnamon 110
Apple-Cinnamon Fritters 102
Apple-Peach Crisp 109
Apple-Peach Crumble with Oatmeal 107
Arancini Balls 151
Artichoke Mushroom Cheese Frittata 24
Asparagus and Goat Cheese Frittata 139
Asparagus and Grits Casserole 138
Asparagus Cheese Strata 14
Asparagus Spears 38
Asparagus with Eggs and Tomatoes 29
Asparagus with Garlic 45
Avocado and Cabbage Slaw Taco 119
Avocado and Egg with Cheese 22
Avocado and Tomato Egg Rolls Wrappers 121

B

Bacon and Cheese Casserole 19
Bacon and Cheese Muffin Sandwiches 9
Bacon and Egg Cheese Cups 15
Bacon-Wrapped Balsamic Turkey with Carrots 72
Bacon-Wrapped Cheesy Chicken Breast 66
Bacon-Wrapped Spiced Chicken Rolls 65
Baked Butter Cake 148
Baked Garlicky Whole Chicken 66
Baked Rice 169
Baked Tofu 40
Baked Turkey and Cauliflower Meatloaf 69
Banana and Chocolate Bread 16
Banana and Oat Bread Pudding 17
Banana and Oat Bread Pudding 21
Barbecue Chicken Drumsticks 65
Basil Salmon with Tomato 56
Beef and Bell Pepper Cheese Fajitas 122
Beef and Cannellini Casserole 141
Beef and Green Chile Casserole 140
Beef and Mushroom Casserole 137
Beef and Red Onion Taco 120
Beer Battered Onion Rings 159
Beer Cod Fillets 56
Beer-Battered Cod Tacos 129
Bell Peppers with Garlic 33
Black and White Chocolate Cake 111
Black Beans Cheese Tacos with Salsa 34
Blackberry Almond Muffins 113
Blackberry Brownie 114
Blackberry Goden Cobbler 111
Blintzes 150
Blistered Cherry Tomatoes 147
Blistered Shishito Peppers 158
Blueberry and Peach Tart 117
Blueberry Chocolate Cupcakes 114
Blueberry Cobbler 20
Blueberry Muffins 22
Bourbon Chocolate Pecan Pie 108
Bourbon French Toast 14
Brazilian Cheese Bread 152
Breaded Catfish Nuggets 59
Breaded Chicken Schnitzel 83
Breaded Eggplant Slices 35
Breaded Fish Strips 53
Breaded Green Tomatoes with Horseradish 91
Breaded Zucchini Chips 32
Breaded Zucchini Tots 91
Breakfast Sausage and Colorful Peppers Casserole 138
Brie Pear Sandwiches 93
Broccoli Cheese Quiche 19
Broccoli with Cheese 38
Broccoli with Cheese 43
Broccoli with Hot Sauce 47
Broccoli with Peppercorn 41
Broccoli with Sauce 28
Broccoli, Tomato, and Carrot Quiche 143
Brown Sugar Butter Rolls 24
Bruschetta Stuffed Chicken 68
Bruschetta with Parmesan Tomato 96
Brussels Sprouts with Cheese 27
Brussels Sprouts with Chili Sauce 37
Brussels Sprouts with Sage 43
Brussels Sprouts with Sauce 45
Brussels Sprouts with Tomatoes 29
Butter Shortbread 105
Buttered Knots with Parsley 162
Buttermilk Banana Cake 146
Buttermilk Biscuits 14
Buttermilk Fried Chicken Wings 88
Butternut Squash Croquettes 45
Butternut Squash with Cheese 30
Butternut Squash with Fried-Hazelnuts 160
Buttery Snack Mix 90

C-D

Cabbage and Peas with Mango 30
Cabbage Wedges with Cheese 39
Cabbage with Red Pepper 47
Cajun Chicken Drumsticks 64
Canadian Poutine 158
Candy Coated Pecans 162
Caramelized Cinnamon Peaches 97
Caramelized Fruity Kebabs 109
Caramelized Peach with Blueberry Yogurt 112
Carrot and Banana Muffins 23
Carrot and Pepper Frittata 18
Carrot and Potato with Thyme 31
Carrot Tofu with Peanuts 30
Carrot with Glaze 46
Carrots with Dill 26
Catfish Fillets with Pecan 58
Cauliflower with Paprika 29
Cauliflower with Yogurt and Cashew 31
Celery Roots with Butter 33
Cheddar Turkey Burgers 79
Cheese Egg Florentine with Spinach 22
Cheese Grits 16
Cheesy Broccoli Gratin 47
Cheesy Broccoli Tots 28
Cheesy Ham Hash Brown Cups 15
Cheesy Hash Brown Casserole 16
Cheesy Vegetable Wraps 131
Cherry Sauce-Glazed Duck 75
Cherry Tomato with Basil 164
Chicken and Cabbage Egg Rolls 128
Chicken and Peppers Skewers with Corn 84
Chicken and Spring Onion Wraps 128
Chicken and Veggies Casserole 142
Chicken Breast Nuggets 70
Chicken Breast with Veggies and Beans 74
Chicken Broccoli Divan 140
Chicken Drumettes with Buffalo Sauce 66
Chicken Goulash 68
Chicken Sausages with Apple 17
Chicken Tostadas with Coleslaw Topping 76
Chile Seasoning 169
Chili Brown Rice Cheese Quiches 21
Chinese Spiced Turkey Thighs 71
Chips with Lemony Cream Dip 165
Chocolate Bread Pudding 103
Chocolate Chip and Oat Cookies 115
Chocolate Glazed Custard Donut Holes 148
Chocolate-Coconut Cake 117
Chorizo, Potato, and Corn Frittata 143
Cinnamon Apple Chips 98
Cinnamon Apple Wedges with Yogurt 99
Cinnamon Candy Covered Apple 104
Cinnamon-Sugar Chickpeas 157
Classic Mediterranean Quiche 141
Coated Pickle Spears 89
Coconut Brown Rice Porridge with Dates 18
Coconut Chocolate Macaroons 150
Coconut Flake-Coated Pineapple Rings 108
Cod Fillet Taco with Salsa 121
Cod Fillets with Parsley 52
Coffee-Coconut Cake 105
Corn and Black Bean Chunky Salsa 100
Corn Cheese Casserole 48
Corn Kernels and Bell Pepper Casserole 138
Corn on the Cob 46
Cornmeal Pancake 17
Crab Meat and Cream Cheese Wontons 130
Cream Cheese Wontons 125
Cream Glazed Cinnamon Rolls 152
Creamy Cauliflower and Pumpkin Casserole 135
Creamy Potato 49
Creamy Sausage and Cheese Quiche 20
Crispy Chili Chicken Skin 64
Crispy Tofu Strips 36
Crispy Zucchini 159
Crunchy Tortilla Chips 158
Cuban Pork and Turkey Sandwiches 95
Curried Chicken and Sweet Potato 79
Curried Shrimp and Zucchini Potstickers 124
Desiccated Coconut-Pineapple Sticks 103
Deviled Eggs wiih Paprika 92
Double Cheese Green Bean Casserole 139
Double Cheese Sausage Balls 91

E-F

Easy Dipping Sauce 170
Edamame 97
Egg and Avocado Cheese Burrito 20
Egg and Spinach with Basil 39
Egg Cheese Bread 11
Eggplant Parmesan Hoagies 122
Eggplant with Basil 33
Eggplant with Yogurt 39
Eggs in Bell Pepper Rings 12
Empanadas de Pollo Verde 133
Enchilada Sauce 168
English Pea and Potato Samosas 125
Fast Corn on the Cob 159
Fish Sticks 88
French Fries with Ketchup 161
Fried Banana with Chocolate Sauce 113
Fried Thai Hens with Vegetable Salad 83
Fudgy Brownies 113

G-H

Garlic Stuffed Mushrooms 40
Garlicky Carrots 37
Garlicky Cod Fillets 58
Glazed Cauliflower 34
Glazed Red Potato and Mushrooms 27
Greek Lamb and Feta Hamburgers 124
Greek Spinach Pie with Feta 161
Green Beans with Sesame Seeds 44
Half-and-Half Frittata 136
Halibut Fillets with Cheese 59

Halibut Steaks with Vermouth 60
Ham and Cheese Stuffed Mushroom 94
Ham and Cheese Toast 13
Ham and Tomato Sandwiches with Cheese 10
Ham Cheese Omelet 15
Ham-Chicken Meatballs with Lemony Mustard 85
Hawaiian Glazed Chicken Bites 67
Hearty Chicken Rochambeau with Mushroom Sauce 76
Herby Turkey with Dijon Sauce 78
Homemade Biscuits 10
Homemade Potato Chips 92
Honey Chicken Thighs on Waffles 77
Honey-Glazed Chicken 73
Hot Chicken Wings 157
Hot Chickpeas 95

I-J

Italian Cheesy Rice Balls 97
Italian Herby Chicken with Tomatoes 64
Jalapeño Cheddar Cornbread 160
Japanese Pork and Cabbage Gyoza 130
Japanese Skewered Chicken (Yakitori) 86

K

Kale Cheese Eggs 19
Kale with Tahini and Lemon 35
Keto Cheesy Quiche 144
Korean Bulgogi Burgers 132
Korean-Inspired Chicken Wings 80

L

Lemony Chickpea Oat Meatballs 36
Lemony Cod Fillets 60
Lemony Wax Beans 26
Lettuce Turkey and Mushroom Taco 82
Lettuce-Wrapped Chicken with Peanut Sauce 77
Lime Avocado Chips 100
Lime Avocado Wedge 166
Lush Veggies Frittata 144

M-N

Manchego Cheese Wafers 165
Maple Bacon Pinwheels 160
Maple Blackberry and Peach Cobbler 112
Maple-Mustard Turkey Breast 70
Marinated Olive Stromboli 149
Mexican Cheese Potato Taquitos 122
Mexican Churros 146
Mexican Spiced Chicken Burgers 133
Mini Crescent Dogs 150
Mixed Berries with Mixed Nuts Streusel 107
Mixed Berry Crisp with Coconut Chips 103
Mixed Berry Pancake 23
Monk Fruit and Hazelnut Cake 116
Montreal Steak Hamburgers 132
Mozzarella Chicken and Yogurt Taquitos 123
Mozzarella Chicken Sausage Pizza 94
Mozzarella Pepperoni and Chicken Pizza 65
Muffuletta with Mozzarella Olives Topping 95

Mushroom and Spinach Cheese Frittata 18
Mushroom and Spinach Frittata 136
Mushroom, Veggies and Noodle Spring Rolls 120
Mustard Sole Fillets 53
Nuggets 151

O

Okra and Cauliflower Casserole 140
Okra Chips 157
Okra with Sour Cream 31
Orange-Balsamic Glazed Duck Breasts 72
Oregano-Balsamic Chicken Breast 81

P-Q

Panko Cheese Asparagus 46
Panko Fish Fillets 52
Panko- Crusted Artichoke Bites 94
Panko-Crusted Cheese Green Beans 41
Panko-Crusted Chicken Fingers 73
Panko-Crusted Chicken Livers 67
Panko-Green Tomatoes Slices 162
Panko-Kale Salad Sushi Rolls 153
Paprika Chicken Skewers with Satay Sauce 80
Parma Prosciutto-Wrapped Pears 90
Parmesan Breaded Chicken Cutlets 67
Parmesan Cauliflower Patties 161
Parmesan Chicken Ciabatta Sandwiches 81
Parmesan Chicken with Roasted Peanuts 73
Parmesan Ranch Snack Mix 88
Parmesan Shrimps 165
Parsnip Fries with Creamy Yogurt Dip 163
Pastrami and Bell Pepper Casserole 136
Pea and Mushroom with Rice 36
Peach and Blueberry Galette 102
Pear Tart with Caramel Sauce 115
Pecan Granola with Maple Syrup 27
Pecan-Coconut Cookies 109
Peppers with Sauce 44
Philly Cheese Steaks 129
Pickle Spears with Buttermilk Dressing 149
Pimento and Turkey Casserole 135
Pistachio and Walnut Baklava 104
Polenta Fries with Tangy Chili Mayonnaise 89
Polenta with Butter 170
Pomegranate-Glazed Chicken with Couscous Salad 75
Pork and Carrot Momos 123
Pork Gratin 143
Pork, Cabbage and Mushroom Egg Rolls 147
Potato and Tuna Nicoise Salad 62
Potato Latkes 163
Potato with Peppers 21
Potato with Yogurt 48
Potato, Spinach and Black Bean Burritos 126
Pound Cake 110
Prawn and Cabbage Egg Wrappers 126
Pumpkin Pudding with Vanilla Wafers Topping 111
Quick Edamame 157

R

Ranch Cheddar Broccoli Casserole 136
Raspberry Muffins 107
Red Snapper with Lemon 60
Ricotta Capers with Lemon Zest 98
Ricotta Cheesecake 104
Risotto Croquettes 155
Ritzy Seafood Casserole 137
Roast Mushrooms 37
Roast Mushrooms with Butter 168
Roasted Chicken and Sausage with Peppers 82
Roasted Walnuts, Pecans, and Almonds 93
Rosemary Beets with Glaze 34
Rosemary Potato 49

S

S'mores 103
Salad Dressing 170
Salmon and Asparagus 57
Salmon Bowl with Salsa 59
Salmon Patties 54
Salmon Patties 56
Salmon Spring Rolls with Carrot 51
Salmon Steaks with Butter 57
Salmon with Asparagus 58
Salmon with Teriyaki Sauce 52
Salsa Bacon and Egg Cheese Wraps 121
Sausage and Apple Patties 13
Sausage and Broccoli Egg Casserole 137
Sausage and Cheese Tater Tots 10
Sesame Kale Chips 93
Shrimp and Baby Spinach Frittata 142
Shrimp and Spinach Rice Frittata 11
Shrimp Toasts with Thai Chili Sauce 98
Shrimp, Sausage and Corn Bake 166
Small Hush Puppies 90
Smoky Sausage and Mushroom Empanadas 92
Smoky Trout and Crème Fraiche Frittata 139
Snapper with Plums 55
Snapper with Tomato and Olives 51
Sole and Cauliflower Fritters 61
Southern Fudge Pie 114
Southwest Lemony Corn and Bell Pepper 163
Spanish Chicken and Sweet Pepper 86
Spice Mix with Cumin 169
Spicy Corn Tortilla Chips 99
Spinach and Bacon Cheese Muffins 12
Spinach and Bacon Cheese Roll-ups 12
Spinach and Mushroom Cheese Calzones 99
Spinach and Tomato Pockets 127
Spinach, Chickpea and Tomato Casserole 142
Squash and Mushroom Mélange 41
Squash and Parsnip 26
Squash with Cinnamon 48
Sriracha Panko-Crusted Shrimp 154
Strawberry and Rhubarb Crisp 106
Strawberry Puréed-Glazed Turkey Breast 72
Strawberry Toast 9
Stuffed Chicken Rolls with Bell Peppers 68
Sweet and Spicy Roasted Walnuts 89
Sweet Chocolate Cookies 116
Sweet Pecan Tart 153
Sweet Potato Chips with Cinnamon 9
Sweet Potato with Lime 44
Sweet-Sour Chicken Nuggets 71
Swiss Chicken and Ham Casserole 141
Swordfish Steaks with Lemon 57
Syrupy Bacon Knots 13

T

Tandoori Drumsticks 85
Tangy Chicken Breast with Cilantro 71
Tangy Coconut Cake 106
Teriyaki Chicken with Lemony Snow Peas 78
Teriyaki Panko-Shrimp Skewers 154
Teriyaki Sauce 168
Thai Curried Pork Burgers 123
Tilapia and Coleslaw Tacos 54
Tilapia Fillet Tacos 119
Tilapia Meunière with Potato 62
Tofu Carrot and Cauliflower Rice 32
Tomato Corn Frittata with Avocado 11
Tomato Marinara Sauce 169
Tomato Stuffed Mushrooms with Cheese 35
Triple Berry Crisp 112
Tuna and Lettuce Wraps with Mayo 54
Tuna and Pineapple Kebabs 53
Tuna Casserole 55
Tuna Cubes over Rice 55
Tuna Melts Sandwiches 96
Tuna Patties with Cheese Sauce 61
Turkey and Leek Hamburger 124
Turkey Bacon-Wrapped Almond Stuffed Dates 96
Turkey Scotch Eggs 69
Turkey Sliders with Chive Mayonnaise 131
Turnip and Zucchini 26

U-V

Ultimate Chocolate Cheesecake 110
Vanilla Chocolate and Coconut Cake 106
Vanilla Cinnamon Toast 164
Vanilla Granola with Syrup 9
Vegetable Spring Rolls 127

W-Z

Walnut and Cheese Stuffed Mushrooms 38
Walnut Butter Pancake 23
Walnut-Coconut Tart 105
White Chocolate Cookies 108
Zucchini and Carrot with Cheese 32
Zucchini and Tomato Ratatouille 40
Zucchini Cheese Quesadilla 28
Zucchini Crisps 49

CPSIA information can be obtained
at www.ICGtesting.com
Printed in the USA
LVHW060519310323
742973LV00003B/284